COLONEL COGGESHALL—
THE MAN WHO
SAVED LINCOLN

Freda Postle Koch

PoKo Press
P. O. Box 14766
Columbus, Ohio 43214

Dedicated

to

My Parents, Fred and Elsie Postle

and

My Children, Robert, Katharine and Mary Lu

Copyright © 1985 by Freda Postle Koch. All rights reserved. No part of this book may be reproduced, except for purposes of review, without permission in writing from the author.

Library of Congress Catalog Card Number: 84-62613

1 2 3 4 5 / 87 86 85

INTRODUCTION

One summer day in 1956 I did it. I gassed up the Studebaker, drove the 50 miles to Springfield, Ohio, and raced in to see cousin Ralph Busbey.

I hadn't known exactly why I'd come but Mother's voice kept ringing in my ear: "Your father's been gone now four years; you hung on his every word about our family (Ohioans since 1800) and the only one left to tell you about his famous uncles is his first cousin Ralph Busbey. Ralph's in his late 60s, not in too good health, so you better get while the getting's good."

Ralph was expecting me. He was a marvelously genteel, polished gentleman, with elegant manners. He escorted me to the back yard where a lavish luncheon was served by Chrystal, the housekeeper. Blanche, his wife, was equally gracious and carried her huge frame with great grace.

After lunch, Ralph launched into detailed accounts about our ancestry. I'd come to hear about my five great uncles, called Ohio's most famous journalistic family. One of them was Ralph's father, T. Addison Busbey.

I heard about them, all right. Then Ralph startled me. He began talking about a man who saved Lincoln *from* assassination. I blinked. The man was his maternal grandfather, Colonel William T. Coggeshall. As a bodyguard to Lincoln en route to the President's first inauguration, Coggeshall saved him from assassination.

On recovering from the shock of the near fatality, Coggeshall swore Lincoln to secrecy. The secret was so well kept that not until 1908, in a column of the *Springfield (Ohio) Daily Sun,* was the incident mentioned briefly by Coggeshall's widow, Mary. Mind you this was almost half a century after his death.

The gripping details had never been printed.

As Ralph unraveled the frightening account of the assassination attempt in 1861 I took copious notes, breathlessly asking him to wait while my pencil caught up. Finally, after sitting back and taking a deep breath and a long, approving look at me, Ralph whispered, "Freda, you're the only one of your generation who's going to know. You have children and I don't. I'm the last of my line. I'm going to make a codicil to my will leaving all my Grandfather Coggeshall keepsakes to you so they will stay in the family."

I drove back to Columbus on flying tires, excited with my discovery. Little did I know how timely the visit was. Within months I was hospitalized from a crippling automobile accident. Visits with Ralph then were by telephone, letter, and his trips to Columbus. Each added a succulent morsel that fed my subconscious for 15 years.

Then on April 22, 1959, Ralph died of a heart attack. Dear Chrystal, his and Blanche's housekeeper, gathered all the Coggeshall memorabilia, packed them in files, and had them delivered to me.

I stashed away the boxes, files, books and albums, and hung the oil portrait of Colonel Coggeshall in the living room. "He looks like Lincoln," people would say. Within three days all the space in the study, three cupboards, closets, and a chest of drawers was overflowing with the data.

The years passed. I was busy rearing three children, being active in the American Council for Better Broadcasts, and helping launch a Christian radio station.

But the Coggeshall story nagged and gnawed. I couldn't get a handle on it. His life story lay dormant in me, yet aching to be told. Finally, a speech about the Colonel for the local Exchange Club got my pen moving onto paper.

The story was true but the proof about his heroism was missing. One sleepless night in February '75, after Mother died, I got up to rummage in the storage room closet. There were boxes untouched since Ralph died: interesting papers . . . folders . . . booklets I'd not seen before. Skim . . . scan . . . a handwritten letter from president-to-be James A. Garfield . . . a pencilled directive from General George B. McClellan, Union Army commander.

Then suddenly! A faded, pencilled letter that began, "Dear Girlie" . . . could it be . . . it must . . . it *was* a letter (written to her daughter Prockie), describing the details of Coggeshall's sparing Lincoln from death, written by his widow, Mary Coggeshall. It was the thread to completing the tapestry about the Colonel.

Now I could start. But were there still other prizes in the house I knew nothing about? I began to search space-consuming containers in idle cupboards and closets.

There were copies of the Colonel's observations of cabinet members and Civil War generals, made in his diary while attending Lincoln cabinet meetings . . . vivid descriptions of the religious, the humorous, the human sides of Lincoln's character . . . books Coggeshall authored, newspapers he published . . . and meticulous quotes from the rare book, *Lincoln Memorial,* the Colonel wrote, chronicling the first and last trips his Commander-in-Chief Lincoln made to and from Washington as President.

And there were diaries—faded, written in pencil, in pen—tiny, medium sized—a reservoir for the flow of Coggeshall's pen. Especially picturesque were those kept while he was U.S. Minister to Ecuador . . . a time of peril and persecution.

The Colonel's story must be told.

ACKNOWLEDGMENTS

ALL AMERICAN AWARDS FOR:

THE COACH'S WHISTLE of my daughter Katharine Koch—oft a tough editor but perceptive; REFEREE, June Wells Dill, who first saw the potential; DRUM MAJOR, spirited history buff, Ernestine Powell; CHEERLEADER, Evelyn Speckman, precision perfect; BAND MEMBERS, Lillian Ebert, Wilma Koch and Yvonne Hardenbrook whose tooting spurred me; DEVOTED FAN, Chrystal Swan; THE RIGHT HAND READERS, Marcene Mallett, always there, indispensable, Julie Estadt, jolly punctuation detective; LEFT HAND READERS, Frank Mallett, Ruth Foster, Marguerite Reiss, Pat Kern and Suzanne Morris; TERRIFIC TYPIST, Sandra Key; LOYAL ARCHIVIST, Gary Arnold of the Ohio Historical Society; CHEERFUL CONSULTANT, newspaperman Ernest Cady; AFFABLE SIDELINERS, Dr. Harold Hancock, Chairman History Department and John Becker, Librarian, Otterbein College, Charlotte Callahan, Ohio State University Library, Sam Roshon, Public Library of Columbus and Franklin County, and Congressman Chalmers P. Wylie and helpful staff; ADVISER ON CATHOLICISM, former Bishop George A. Fulcher, Diocese of Lafayette, Indiana; MAP ARCHITECT, James Key; TIMEKEEPER AND TICKET TAKER, husband Melvin Koch; ENDURERS OF A TOPSY-TURVY HOUSEHOLD FOR SEVEN YEARS—Team-playing family members Mary Lu and Dan Williams, Robert and Diane and grandchildren Kathy and Carol Koch; and FAMILY-LOVING COUSIN Ralph Coggeshall Busbey, without whose generosity and memorabilia this biography would have been impossible.

CONTENTS

PART I—THE LINCOLN YEARS

1	Come with Me	1
2	Lincoln's Inaugural Train	11
3	Mary's Secret	33
4	Lincoln War Years	51
5	Coggeshall's Emancipation Proclamation	75
6	First Absentee Ballots	79
7	Twenty Days	83

PART II—THE DIPLOMATIC YEARS

8	U.S. Minister to Ecuador	101
9	Diplomatic Duties	123
10	Letters from Quito	131
11	Prejudice Begins	141
12	Dear Little Folks	161
13	Diplomatic Social Life	173
14	Buried Treasure	187
15	Prejudice Continues	191
16	Persecution	217
17	Double Burial	227
	Epilogue	235
	Bibliography	247
	Appendices	
	Index	

PART I
THE LINCOLN YEARS

William T. Coggeshall at age 36
Bodyguard to Lincoln, 1861

CHAPTER 1
COME WITH ME

It was Wednesday, February 13, 1861. Columbus, Ohio, twittered with excitement. President-elect Abraham Lincoln was coming to town on his triumphal, whistle-stop journey to Washington, D.C., to be inaugurated 16th president of the United States. His train was due at 2:00 p.m.

All day, under a light rain, carriages deposited crinoline-gowned ladies and top-hatted gentlemen at the grounds of the Ohio State House. People poured out of jammed clapboard boarding houses and packed hotels to get a good viewing space on the State House steps and Rotunda. Wagons crowded with farm families in hooded coats, wool caps and shawls, boots and blankets rolled in from the countryside. Trainloads of spectators arrived in the morning at the large, frame barn-like Union Station. The great crowd was gathering for a glimpse of the new President-elect who would address Ohioans and meet them at an afternoon reception.

This would be the third stop on Lincoln's journey to Washington since leaving his home in Springfield, Illinois. Already, crowds in Indianapolis and Cincinnati had greeted him.

The William T. Coggeshall family was probably one of the most excited that afternoon. William, his wife Mary, and nine-year-old daughter Jessie would meet Mr. Lincoln. As their carriage rolled toward the station the Coggeshalls could hardly know that Lincoln would drastically change their lives that day. William was the 36-year-old, brown-curly-haired, bearded secretary to Ohio Governor William T. Dennison. Coggeshall was eager to meet the President-elect at the train and help escort him to the State House. He also was to report the event in a story for the *Ohio State Journal*. Mary, 34, would describe the day's events to the three children left at home. And little Jessie would get to meet a President! What an honor!

As the crowd waited for the Presidential train, some of the Ohioans' thoughts might have flashed back to the role their state had in making Lincoln the President.

LINCOLN ELECTED PRESIDENT

At the 1860 Republican Convention in Chicago, delegates were in high gear to choose their nominee for president. On the first ballot, Lincoln had trailed behind New York Senator William E. Seward. But on the third roll call, Lincoln surged ahead. He lacked only 1½ votes to win the 233 needed for nomination.

"Joseph Medill (of the *Chicago Tribune*), who had seated himself quietly in the Ohio delegation, leaned over to whisper to David Cartter, chairman of the Ohioans: 'If you can throw the Ohio delegation to Lincoln, Chase can have anything he wants.' Cartter, a stammerer, bounded up exclaiming excitedly: 'I-I a-a-rise, Mr. Chairman, to a-a-nounce the c-ch-change of f-four votes from Mr. Chase to Mr. Lincoln.' There was a moment of silence. Then the wildest yell of all was loosed."[1] That announcement put "Honest Abe" over the top. Ohio had clinched the nomination for Lincoln.

Gradually, other states followed Ohio's lead until New York, Seward's home state, moved that Lincoln's nomination be unanimous.

Many Ohioans were partial to the lanky Illinoisan. He appealed to them because of his honesty and concern for his fellow man. Slavery was the burning issue in the presidential campaign of 1860. The Democratic party had split over the issue and produced two nominees. Northern Democrats chose a Senator from Lincoln's own state, brilliant orator Stephen A. Douglas, who advocated that each territory, not yet a state, should decide its own slavery question. Southern Democrats (the Seceders), in total support of slave trade, nominated John C. Breckenridge of Tennessee. A small third party emerged with candidate John Bell, the Constitutional Union Party, which hoped the slavery issue could be resolved without conflict.

Abraham Lincoln championed "Preserve the Union and Abolish Slavery" on his campaign across the country.

The nation elected Lincoln by only 39% of the popular vote but he obtained 180 of the total 303 electoral votes. Lincoln swept New England, New York, New Jersey, Pennsylvania, Ohio, Indiana, Illinois, Michigan, Iowa, Wisconsin, California, Minnesota, and Oregon.

---

[1]Benjamin P. Thomas, *Abraham Lincoln*, Alfred A. Knopf, New York City, 1952, p. 213.

The President-elect's determination to preserve the Union was already being put to the test. On February 4, 1861, just nine days before his appearance in Columbus and one month before his inauguration, seven states had seceded from the Union and formed the Confederacy of Southern States. The fear of war was spreading through the land.

Ohioans felt Lincoln could save the nation and they were more than curious to see the new leader whom they felt they had helped catapult into office.

It was nearly two o'clock. The train whistle brought a hush over the crowd of hundreds. They turned to watch the puffing steam engine chug slowly to a halt. Thirty-four guns boomed salute to the new chief. Hatless, the President-elect stepped onto the rear platform, his black hair catching the light rain. A loud cheer went up. Then Mrs. Lincoln, teenage sons Willie and Robert, and young Tad emerged. The Coggeshall's daughter, Jessie, met Lincoln's sons but not the President, for her father and the reception committee moved in upon Lincoln, escorting him to a waiting carriage for the five-block ride to the State House.

The President waved to the hallooing people who lined North High Street. At the State House his 6'4" frame, with his face of chiseled features, towered over the cheering throng as he climbed the west front steps of the Capitol building where Ohio Governor William Dennison greeted him. Inside, Lincoln was led up the wide marble staircase to the House of Representatives to address the Ohio Legislature.

Constantly at Lincoln's side, the agile William Coggeshall steered a path through the buzzing hive of well-wishers. In his role as escort and unofficial, self-appointed bodyguard, Coggeshall was intent on protecting the 52-year-old President-elect from harm.

At 3:45 p.m. Lincoln left the Legislative Hall, returned to the front steps to address the thousands outside, then indoors to greet the people in the State House Rotunda.

LINCOLN NAMES A BABY

Years later, Mary Coggeshall would describe, in a letter to daughter Prockie, the official reception Ohioans gave the President-elect.

> ". . . Thousands of people came. The President stood in the centre of the Rotunda surrounded by state officials and prominent men. People entered the house through the east entrance from Third Street. The people marched six abreast and as close as they [could] step. After a short time, the President was crowded from the Rotunda. . .

"I stood on the third stair, Jessie on the fourth leading to the library. . . .

"As the President was crowded from the Rotunda, Governor Dennison suggested his stepping on the stairs. I heard the remark and stepped onto the fourth stair behind Jessie.

"Mr. Lincoln took my place and from that point could easily reach the hands of the people as they passed out of the building.

"As we looked through to the east entrance, we saw something very strange approaching.

"The President looked earnestly and as the crowd arrived at the stairs, we discovered a man carrying on his upheld hands—his arms held upwards by a woman on one side and a man on the other—a beautiful babe about six months old.

"As they drew near, President Lincoln waved his hand and the crowd stopped and all were still. Then the President leaned over and took the child from his father's arms and kissed it on the forehead, then asked its name.

"'It has no name and we want you to name it,' replied the father. President Lincoln replied, 'Abraham is too long for such a wee mite of humanity and we'll call him Abram.' He then kissed him and placed him in the arms of his mother who said, 'We call him Abraham because he saved his people.'

"As she said [this] the President looked upward and a light shone in his face as he said, 'God knows best.'

"Silence reigned for a moment—then the crowd moved on, many of them with streaming eyes and heads bowed.

"As soon as all were gone, the President retired to the room of the Secretary of State to rest."[2]

COGGESHALL DESCRIBES THE DAY

William Coggeshall described that historic day, too. Besides escorting Lincoln as the governor's secretary, he was also reporting, as state librarian, for the *Ohio State Journal*. He wrote in impeccable detail.

"On the 13th, propitious weather and enthusiasm drew thousands of people together to pay their respects to the President-elect. At an early hour High Street was swarming with excited humanity. The people continued to arrive till noon, when not less than five thousand strangers were in the city.

"At about one o'clock, the military of the city, headed by Goodman's band, formed and marched to the (train) depot. Here the crowd was immense. Every eligible spot in the vicinity of the

---

[2] Mary Coggeshall, February 25, 1908, letter to daughter, Prockie, which letter is in the collection of the author.

depot buildings was black with men, women and youths, who were painfully anxious to get a glimpse of the distinguished guest whom they had assembled to honor.

"As the time for the arrival of the special train drew near, the excitement grew intense; it could be felt rather than observed through the ordinary channels; and when the train was signalled from the first bridge, and the first of the thirty-four-gun salute fired, this excitement found vent in a vigorous huzza.

"The train drove slowly up, and was at once besieged by hundreds of men wild with enthusiasm, who demanded that the President-elect should show himself. A minute or two only elapsed after the train came to a halt, when Mr. Lincoln appeared on the rear platform of the train, and with head uncovered and a pleasant smile, bowed acknowledgment of the manifestations of consideration and respect which met him on all hands. The air was rent with deafening shouts, as the President-elect passed from the train to the open carriage in waiting."[3]

A military escort and band led the march to the State House. They were followed by the President's entourage and the Ohio reception committee.

"This cavalcade," Coggeshall's article continued, "was flanked by great crowds of the excited populace, while the more staid, in buggies, with foot passengers who could not find room on the flanks, brought up the rear.

"The band discoursed the national airs with great vigor, the crowd huzzahed their irrepressible enthusiasm, and the ladies and children waved their respect from the sidewalks and windows with handkerchiefs and miniature flags.

"The western steps and portico of the State House were densely packed with an expectant throng, while the broad walks leading from the western entrance of the yard to the building, and the space immediately in front, were jammed.

"Through this dense mass of humanity, the President-elect, escorted by the reception committee, directed his way, preceded by the military, who opened up a path to the vestibule of the Capitol.

"Cheer upon cheer, hearty and deafening, followed the distinguished guest as he passed into the State House to receive the respects of the Governor and Legislature."

People on the State House lawn were "packed together as closely as pickles in a jar" but remained good natured, hoping for a speech from the President.

---

[3]William T. Coggeshall, *Lincoln Memorial,* Ohio State Journal, Columbus, Ohio, 1865, p. 44.

While the outdoor crowd waited for the indoor proceedings to conclude,

> "... one incident worthy of record occurred. The stars and stripes were elevated above the State House, and as they danced gaily in the breeze, three loud cheers were given with a will."[4]

LINCOLN ADDRESSES OHIO LEGISLATURE

In addition to members of the Ohio Senate and House, a few fortunate people had obtained passes to hear Lincoln address the State House of Representatives and swarmed in when the doors opened. "Lovely women, with the promptness of the sex on public occasions, took possession of the galleries; and when these were inundated with successive waves of crinoline," the House sergeants-at-arms bowed to the feminine floodtide and suspended the rules prohibiting entrance to women.

> "A tumult near the door of the Hall signaled the arrival of the President," Coggeshall wrote. "Mr. Lincoln entered the room, attended by Governor Dennison and the legislative committees. The legislators and spectators rose while the party advanced to the podium."[5]

Coggeshall's description in the *Ohio State Journal* continued:

> "The impression which the appearance of the President-elect created was most agreeable. His great height was conspicuous even in that crowd of goodly men, and lifted him fully in view as he walked up the aisle."

It was as he took the Speaker's stand that the crowd had a better look at the man

> "... upon whom more hopes hang than upon any other living. At first the kindness and amiability of his face strikes you; but as he speaks, the greatness and determination of his nature are apparent.
>
> "Something in his manner, even more than in his word, told how deeply he was affected by the enthusiasm of the people; and when he appealed to them for encouragement and support, every heart responded with mute assurance of both.
>
> "There was the simplicity of greatness in his unassuming and confiding manner, that won its way to instant admiration.
>
> "He looked somewhat worn with the travel and the fatigues of popularity, but warmed to the cordiality of his reception."[6]

---

[4]William T. Coggeshall, *Lincoln Memorial,* Ohio State Journal, Columbus, Ohio, 1865, pp. 44, 45.
[5]Ibid., p. 45.
[6]Ibid., pp. 47, 48.

Governor Dennison introduced Mr. Lincoln to the Legislature, and the President of the Senate gave a stirring welcoming speech.

"Mr. Lincoln responded:

"'Gentlemen of the Senate, and Citizens of Ohio: It is true, as has been said by the President of the Senate, that very great responsibility rests upon me in the position to which the votes of the American people have called me. I am deeply sensible of that weighty responsibility.

"'I cannot but know, what you all know, that without a name—perhaps without a reason why I should have a name—there has fallen upon me a task as did not rest upon the Father of his Country. And so feeling, I cannot but turn and look for the support without which it will be impossible for me to perform that great task. I turn, then, and look to the American people, and to that God who has never forsaken them.

"'Allusion has been made to the interest felt in relation to the policy of the new administration. In this I have received from some a degree of credit for having kept silence, from others some depreciation.

"'I still think I was right. In the varying and repeatedly shifting scenes of the present, without a precedent which could enable me to judge for the past, it has seemed fitting that before speaking upon the difficulties of the country I should have gained a view of the whole field. To be sure, after all, I would be at liberty to modify and change the course of policy as future events might make a change necessary.

"'I have not maintained silence [about policy of my administration] from any want of real anxiety, for there is nothing going wrong.

"'It is a consoling circumstance that when we look out, there is nothing that really hurts anybody.

"'We entertain different views upon political questions, but nobody is suffering anything. This is a most consoling circumstance, and from it, I judge that all we want is time and patience and a reliance on that God who has never forsaken this people.

"'Unless sustained by the American people and by God, I cannot hope to be successful.'"

"The speeches were listened to with attention," Coggeshall reported, "and received with deep feeling. At the conclusion of Mr. Lincoln's remarks the applause was quick and hearty."[7]

Reporter Coggeshall went through a pocketful of freshly sharpened pencils in jotting down Lincoln's every word.

---

[7]William T. Coggeshall, *Lincoln Memorial,* Ohio State Journal, Columbus, Ohio, 1865, pp. 46, 47.

"HONEST ABE" ADDRESSES THE PEOPLE

After his speech in the House, the President went to the front steps of the Capitol to address the thousands of people still waiting in a light mist. The President-elect referred to the "few broken remarks" he had just made to the "General Assembly of the great state of Ohio." Then Lincoln, obviously impressed by the size of his welcome, told his outdoor audience:

"'Judging from what I see, I infer that the reception was one without party distinction, and one of entire kindness—one that had nothing in it beyond a feeling of the citizenship of the United States of America.

"'Knowing, as I do, that any crowd drawn together as this has been, is made up of the citizens near about, and that in this county of Franklin, there is great difference of political sentiment, and those agreeing with me having a little the shortest row; from this and the circumstances I have mentioned, I infer that you do me the honor to meet me here without distinction of party. I think this is as it should be.

"'Many of you were not favorable to the election of myself to the Presidency, were favorable to the election of the distinguished Senator [Douglas] from the State in which I reside. If Senator Douglas had been elected to the Presidency in the late contest, I think my friends would have joined heartily in meeting and greeting him on his passage through your Capitol, as you have me today.

"'If any of the other candidates had been elected, I think it would have been altogether becoming and proper for all to have joined in showing honor quite as well to the office and the country as to the man . . .

"'We have a large country and a large future before us, and the manifestations of good will towards the Government, and affection for the Union, which you may exhibit, are of immense value to you and your posterity forever.'"[8]

RECEPTION IN THE ROTUNDA

With his breast pocket full of dulled pencils, Coggeshall returned behind the outdoor rostrum to break a path through the dense crowd for the President-elect to attend the Reception inside the Rotunda. His story in the *Ohio State Journal* continued:

"The speaking concluded, hand-shaking commenced. Mr. Lincoln took his position in the Rotunda near the stairway leading

---

[8]William T. Coggeshall, *Lincoln Memorial,* Ohio State Journal, Columbus, Ohio, 1865, pp. 48, 49.

to the Library, and the people admitted at the south door, passed through and out at the north door.

"Almost immediately the vast Rotunda was crowded with eager, turbulent, pushing, crowding, jostling sovereigns, frantic to wrench the hand of the President-elect.

"An attempt was made to preserve a lane through which the hand-shakers might pass to Mr. Lincoln, and furious and heroic were the struggles to keep this avenue open. With a sublime devotion which demands highest praise, a few spartans held back the crowd, which heaved and surged to and fro.

"For a while the President greeted the people with his right hand only, but as the officers gave way before the irresistible crowd, he shook hands right and left, with astonishing rapidity.

"The physical exertion must have been tremendous. People plunged at his arms with frantic enthusiasm, and all the infinite variety of shakes, from the wild and irrepressible pump-handle movement to the dead grip, was executed upon the devoted sinister and dexter of the President.

"Some glanced into his face as they grasped his hand; others invoked the blessings of heaven upon him; others affectionately gave him their last gasping assurance of devotion; others, bewildered and furious, with hats crushed over their eyes, seized his hand in a convulsive grasp, and passed on as if they had not the remotest idea who, what, or where they were, nor what anything was at all about.

"But at last the performance became intolerable to the President, who retired to the stair-case in exhaustion, and contented himself with looking at the crowd as it swept before him. It was a very good-natured crowd, nothing occurred to mar the harmony of the occasion, and the utmost enthusiasm prevailed."[9]

"Late in the afternoon Lincoln learned that the electoral votes [had] been counted and that he [was] now president."[10]

LINCOLN KISSES JESSIE

Coggeshall's wife Mary, who had given her place on the third step of the staircase to Mr. Lincoln, would continue her letter to Prockie, written years later, describing the Reception and its ending:

"As soon as all were gone, the President retired to the room of the Secretary of State to rest.

---

[9] William T. Coggeshall, *Lincoln Memorial,* Ohio State Journal, Columbus, Ohio, 1865, pp. 49, 50.
[10] Paul M. Angle, *Lincoln Day By Day 1854-1861,* Abraham Lincoln Association, Springfield, Ill., 1933, p. 372.

"*[Daughter] Jessie and I were going home but she wanted to shake hands with a President. Her father [Coggeshall] took us to see him. When her father presented her, [the President] bowed and, taking her hand over to kiss her said, 'My dear, when you grow to be a young lady, you can say that Abraham Lincoln bowed himself half way to the ground to kiss you.'*

"*Looking up in his, her beautiful eyes filled with tears, and he, still holding her hand, she replied, 'Yes sir, and I promise you that no one shall ever kiss me where you have just left your kiss.'*

"*He looked at her a moment then said while his eyes were looking upward, 'God knows best.'*

"*Immediately he turned to Mr. Coggeshall and said, 'Come with me to Washington and I shall go safely.'*"[11]

---

[11] Mary Coggeshall February 25, 1908, letter, in the collection of the author.

CHAPTER 2
LINCOLN's INAUGURAL TRAIN

On the morning of Thursday, February 14, 1861, William Coggeshall was aboard the flag-draped, flower-trimmed train taking President-elect Abraham Lincoln to Washington.

The happy Ohio official settled into his green velour, straight-backed seat as the steam engine puffed slowly out of Columbus' Union Station. We can imagine he might have put together the pieces of his life, trying to understand why Lincoln had impulsively invited him to Washington. "Come with me and I shall go safely," Lincoln had said.

It had been so simple and fast.

As the train lurched toward Pittsburgh, Coggeshall would travel back into the state of his birth.

COGGESHALL'S HERITAGE

William was born September 6, 1824, in Lewistown, Pennsylvania. Those were the frontier days of Indians, coonskin caps and hard cider. There were no railways then. It was travel by horseback, canal boat, wagons, horse and buggy, carriages and dirt roads. Communication was by long-delayed letters carried in saddlebags on horseback.

Men felled the trees of the forests to build wood settlements for their families. Women swished around in long, homespun dresses, cooked on wood-burning stoves or at the open hearth, and nourished their families from their own vegetable gardens. They washed clothing by hand on a scrubboard and carried water by bucket from a well or spring, heating it on an open fire for laundry and Saturday night baths. Children studied by candlelight or by the light of the open fire.

Pioneers and frontiersmen had conquered a wilderness, won a revolution, and formed a new nation, the United States. In the year of

William's birth, 1824, brave men were still exploring, opening up virgin territories, and carving their own kinds of free government in a developing nation.

Coggeshall doubtless had fond memories of the Saturday night baths shared with many brothers and sisters. The third of twelve children, he was named for his father, William. Proudly, father William told his offspring they were "descended from the first president of the State of Rhode Island, John Coggeshall. John had come to America in 1632 and suffered some persecution in Massachusetts Bay because of his support of Anne Hutchinson" who was "banished from the colony for religious heresy."[1]

Father William had married a woman of German descent, Eliza Grotz. When young William was born, the father was a promising businessman who owned a "carriage manufactory."

Little William was an obviously precocious boy, so his parents placed him in boarding school early. A biographer would later note that "by some [William Coggeshall] was considered rather truant than studious until time had passed and he had numbered 13 years."[2] The parents apparently sensed an insatiable appetite for learning in the boy's curious questioning and constant jotting of notes on what he saw. They decided to prepare their 13-year-old for a thorough college education. William's father had acquired a partner and enlarged his wagon and carriage factory to include an iron foundry and could afford to educate his son. The prospect encouraged William and he commenced devoting himself "continually and industriously" to his studies.

The foundry did not do well, however, and William soon had to leave his books and go to work in the paint shop of the "manufactory." The boy didn't enjoy painting, but did his job well.

In time, his father was again able to afford a formal education for the lad and sent William to an "advanced school" [academy] about 150 miles north of Lewistown in Chenango County, New York. He was there only four months when his father's business again dropped and he had to return home.

The ups and downs in his early life may have helped prepare William Coggeshall for the adventure that began abruptly when he agreed to board the Inaugural Train carrying Lincoln to Washington.

---

[1] Anne Hutchinson, English-born religious teacher, taught that salvation came through God's Grace, not good works. Most colony clergy disagreed, tried her, and banished her in 1637. She moved to Rhode Island, then New York. Killed by Indians.
[2] T. Herbert Whipple, *Chicago Budget*, 1852.

The Inaugural Train had started its journey in Lincoln's home city of Springfield, Illinois, on Monday, February 11.

The train arrived in Pittsburgh in a downpour on Thursday, February 14, and Coggeshall kept eyewitness notes. He recorded:

> "In a pelting rain . . . the party proceeded in carriages to the Monongahela House where Mr. Lincoln addressed a huge crowd. . . . He remarked that if all these energetic, whole-souled people whom he saw before him were for the preservation of the Union, he did not see how it could be in danger."[3]

The crowd cheered this optimism, Coggeshall noted, replying with the chant, "Union and No Compromise."

In Pittsburgh, Coggeshall overheard Lincoln express an attitude typical of the leader fondly known as "Honest Abe:"

> "'There is really no crisis springing from anything in the Government itself,'" the President-elect said. "'There is no crisis except such a one as may be gotten up at any time by turbulent men, aided by designing politicians. My advice, then, under such circumstances, is to keep cool. If the American people will only keep their temper on both sides of the line, the trouble will come to an end.'"[4]

The steam engine puffed back across the Ohio border and headed for Cleveland. At Alliance, Ohio, a Mr. McCullough, president of the railroad,[5] gave the inaugural party "an elegant dinner. Salutes were fired, smashing windows including the one at which Mrs. Lincoln sat during dinner. The band played national airs and an elegant company of Zouaves [Union soldiers wearing brightly colored French-style uniforms with flowing jackets] stood guard."[6]

This incident indicated to Coggeshall a reason why he might be on the train. A president-elect always needed protection and wanted men around him with whom he felt safe. Lincoln most certainly must have felt safe with William Coggeshall. When he invited the young man to go to Washington, Lincoln had said, "Come with me and I shall go safely." Coggeshall was a hand-picked bodyguard.

---

[3]William T. Coggeshall, *Lincoln Memorial,* Ohio State Journal, Columbus, Ohio, 1865, p. 52.
[4]Ibid. p. 54.
[5]This was taken from Coggeshall's own writing. The railroad official was probably J. N. McCullough of the Pittsburgh, Ft. Wayne and Chicago Railway.
[6]William T. Coggeshall, *Lincoln Memorial,* Ohio State Journal, Columbus, Ohio, 1865, p. 55.

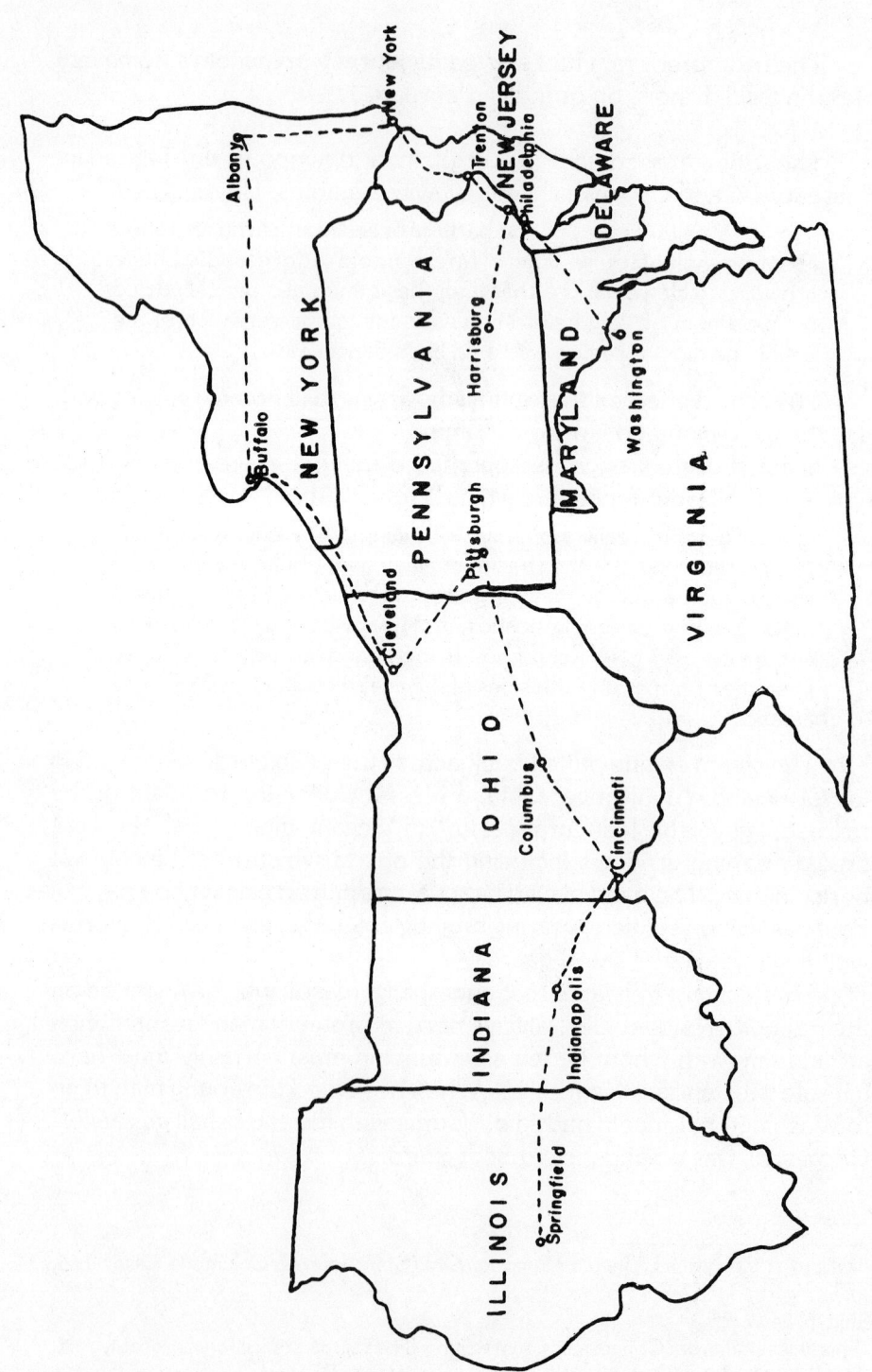

Lincoln's inaugural trip, February 11–23, 1861.

As the train steamed through northeastern Ohio, windmills, barns, blacksmith shops, and snowswept fields dotted the landscape. And one-room schoolhouses like the one where Coggeshall had taught.

TEACHER AT 19

When William was 18 his father had moved the family to Akron, Ohio, to start anew. At 19, young Coggeshall struck out on his own to teach in an Akron District School. But he was more fascinated with recording his trials and tribulations of "teaching young minds how to shoot" than in the doing. The young schoolmaster kept numerous diaries full of memos signed with his initials, W.T.C. He put his daily reflections in "A Leaf From the Portfolio of a District School Teacher, Akron, February 20, 1843" and signed it "by V.G.," one of the youthful pretentious pseudonyms he used.

The teenage teacher had been tall and thin—and the same age as some of his students. But they quickly learned who was in command. On the very first day of school Coggeshall cured one tough, brutish lad of obstinacy. The boy had refused to read. Coggeshall gave him three minutes to start "and he read not. Grabbing him by the collar I twitched him from the bench and soon made him utter forth sounds expressive of the most heartfelt anguish. I then told him to read, which he seemed perfectly willing to do—and amid sobs and snuffles we murdered another verse. *That boy never refused to read afterwards for me and the rest profited by his example.*"[7]

How different the last day of school that year had been. Young freshly scrubbed swains wearing collars stiffly starched to their ears and giggly, ribboned, pig-tailed girls in Sunday School best shed tears at bidding the young schoolmaster farewell. "I gazed upon these symbolic prattlers . . . but felt that with the weeping crowd I could not sympathise [sic]. One by one the mourners withdrew and as the sound of the last goodbye fell upon my ear, my heart leaped for joy. I now bade the old palace a long lasting farewell—and turned my footsteps toward the director's house with whom I was to settle for duties during the last three months. . . . The next day I took my last look of the seat of my pedagogic apprenticeship, bid a long farewell to friends and enemies— and with a heart much lighter than I had had three months previous, strolled over the hills, and through the vales on my homeward route."[8]

After just three months, the erstwhile teacher became restless and moved back into town to pursue his own education.

---

[7] William T. Coggeshall Papers, Ohio Historical Society.
[8] Ibid.

Coggeshall had decided to study law and arranged his own program in the Akron law office of L. V. Beirce. There he could pore over pages of legal authorities. But after three months in the annals of Coke and Blackstone, he concluded that he could not "assimilate the dry logic of one and the acute syllogisms of the other." So he "threw legal quips and quiddities to the winds."[9]

PUBLISHER OF TEMPERANCE NEWSPAPERS

The young man then turned to writing, to couple his favorite pastime with a growing sense of moral outrage at what he termed the disgrace of his time—alcohol. He became a crusading moralist.

> "The 18th century had been a hard-drinking century. Alcoholic over-indulgence was more or less socially acceptable. There were well-known alcoholics in positions of public trust. Cider, beer, wine, and whiskey were cheap. . . . Belief in liquor's medicinal values made it a common household remedy for many ills."[10]

In the 19th century, alarm over the social abuses resulting from alcohol spread quickly. Liquor was destroying family life, attacking human rights and, because of absenteeism, affecting production in factories. Alcohol lured men to corner saloons after work, during work, nighttimes. It was their milk and honey. It kept them from their families. It took their money. It affected their ability to vote. Alcohol left many males in a drunken stupor. They abused their wives, their children. They cursed them. They battered them. Their wages intended for food and clothing went to drink. Sometimes children had to steal to eat.

Women began temperance crusades in their homes and communities. They took up banners and marched into saloons. They prayed in saloons. They chanted, "Lips that touch liquor shall never touch mine." They were kicked, abused, and drenched with slop. Women generally found unresponsiveness in saloons, so began approaching local lawmakers and legislators.

Temperance groups began springing up. By the early 1830s there were 5,000 Temperance Societies in the United States. Some were The Sons of Temperance, The Washington Temperance Society, and Total Abstainers. Much of their motivation came from the churches. They conducted their crusades with missionary zeal, held revival meetings,

---

[9]T. Herbert Whipple, *Chicago Budget*, 1852.
[10]Russel Blaine Nye, *Society and Culture in America, 1830–1860*, Harper & Row, New York, Evanston, Ill., San Francisco, London, 1974, p. 48.

published pamphlets, gave essay prizes, established "Temperance Hotels." Converted drunkards were popular speakers.

But this was not enough. Besides the moral approach, temperance societies sought political help. In 1838, Massachusetts passed an act regulating liquor sales and several states instigated local-option laws, but enforcing them was difficult. In 1840, Massachusetts repealed its liquor sales law of 1838.

The abuses resulting from alcohol were contrary to the way William Coggeshall had been reared. He wanted to help the victims of drink. He started raising his voice—and his pen.

In Akron, he had drafted the Constitution of the Juvenile Temperance Society for the Methodist Church Sabbath School and had spoken against the "devil" drink at town meetings where he was thunderously applauded.

Eager Coggeshall got a job as head clerk and assistant editor of the Akron temperance paper, *A Wit, a Wag and a Painter*. At age 21, he bought an interest in the paper, which was owned by a man named Samuel A. Lane. It flourished and, as the list of subscribers grew, he and Lane gave speeches all over northern Ohio about the "evil of the 19th century—liquor."

That same year of 1845, young Coggeshall met and fell in love with 19-year-old Mary Maria Carpenter, the daughter of Dr. Jesse Page Carpenter and Phoebe Girard Carpenter, who had moved to Ohio from Vermont. William and Mary were married in Akron on Sunday, October 26, 1845.

Mary was a refined young woman with delicate features and long black hair which she would sometimes "crimp." William loved that she was compassionate, stable, and of strong will. His young bride brought a balance to his own restless desire to create, his dreaminess, and often fiery nature.

After just a year and a half at the *Wig, Wag, and a Painter*, Coggeshall bought out his partner, hired a co-worker named Drew, and changed the name of the paper to *Teetotal Mechanic*, a workingman's temperance paper.

In a few months, the 22-year-old editor moved to the larger city of Cleveland. There, with B. F. Pinkham, he started *The Ohio Temperance Artisan* on the promise of backing from wealthy teetotalers. But when loans matured in a few months, Coggeshall's wealthy friends bowed out.

He was thoroughly disgusted and disillusioned that his "friends" could leave the cause against alcohol. Hope for the campaign came from New England. Maine passed a state prohibition law in 1846, the first state to do so. There was crying need for his temperance journal,

Coggeshall felt. He decided to leave the *Artisan* in his partner's control while he set out on a lecture tour to earn his own money for the paper.

Coggeshall's lectures on temperance were filled with glittering similes. Excerpts from one example of his outlines show his line of attack:

"TEMPERANCE LECTURE

Ladies and Gentlemen:

Progress of Temperance
Change of Customs—Fireside—Parties, etc.
Operation of Alcohol
Educational View
Physical, Moral and Intellectual Effect
Perfectly Indigestible
Slow But Sure Poison
Tobacco Illustration
Alcohol the Same
. . . . .
No man wishes to become a drunkard, etc.
It is like the approaches of death
. . . . .
Fire good in its place—Swallowing it
No man ever benefitted
. . . . .
Destroys the seller as well as the Drinker
Rumsellers in the Penitentiary—Squire Wells
The Kind of System
Playing with fire—The Corpse
Beating a neighbor—Horse Stealing
Counterfeiting—coin as well as men
The right to legalize—villainy
. . . . .
Effect of Legislation on Rumsellers
'Laugh but you're hit'
Objections to—flaws in all laws
Too big a boo! for such a little house
Rumies objections—Hypocrisy
. . . . .
If all who profess good citizenship
Influence of wealth, fashion, etc.
Want Consistency
. . . . .
Let the cry go forth!"[11]

---

[11]William T. Coggeshall Papers, Ohio Historical Society.

Coggeshall was an impressive speaker. A Chicago newspaperman of the period reported that the crusader was "a gentleman, every inch of him—about five feet ten inches in stature—slim—dark hair, that inclines to curl—light beard and moustache—dark eyes—rather delicate features—quick and nervous in his motions—walks rapidly—dresses plainly, usually in black, and wears no jewelry or other 'fancys' [sic]—smokes no cigars—drinks no rum—belongs to no organized society, of a religious, reformatory or political character—and, although not a graduate of any college or academy, writes down his name as 'SCHOLAR.'"[12]

Though not a diplomaed scholar, Coggeshall had the ability to observe, in vivid detail and with some moralizing, the life in his developing nation.

The itinerant temperance advocate lectured his cause for several weeks for the *Poughkeepsie (N.Y.) Blacksmith* and was warmly received. But because the lecturing kept him moving and was unprofitable, he abandoned it for a more stationary way of life and more time with his young bride.

Coggeshall congratulated himself on his choice of a wife. At first, Mary remonstrated at what she called her husband's "awayness" but soon learned to accept his early life as an itinerant reporter and lecturer and came to encourage it. Like his parents earlier, she saw his thirst for knowledge, recognized his moral verve and enabled him to grow. Early, she coped with the demands on her lecturer-publisher husband. She would send William off on assignments at a moment's notice, often not knowing when she would see him again. She knew he was only struggling to make a living and a career. In their early years the Coggeshalls were often so plagued with financial problems that at times, William once said, the couple was "near starvation."

Mary spent many lonely nights beside her open fire. She waited patiently for William to return. She knew he had trials along with much ambition. She was eager to support him and his special talents.

EXPANDING JOURNALISM CAREER

Journalism was flourishing in the important midwest city of Cincinnati, Ohio, in the mid-1800s so William and Mary moved there in 1847. He was 23. But many other striving writers were also there. Painfully, William recalled that it took "six weeks of dodging of want and starvation" before he was hired as assistant editor of the *Daily Queen City*. For eleven months he worked hard to earn six dollars a week.

---

[12]T. Herbert Whipple, *Chicago Budget*, 1852.

Then he moved to the *Cincinnati Daily Times* where he became a "local" (columnist) at nine dollars a week.

While working at the *Queen City* the aspiring author began one of the most enjoyable periods of his writing career. He wrote personal sketches and stories under the name of "Lucius Markham." Of all of Coggeshall's pseudonyms, this was his favorite and he used it for many years at many newspapers. He sent copies of his stories to the *New York Tribune* and to other journals including the *Boston New Englander*. They printed his pieces.

Sometimes his stories were happy, sometimes sad, but most always, moralistic. One true story was about Ellen Artain. She was the slimmest girl in town—an hourglass figure—the envy of all. She kept her slim waist by removing her tightly laced corset only on Saturday night to bathe. Ellen got the strings pulled super-tight by fastening them to a heavy cord hooked to a window frame, throwing her weight upon the cord and then—squash! She was laced in—hardly able to breathe—but thin, thin. Ellen caught the most eligible bachelor in town. On her wedding day she resorted to the same window-cord, tight-lacing technique when suddenly her corset strings broke and she fell to the floor. Weeks later she was able to be married but because of her injury and near starvation from her obsession with tight-lacing, she never regained strength and died in two years.

Coggeshall wrote, "This is a true tale. The circumstances were told by the Mary who is one of its characters, and who is now a respectable old maid, with a thick waist, but who might have been a bride had she been willing to take the place Ellen Artain left vacant. . . . This pernicious practice . . . has not been entirely abolished. In various forms it is yet destroying the health and strength of mothers and daughters; and those facts which illustrate its great evils should be reiterated till its complete abolition is accomplished."[13]

Coggeshall's stories were widely printed. Soon, his newspaper salary was increased to a fat ten dollars a week. The eager writer then joined the *Cincinnati Gazette* whose associate editor was the famous William D. Gallagher.[14] The *Gazette* published his first story of any length and literary merit. Entitled "Oakshaw: A Tale of Avarice," it won

---

[13] William T. Coggeshall, *Easy Warren and His Cotemporaries* [sic], Redfield, 110–112 Nassau St., New York, 1854, p. 184.

[14] Gallagher (author, editor, publisher, poet) championed the importance of Western writers and poets. Was once secretary to Salmon P. Chase; associate editor *Ohio State Journal* (1838); editor/owner *Louisville Daily Courier;* and publisher of three volumes of collective poetry.

the third-place $50 prize in a contest sponsored by the *Louisville Courier*. Coggeshall's career star was climbing.

The Inaugural Train jolted. It puffed through crossroads, hamlets, and towns en route to Cleveland. Hundreds of people lined the railroad tracks and waved.

Delight! Delight! William and Mary's first child was born in Cincinnati on June 22, 1849. It was a boy, Willie West. With the new responsibilities of fatherhood, the happy author pushed his short story pen even harder!

Alarmed over what he saw as the spreading moral decadence in the midwest and the need for social reforms in 1850, Coggeshall accepted the post as editor of *The Western Fountain* which he described as an "excellent Temperance paper" in Cincinnati.

Coggeshall's appointment won the notice of other journalists. "This gentleman has wide popularity, is an energetic and fine writer over the nome de plume of 'Lucius Markham' and will be a favorite with readers," the *Columbian and Great West* reported on the appointment. But after a year, *The Fountain* failed due to lack of funds.

Coggeshall was distressed at closing the doors on a temperance newspaper for the second time. Such failure only spurred him to try harder to heighten public awareness of what he felt were society's ills—liquor, child labor, inadequate education, youth begging and thievery, dishonesty in politics, poor working conditions, and slavery. He hoped that some day, besides writing commentary on such conditions, he could become part of the political process and do something about them. For the time being, however, he contented himself with directing his views toward helping young people establish moral values. His writings became very popular.

Coggeshall was heartened in his temperance efforts when, by 1855, all of New England and every state from Ohio to Iowa was dry. New York passed a law which was immediately tied up in litigation. New Jersey and Maryland held out and it was never an issue in the South. . . . "The American conscience was never again easy with liquor; drinking habits changed, control was established over the trade, and social acceptance of the drinker was never so certain again."[15]

Some temperance efforts slipped during the Civil War, but afterwards, a federal law requiring a license to sell liquor was passed in 1866.

---

[15]Russel Blaine Nye, *Society and Culture in America, 1830–1860,* Harper & Row, New York, Evanston, San Francisco, London, 1974, p. 50.

And the struggling Women's Christian Temperance Union (WCTU) gained enough strength to become national in 1874.

MORALIST

Coggeshall had grown up with 11 brothers and sisters and appreciated his parents' recognition of each child's worth. Through the ups and downs of the father's carriage business, the parents always managed to instill a sense of social consciousness in their children.

In addition to the temperance issue there were other social ills the committed crusader saw and felt his duty to pierce with the point of his pen. One of his concerns was for the plight of children in the mid-1800s. In "My Ragged School," circa 1851, he criticized public education:

> "The ragged school of the court, under my window, is where boys and girls learn to shoot marbles, to fly kites, to steal store-boxes for firewood, to swear, to pitch pennies, and to cheat dexterously.... Some sell matches, some gather rags and papers out of the sewers, some sell oranges and apples, others toothpicks or envelopes. They are all sharp at a bargain and know how to make change—that is their only book learning....
>
> "I sometimes ask myself whether it were not *cheaper* for society to protect these children now, than be obliged to sustain criminal courts and prisons to protect society from their sharpness when they have grown up....
>
> "It is the duty of government to provide that all children *may* be educated—it is the duty of society to provide that all children *can* be educated."[16]

For the births of their next two children, Mary returned to the Akron area for care by her father, Dr. Jesse Carpenter, while Coggeshall was on a cross-country assignment with noted Hungarian patriot, Louis Kossuth. Jessie Austrace, the Coggeshall's first daughter, was born in Medina County September 22, 1851. She was named for Mary's father. (In her teens, Jessie would become an international hostess.)

Eighteen months later, Mary bore a second son, Turner, in Medina County on April 14, 1853. During this time Coggeshall was completing one of his first books, *Easy Warren and His Cotemporaries*[17] [sic], a group of short stories painting the hardships, hazards, and happiness of frontier life. It was published in 1854 under his favorite pen name, Lucius Markham, and he dedicated it "TO WILLIE, JESSIE, AND TURNER."

---

[16]William T. Coggeshall, *Home Hits and Hints*, Redfield, 34 Beekman St., New York, 1859, pp. 333-338.

[17]*Easy Warren* was widely published in England.

But Turner died at age two (cause of death unknown) and, despite the arrival of a fourth baby, Mary Maria (Mamie), born in Cincinnati February 17, 1856, Coggeshall still grieved the loss of little Turner. In the frontispiece to his next book of short stories, *Home Hits and Hints,* 1859, Coggeshall memorialized his lost son:

> "A gap is in our fireside ring,
> The wideness of a little tomb;
> A prattle such as robins sing,
> Has faded out of every room."

The death of baby Turner was a sad day for William and Mary. He wrote tender pieces about their loss.

Coggeshall undoubtedly reflected more about the reason "why" he was on the Inaugural Train. It is not beyond belief that, winding through the crowd on the State House steps of Columbus, Lincoln might have felt the young man leading him bore a personal loyalty to him.

CORRESPONDENT FOR PRESTIGIOUS NEWSPAPERS

Coggeshall's cross-country train ride in 1861 was not his first. In 1852, at age 28, he had gone to Cleveland for the *Cincinnati Daily Times* to cover the visit of Louis Kossuth, the revolutionary leader and first president of Hungary (April-August, 1848). Kossuth was visiting the United States to solicit aid for Hungary's continuing battle for independence from Austria, which was aided by the Russians. Kossuth was a big man and great orator with booming voice. He attracted huge crowds wherever he spoke. Coggeshall's reporting was so good that Kossuth asked him "to be his secretary" and to cover the rest of his American tour. During the tour, the young journalist's reports were also filed in the *New York Times, New York Tribune, Boston Commonwealth, The St. Louis Republican, Ohio Statesman,* and *Cincinnati Columbian and Great West.*

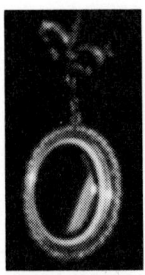

Tiger eye brooch, gift to Mary Coggeshall from Louis Kossuth, ex-president of Hungary.

After the tour, Kossuth sent the young man gifts he would always prize: a gold pen which Kossuth invited Coggeshall "to use in Hungary" if the country had to fight for freedom again; a letter of praise for Coggeshall's reporting with "untiring assiduity and rare intellectual skill" and a stunning brooch with a 1½" tiger eye stone, for Mary. It was inscribed: "SOUVENIR—To Mrs. W. T. Coggeshall, Kossuth & Suite 1852."

That train trip gave the ambitious journalist a chance to see the United States. He compiled a lengthy biography about Kossuth but never found time to organize and publish it.

A fulfilling job Coggeshall had in Cincinnati was as editor and publisher of the monthly magazine, *Genius of the West,* 1853-56. He loved printing stories and poems by Western authors. They needed more exposure, he felt, and *Genius* provided a vehicle for them. He wrote articles for it using his favorite pseudonym, Lucius Markham.

LIBRARIAN FOR OHIO

In 1856, at age 32, Coggeshall became part-time secretary to Governor Salmon P. Chase and was appointed official librarian of Ohio, one of his most important career achievements. Governor Chase rewarded the young journalist who had portrayed the life of the times with fastidious attention to detail. Coggeshall's new duties were to keep the official records for the State of Ohio and acquire writings by Ohioans to add to the cultural heritage of the state.

Eager at his official post, the happy author-librarian roamed the meager stacks of his new domain on the second floor of the State House in Columbus.

Now William Coggeshall was in politics. Now he might get a chance to correct society's ills.

The official records were sorely lacking in works about the West or by Western authors. Coggeshall determined to increase the size of the library. Most writings in his time, whether fiction, poetry, or historical, were credited to the authors from the Eastern United States. Coggeshall agreed with his former employer, *Cincinnati Gazette* editor William D. Gallagher, that Western writers were ignored because an eastern clique dominated publishing and critical circles.

Young Coggeshall resolved that now he would do something to highlight Western authors and "get a rise out of those east coast journalists dominated by Griswold and Duyckincks."[18]

---

[18]Ralph Coggeshall Busbey Papers, in the collection of the author.

GENIUS OF THE WEST.

VOL. III. CINCINNATI, OCTOBER, 1854. NO. 4.

A LITTLE HISTORY—WITH A LITTLE COMMENT.

BY LUCIUS MARKHAM.

It may often be profitable to rehearse familiar history and deduce reflections therefrom, on little themes. Be not driven then, considerate reader, to fling the book in a corner, when I announce that I have a little history and a little comment to give you on a theme which very many people think 'flat, stale and unprofitable.'

Intemperance is an ancient 'invention.' We can trace manifestations of the uncareful use of that which will intoxicate, to a period so remote that mists fall thick around the deeds of all men, except those who were Kings, Leaders or Representative Heroes.

Savage nations, from which modern navigators and travelers have lifted the veil of obscurity, are found to have among *them*, customs which 'come down from former generations,' that bear striking relations to those habits civilization encourages for the promotion of social sympathy—which the fashions of our times permit, that the heart may be glad an hour, though at the risk of life-time regrets. Distillation, however, is not a discovery heavily hoary with age.

The venerable men of Israel—the ancient Egyptians—the sedate Romans—the learned Greeks who grew 'mellow' on festive occasions, or during the excitement of State Ceremonies, knew no more, philosophically, of that subtile principle, which lurked in the ruby draughts they imbibed—that principle we call Alcohol—than they did of the capacity for wonder-working, belonging to that mysterious agent by which we talk to our friends, thousands of miles distant, and receive their answers with the instant they are spoken.

Assuredly the Shepherds of ancient Isreal heard the thunder, and saw the lightnings flash, but they watched their flocks with tender care, and entertained no speculations whether the terrifying commotion in the heavens might be turned to practical account.

Not any of them, I'll venture, had even the remotest leaning toward an idea that he might fly a kite into the storm-cloud and take the lightning in his hand, and make it talk for him to his fellow shepherds on remote hills. When the storms were pent up these men of simple wants had their feasts and they were 'mellow;' yet they sought out no inventions by which they might intensify the power of their '*good wine*' *to drown care.*

They were satisfied with natural processes, and among them the warnings of the wise Poet of the Proverbs were sufficient:

"Who hath woe? who hath sorrow? who hath

William T. Coggeshall (standing)—Librarian, State of Ohio, 1856–1861.

LITERARY LIGHT OF HIS TIME

In 1860 Coggeshall became private secretary to newly elected Ohio Governor William Dennison. The same year, two of the journalist's dreams came true. Dream One, to improve education, bore fruit when he was chosen editor of the *Ohio Education Monthly,* publication of the Ohio Teacher's Association. Dream Two, to highlight Western authors, came true when his *Poets and Poetry of the West* was published. In the 688-page volume he included poems covering half a century from 1789 to 1860. He incorporated brief biographical sketches and some critical analysis of 152 "Western" poets—97 men and 55 women—from Michigan, Ohio, Indiana, Wisconsin, Illinois, Kentucky, Missouri, Minnesota, and Kansas.

The ambitious anthology included poems by Coggeshall's mentor, newspaper editor William D. Gallagher, and Frances Dana Gage, daughter of one founder of Marietta, Ohio, woman's activist, mother of eight, with six sons in the Civil War, and first woman journalist to become a nurse in the War. Her poems were jewels, in both form and fact. After her husband, a Congressman from Zanesville, Ohio, suffered a concussion and disability from a silver-headed cane wielded by a pro-slavery Congressman from the South, Mrs. Gage's poems for *The Ladies Repository* and editorship of the *Ohio Cultivator* supported her family.

Poets and Poetry of the West, a massive compilation, had taken the persistent author years to collect. It is a fascinating mirror of pioneer and frontier life. The *Dictionary of American Biography* calls the work "a valuable record of poets . . . for what in those days was called the West."[19] It made Coggeshall a literary light of his time.

The year 1860 was full of blessings for William Coggeshall. Besides the two career achievements, he and Mary had a fifth child, Harriet Eliza (Hattie), born in Columbus, May 25.

LECTURER OF NOTE

As librarian for Ohio, Coggeshall increased the number of volumes on the shelves, a portion being his own lectures. He received many speaking engagements. Besides talking about the contents of the library and the need for preserving Western literature, each speech gave Coggeshall another opportunity to continue his social crusade and to provide more income for his growing family. One newspaper report

---

[19]*Dictionary of American Biography,* Vol. II, Brearly to Cushing; edited by Allen Johnson and Dumas Malone, Chas. Scribner's Sons, New York, 1957, p. 272.

Now Ready.

THE POETS AND POETRY

OF

THE WEST.

With Biographical and Critical Notices.

WM. T. COGGESHALL
OHIO STATE LIBRARIAN, EDITOR.

This volume, which will be printed from new type, on heavy calendered paper, has been in course of preparation for several years, and is the first of a series designed to afford a complete survey of the Literature of the Great West.

"The Poets and Poetry" will not only contain the gems of poetry produced in the West, but it will fairly represent the respectable poetical literature of Kentucky, Ohio, Indiana, Illinois, Michigan, Missouri, Wisconsin, Iowa, Minnesota and Kansas.

The biographical notices of leading poets are elaborate, and are from the pens of well-known writers. The book will, therefore, present important materials for a literary history of the Western States.

More than one hundred and fifty poets are represented.

The publishers feel confident that a work of so much intrinsic importance, and relative interest, cannot fail to receive general attention. Every Western man of intelligence desires some such compendium of Western Poetry; and the book should be in all the public libraries of the vast region from which its materials have been drawn.

It will contain about 700 royal octavo pages, handsomely bound in half Roan. Price $3.25.

Agents Wanted in every County in the "Great West."

Applications for agencies should be made immediately. Address

FOLLETT, FOSTER & CO., Columbus, O.

Ad from the publisher for *Poets and Poetry of the West.* For this volume, Coggeshall was deemed "Literary light of his time."

describes him as "having an electrifying effect on audience; he received a $20 stipend for a speech to which admission.

On Friday, February 15, 1861, the train stopped in Cleveland. There, Coggeshall noted, Lincoln was greeted by a parade that included a "full-rigged ship decorated with national flags, and manned by stalwart tars, the representatives of the lake shipping interest."[20]

The fiery orator's lectures were widely copied and reprinted from New York to San Francisco on a wide range of topics. A few were: "Cash and Character," on the conduct of persons in high positions, 1855; "Temperance;" "The Need and Availability of the Writing and Spelling Reform" in 1857; "The Protective Policy in Literature," 1858; and "The Issue of the November Election" delivered in October, 1860, one month before Lincoln was elected president. In this lecture Coggeshall strongly supported Lincoln's effort to preserve the Union and abolish slavery. He spoke out boldly for these goals.

Other of Coggeshall's works were well known. *The Newspaper Record of 1856* was a complete list of newspapers and periodicals in the United States, Canada, and Great Britain and included a sketch on the origin and progress of printing and facts about newspapers in Europe and America.

Coggeshall compiled an *Index to Ohio Laws and Resolutions, 1845-57.* It was a 302-page listing of documents in the journals of the Ohio House and Senate from 1802-1836 and was a valuable encyclopedia for the state.

In *Frontier Life,* 1860, Coggeshall published a collection of his own short stories, both fictional and fact. In it, he used the plot of a murder mystery, "Everglade Heroes—A Tale of Florida," to present his solution to the increasingly explosive slavery problem. Coggeshall's young heroine determined, after her father's double-dealing life, to sell her Florida plantation, set free the slaves, and provide homes for them where they chose—in Africa or America.

As the train left familiar country, Coggeshall must have anticipated the new venture ahead. During long stretches between cities he must have conversed freely with President-elect Lincoln and finally crystallized the "why" of his presence. Lincoln must have felt safe with him. For, had Lincoln not said, "with you with me I shall go safely?"

---

[20]William T. Coggeshall, *Lincoln Memorial,* Ohio State Journal, Columbus, Ohio, 1865, p. 57.

There was perhaps another reason why he was asked on the trip. Coggeshall, and others who knew him, left many documents to show he was a reporter who recorded events accurately and we can only conjecture that Lincoln knew it at the time.[21]

In the next six cities Coggeshall continued his notetaking. He captured Lincoln's deep dedication and his flair for humor as well as the liberator's realization of the risks involved in his presidency.

The train went to Buffalo, New York, where Lincoln's oft-referred-to religious faith shone:

> "'For the ability to perform my task I trust in that Supreme Being who has never forsaken His favored land.'"[22]

And on February 18 in Albany, Lincoln told the crowd:

> "'It is true, that while I hold myself, without mock modesty, the humblest of all the individuals who have ever been elected President of the United States, I yet have a more difficult task to perform than any of them has ever encountered. . . . I have confidence that the Almighty Ruler of the Universe . . . can and will bring us through this difficulty, as He has heretofore brought us through all preceding difficulties of the country.'"[23]

In New York City the reception was enormous. This was unexpected in Senator William Seward's state—Seward who had opposed Lincoln for the presidential nomination and led the first-vote balloting at the Republican Convention of 1860; Seward, the pronounced Republican who would gladly have voted to reinforce the Constitution's guarantee to slavery in the slave states.[24]

Coggeshall was at a loss to describe the resounding reception. "New York City was a *most promising* demonstration. Places of business were closed. Hundreds of thousands [thronged] the streets.

> ". . . Lincoln said, 'It is with feelings of deep gratitude that I make my acknowledgements for the reception given me in the great commercial city of New York. I cannot but remember that this is done by a people who do not, by a majority, agree with me in political sentiment. It is the more grateful, because in this I see that,

---

[21] After Lincoln asked Coggeshall to join the Inaugural Train, it gave him an opportunity to cover, as a reporter, more of the inaugural story than he had planned for. Now that he was committed to protecting Lincoln, loyalty would require him to be circumspect in what he reported.

[22] William T. Coggeshall, *Lincoln Memorial,* Ohio State Journal, Columbus, Ohio, 1865, p. 64.

[23] Ibid., p. 68.

[24] E. Benjamin Andrews, *History of the United States,* Vol. III, Chas. Scribner's Sons, New York, 1926, p. 326.

for the greatest principles of our Government, the people are almost unanimous.'"[25]

An infusion of strength came in Lincoln's speech in Trenton, New Jersey, the following day:

"'Received, as I am, by the members of a Legislature, the majority of whom do not agree with me in political sentiments, I trust that I may have their assistance in piloting the Ship of State through this voyage, surrounded by perils as it is; for if it should suffer shipwreck now, there will be no pilot ever needed for another voyage.'"[26]

Lincoln's train chugged onward to Philadelphia where he said:

"'I promise you in all sincerity, that I bring to the work a sincere heart. Whether I will bring a head equal to that heart, will be for future times to determine.'"[27]—February 20, 1861.

Lincoln made an even more unexpected confession one day later when the tired President addressed a crowd at Independence Hall. His face lit up as he said to the solemn assemblage:

"'. . . the Declaration of Independence gave liberty, not alone to the people of this country, but, I hope, to the world for all future time. . . . If this country cannot be saved without giving up that principle, I was about to say I would rather be assassinated on this spot than surrender it.

"'Now in my view of the present aspect of affairs, there need be no bloodshed or war. There is no necessity for it. I am not in favor of such a course; . . . there will be no bloodshed unless it be forced upon the Government, and then it will be compelled to act in self-defense.

"'My friends, this is wholly an unexpected speech, and I did not expect to be called upon to say a word when I came here. I supposed it was merely to do something towards raising the flag. I may, therefore, have said something indiscreet. I have said nothing but what I am willing to live by, and if it be the pleasure of Almighty God, to die by.'"[28]

So the journey proceeded . . . from whistle stop to whistle stop . . . dust eddies blew past the windows as the train puffed along. Coggeshall

---

[25]William T. Coggeshall, *Lincoln Memorial,* Ohio State Journal, Columbus, Ohio, 1865, p. 70.
[26]Ibid., p. 73.
[27]Ibid., p. 74.
[28]Ibid., p. 76.

kept meticulous notes of Lincoln's speeches and conferred frequently with the President for whom he had by now become a confidante.

In Harrisburg, Pennsylvania, on February 21, Lincoln reiterated his concern:

> "'I hope it will never become [a] duty to shed blood; and most especially never to shed fraternal blood.'"[29]

---

[29]William T. Coggeshall, *Lincoln Memorial,* Ohio State Journal, Columbus, Ohio, 1865, p. 79.

CHAPTER 3
MARY'S SECRET

The last leg of Lincoln's inaugural journey was to begin on the birthday of the man Lincoln so admired, George Washington, February 22. But, disturbing news prompted a change in the President-elect's schedule from Harrisburg, Pennsylvania, to Washington City, as Coggeshall would later reveal:

> "At Harrisburg information from friends at Washington, was communicated to Mr. Lincoln that a plot to assassinate him had been discovered at Baltimore, and therefore that it would not be wise to follow out the programme . . . to that city. Consequently, the President-elect, with a confidential friend, took a special train from Harrisburg."[1]

To outwit the reported assassination plot, Lincoln left with "one friend"[2] on a train from Harrisburg 12 hours before schedule in order to pass secretly through Baltimore. The train digressed to Philadelphia where the Lincoln party would take a direct train to Washington. A dispatch from Harrisburg to the *New York Times* dated February 23, 1861, 8:00 a.m. informed:

> "On Thursday night after he retired, Mr. Lincoln was aroused and informed that a stranger desired to see him on a matter of life or death. . . . After clearance of the informant's name by Lincoln, a prolonged conversation elicited the fact that an organized body of men determined that Mr. Lincoln should not be inaugurated and

---

[1] William T. Coggeshall, *Lincoln Memorial,* Ohio State Journal, Columbus, Ohio, 1865, p. 80.
[2] *The Rebellion Record, A Diary of American Events,* edited by Frank Moore, Arno Press, a New York Times Co., New York, 1977, Documents, p. 33.

that he should never leave the city of Baltimore alive, if indeed he ever entered it.

"The murder plan was hatched by both Southerners and some foreigners. [These were people who sympathized warmly with the Secessionists.] Statesmen laid the plan, bankers endorsed it, and adventurers were to carry it into effect. . . . The leader of the conspirators was an Italian refugee, a barber, well known in Baltimore, who assumed the name of 'Orsini,' as indicative of the part he was to perform. . . . They understood Mr. Lincoln was to leave Harrisburg at 9 o'clock this morning by special train . . . the idea was, if possible, to throw the cars from the road at some point when they would rush down a steep embankment and destroy the lives of all on board. In case of failure of this project, their plan was to surround the carriage on the way from depot to depot in Baltimore and assassinate him with dagger or pistol shot . . . or hand grenade.

"So authentic was the source of this information that Mr. Lincoln . . . was compelled to make arrangements which would enable him to subvert the plans of his enemies. At 9 o'clock p.m. Mr. Lincoln left Harrisburg on a special train. He wore a scotch plaid cap and a very long military cloak, so that he was entirely unrecognizable.

"Accompanied by Supt. Lewis and one friend, he started, while all the town, with the exception of Mrs. Lincoln, Col. Sumner, Mr. Judd, and two reporters,[3] who were sworn to secrecy, supposed him to be asleep. . . . The telegraph wires were put beyond reach of anyone who might desire to use them."[4]

There is some controversy about the identity of the "one friend," referred to by the *New York Times,* with whom Lincoln escaped. It is popularly believed that it was Colonel Ward Lamon who accompanied Lincoln from Harrisburg to Washington. *The Rebellion Record* says Lamon entered the carriage with Lincoln which took Lincoln from the Jones Hotel to the special train in Harrisburg. But, Lamon is not mentioned again.

Another source, *Lincoln the President—Springfield to Gettysburg,* quotes Congressman Washburne of Illinois as saying he met Lincoln and Lamon when they "got off the train in Washington" though there are "conflicting claims as to this detail."[5]

---

[3]In addition to being a bodyguard for Lincoln, Coggeshall himself was also covering the Lincoln inauguration for the *Ohio State Journal.*
[4]*The Rebellion Record, A Diary of American Events,* edited by Frank Moore, Arno Press, a New York Times Co., New York, 1977, Documents, pp. 33, 34.
[5]J. G. Randall, *Lincoln the President—Springfield to Gettysburg,* Dodd, Mead & Co., New York, 1946, p. 289.

In *The Life of Abraham Lincoln,* Lamon himself says he was on the train from Harrisburg to Washington—that he got on the train at Harrisburg, left Harrisburg, went to Philadelphia, and was met by a detective. Lincoln and Lamon and the detective got in a carriage and were joined by Mr. Linney, an under-official of the Philadelphia-Wilmington-Baltimore Railroad. They left Philadelphia, went to Baltimore, and both Lincoln and Lamon were on the train to Washington.

COGGESHALL SAVES LINCOLN FROM ASSASSINATION

William T. Coggeshall, however, provided a different version of the escape, to his wife, Mary. Years later in a letter to Prockie, dated February 25, 1908, Mary described the episode as her husband had told it to her years before. She revealed her secret.[6]

". . . Upon reaching the point near Harrisburg, where their car would be switched off for Baltimore . . . the officials told him [Lincoln] that he and his party would be placed in another [railroad] car by themselves, in the front of his [presidential] car and upon reaching Baltimore, a car would be in waiting and they must get into it instantly, he [Lincoln] being among the last.

"A great crowd was awaiting him [Lincoln] near his own car and the party in the front car passed out and out, waiting, Mr. Lincoln and Mr. Coggeshall being the last to go out.

"As they neared the door, they heard a hissing sound and discovered a Hand Grenade just ready to explode.

"As Mr. Lincoln reached the door, Mr. Coggeshall grasped the shell and hurled it through the open window where it [had] been dropped into the car. As it struck beyond the tracks and exploded, no one was hurt. He sprang upon the car where the president awaited him.

"They took a seat together and with a bound the car leaped forward. Neither spoke for some minutes. Then the President leaned forward and said, 'Did I not tell you I should go safely if you went with me.'"

Both the *Springfield* (Ohio) *Daily Sun* and the *Cincinnati Star* interviewed Mary Coggeshall in February 1908 and published lengthy stories about Coggeshall's life. Both papers briefly mentioned the assassination attempt and the *Star* added a detail not in Mary's letter to Prockie:

---

[6]The following material is based upon heretofore unpublished information obtained from family papers, particularly a letter written by Coggeshall's widow, Mary, to a daughter Prockie, February 25, 1908.

> "Mr. Coggeshall gave Mr. Lincoln a shove that sent him out onto the platform."

Coggeshall had thus been "the friend" who accompanied Lincoln and saved him from the assassin's grenade attempt.

Mary Coggeshall's letter also explains why the incident had remained secret.

> "Mr. Coggeshall asked him [Lincoln] not to mention it [the assassination attempt] to anyone for he felt that God's hand had been laid upon them in a miraculous manner, and they had been close to the Gate leading to the upper world and it was too solemn for the world to discuss.
>
> "[Coggeshall] said he should tell his wife [Mary], as he never kept anything from her, and she would not refer to it while they were living.
>
> "The President consented but wished Mr. Coggeshall to remain near him until after the Inauguration which passed off pleasantly, and Mr. Coggeshall left for home with the parting words, 'God knows best.'"[7]

Of the incident, Coggeshall himself would write in the *Lincoln Memorial* that, after addressing the Pennsylvania Legislature,

> "The President-elect, with a confidential friend, took a special train from Harrisburg to Philadelphia, and early on the morning of the 23rd of February, reached Washington."[8]

"W.T.C." is written in Coggeshall's handwriting, in the margin of the above account, beside the words "with a confidential friend," indicating William Coggeshall himself was the "one friend" who acted with the President-elect to avoid the murder plot.

When Lincoln and his party arrived at Washington on February 23, 1861, "very decided surprise was manifested ... when it became known that the President-elect had reached the Capitol in advance of his escort. The manner of his coming was severely denounced by both friends and foes, but subsequent developments established the fact of an organized movement to prevent Mr. Lincoln's inauguration by assassination at Baltimore, and the wisdom of the manner in which it was defeated was vindicated."[9]

---

[7]Mary Coggeshall Papers, in the collection of the author.
[8]William T. Coggeshall, *Lincoln Memorial,* Ohio State Journal, Columbus, Ohio, 1865, p. 80.
[9]Ibid., p. 80.

"Some of Mr. Lincoln's friends having heard that a conspiracy existed to assassinate him on his way to Washington, set on foot an investigation. . . . They employed a detective of great experience who was at Baltimore in the business some three weeks prior to Mr. Lincoln's expected arrival there, employing both men and women to assist him. The detective discovered a combination of men banded together under solemn oath to assassinate the President-elect. Their characters and pursuits . . . were various. Some were impelled by a fanatical zeal which they termed patriotism, and justified their acts by the example of Brutus, in ridding his country of a tyrant. . . . Others were stimulated by the offers of pecuniary reward. These, it was observed, stayed away from their usual places of work for several weeks prior to the intended assault. Although their circumstances had previously rendered them dependent on their daily labor for support, they were during this time abundantly supplied with money, which they squandered in bar-rooms and disreputable places.

"After the discovery of the plot, a strict watch was kept by the agents of detection over the movements of the conspirators, and efficient measures were adopted to guard against any attack which they might mediate upon the President-elect until he was installed in office. . . .

"Some of the women employed by the detective went to serve as waiters, seamstresses, etc., in the families of the conspirators, and a record was regularly kept of what was said and done to further their enterprise. A record was also kept by the detective of their deliberations in secret conclave, but for sufficient reasons, it is withheld for the present from publication. The detective and his agents regularly contributed money to pay the expenses of the conspiracy."

—"*Albany Evening Journal*"[10]

LINCOLN'S FIRST INAUGURAL ADDRESS
MARCH 4, 1861

After William Coggeshall saved Lincoln from possible death, the President appointed him an official presidential bodyguard. Coggeshall had the rank of Colonel and was a member of the Secret Service.[11]

---

[10]*The Rebellion Record, A Diary of American Events,* edited by Frank Moore, Arno Press, a New York Times Co., New York, 1977, pp. 34, 35.

[11]It was not the Secret Service as we know it today but at the time a group of bodyguards appointed by the President and paid for by the presidential discretionary fund. The Secret Service was not established until July 1865.

"Inauguration day, unlike the usual Washington weather, was bright and clear. Great multitudes thronged the plaza in front of the Capitol. Senator Baker of Oregon introduced Mr. Lincoln to the crowd, and the latter, stepping forward, handed his silk hat to Senator Stephen A. Douglas, who held it during the inaugural address."[12]

Young Colonel Coggeshall stood on the steps of the Capitol as his new Commander-in-Chief, President Lincoln, appealed to "avoid war" and "build a friendly, united nation."

"'. . . no State, upon its own mere motion, can lawfully get out of the Union,' Lincoln argued . . . "acts of violence within any State or States against the authority of the United States are insurrectionary or revolutionary, according to circumstances. . . . I, therefore, consider that, in view of the Constitution and the laws, the Union is unbroken, and, to the extent of my ability, I shall take care, as the Constitution itself expressly enjoins upon me, that the laws of the Union shall be faithfully executed in all the States.

"In your hand . . . is this momentous issue of civil war. . . . I am loath to close. We are not enemies. Though passion may have strained, it must not break our bonds of affection.'"[13]

"At the close of his speech, Chief Justice Taney administered the oath of office. Then in the presence of the people, President Lincoln kissed each of the 34 young ladies representing the 34 states."[14]

William Coggeshall listened intently, remembering Lincoln's invitation to go to Washington: "Come with me and I shall go safely." The man now sworn in as 16th President of the United States had predicted precisely.

---

[12]Mary Coggeshall Papers, in the collection of the author.
[13]William T. Coggeshall, *Lincoln Memorial,* Ohio State Journal, Columbus, Ohio, 1865, pp. 87, 94.
[14]Mary Coggeshall Papers, in the collection of the author.

Feby 25 1908

Dear Prockie
 My precious Gertie
It is storming outside and I feel pretty blue inside, but am going to drive them all away by writing to you. Do hope you are all well or at least are improving. Have been thinking I gave you all about the Library and guess said nothing about the pictures. They were taken by an artist on High St. and One of them is Mr Bascom the other is the old Librarian. I do not remember his name
Another thing
 There were no more festivities held in the State house until Gov. [???] was inaugurated

Excerpt from Mary Coggeshall letter to daughter Prockie, February 25, 1908.

Then there was a big crowd for Dennison was a great favorite

Mrs Governor Cox used to say he was the handsomest man both in looks and manners that she ever saw.

The next reception was given by the State of Ohio to President when he was on the way to his first Inauguration

Governor Dennison entertained the President & party two nights and one day. Thousands of People came to that reception. The President stood in the centre of the Rotunda surrounded by State Official Officials and prominent men from all parts of the State

No 2

People entered the house through the East entrance from Third street

The people marched six abreast and as close as they step. After a short time the President was crowded from the Rotunda close to the steps leading the west entrance on High street. I stood on the third stair Jessie on the fourth leading to the Library where we could come in from the East entrance

As the President was crowded from the Rotunda Governor Dennison suggested his stepping on the stairs. I heard the remark and stepped onto the fourth stair behind Jessie. Mr Lincoln took my place and from that point could easily reach the hands of the people as they passed out of the building

As we looked through to the East entrance we saw

Something very strange approaching. The President looked earnestly,
and as the crowd arrived at the
stairs he discovered a man
carrying on his upheld hands
his arms held upwards by a
a woman on one side and a man
on the other a beautiful babe about
six months old
As they drew near President
Lincoln waved his hand and
the crowd stopped and all were
still. Then the president leaned
over and took the child from
his fathers arms and kissed it
on the forehead, then asked
its name. It has no name and
we want you to name it
replied the Father. President
Lincoln replied Abraham is too
long for such a wee mite of
humanity and will call him
Abram. He then kissed him
and placed him in the arms
of his mother who said we
call him Abraham because "He
saved his people."

As she said the President
looked upward and a light
shone in his face as he
" Said God knows best."
Silence reigned for a moment
then the crowd moved on
many of them with streaming
eyes and heads bowed.
As soon as all were gone
the President retired to the
room of the Secretary of State
to rest while Governor Dennison
held a reception in his rooms,
for the strangers from all parts
of the state.
Jessie and going home
but she wanted to shake hands
with a President her father
too as to see him when her
father presented her to him
he bowed and taking her
leaned over to kiss her then
said My dear when you grow
to be a young Lady you can say

that Abraham[5] Lincoln bowed himself half way to the ground to kiss you. Looking up in his her beautiful eyes filled with tears and he still holding her hand she replied, Yes sir and I promise you that no one shall ever kiss me where you have just left your kiss. He looked at her a moment then said while his eyes were looking upward "God knows best."

Immediately he turned to Mr Coggeshall and said Come with me to Washington and I shall go safely. Mr C said he was on the Governors staff and must speak to him. Do so was the reply. When Mr Coggeshall returned with the Governors consent the President again looked up and said "God knows best and I shall go safely."

That evening they gave a reception for the President as he was the guest of Ohio

and special Guest of
Governor Hermiston.
They left the next morning
for Washington. The President's
Car was decorated with
flags and flowers. Quite a
number of Gentlemen from
Illinois and Ohio accompanied
him. Upon reaching the point
near Harrisburg where their Car
would be switched of for
Baltimore the officials told him
that he and his party would
be placed in an other Car
by themselves in front of
his car and upon reaching
Baltimore a car would be
in waiting and they must get
into it instantly, he being
among the last.
A great Crowd was awaiting
him, near his own Car

and the party in the front car passed out without waiting Mr Lincoln and Mr Coggeshall being the last to go out.

As they neared the door they heard a hissing sound and discovered a Hand Grenade just ready to explode.

As Mr Lincoln reached the door Mr Coggeshall grasped the shell and hurled it through the open window where it been dropped into the car. As it struck beyond the tracks and exploded no one was hurt. He sprang upon the car where the president awaited him

They took a seat together and with a bound the car leaped forward. Neither spoke for some minutes.

then the President leaned forward and said "Did I not tell you I should go safely if you went with me."

Mr Coggeshall asked him not to mention it to any one for he felt that Gods hand had been laid upon them in a miraculous manner and they had been close to the gate leading to the upper world and it was too solemn for the world to discuss. Said he should tell his wife as he never kept any thing from her and she would not refer to it while they were living

The President consented but wished Mr Coggeshall to remain near him until after the Inauguration which passed off pleasantly and Mr C D in fact with the parting words "God knows best."

President Lincoln often referred to Mr Coggeshall and reccommend him as the best man to head the Secret service of the government At the time of his second inauguration Mr Coggeshall was especially invited to be present. Mr C was in the east until the evening of April when he bade the President and wife good bye reaching Columbus in the early morning he news of his assassination

~~Lincoln's last remains~~

~~That~~

The Remains of President ~~Lincoln~~ were received the last of April and placed in ~~the~~ Rotunda of the State House where he had met the People and seemed very happy~~y~~.

I cannot write more of this sad Memorial Service

CHAPTER 4
LINCOLN WAR YEARS

LINCOLN RELIGIOUS FAITH

Religious faith and a sense of humor helped the President survive the stress of keeping this disintegrating nation together. Coggeshall's diaries refer to Lincoln as a "religious man" who vowed to carry out the deathbed wish of his mother to "love your kindred, and worship God." His faith shines through his speeches and one-to-one conversations.

Early in the Civil War one minister asked the President why he, such a religious man, belonged to no denomination.

"Show me the church," Lincoln replied, "which writes over its portals, 'Thou shalt love thy God with all thy strength of heart and mind and thy neighbor as thyself'—and I will join that church."[1]

Another clergyman said to Lincoln: "Let us have faith, Mr. President, that the Lord is on our side in this great struggle." Again, Lincoln quietly replied: "I am not at all concerned about that, for I know the Lord is always on the side of the right; but it is my constant anxiety and prayer that I and this nation may be on the Lord's side."[2]

LINCOLN HUMOR

Lincoln's humor often riled his associates, but it was one of the keys to his success. Despite his troubles and his worries, he looked upon laughter as the "joyous evergreen of life." Many were shocked that the President would tell funny little stories in a time of such daily tragedy, but each of his stories had a point illustrating the matter at

---
[1] Ralph Coggeshall Busbey Papers, in the collection of the author.
[2] Ibid.

hand. His critics thought the country was in the care of a man who could not save it.

But Lincoln knew the value of laughter. During one tense session in the Cabinet, Lincoln said: "Gentlemen, why don't you laugh? With the fearful strain that is upon me day and night, if I did not laugh I should die, and you need the same medicine as much as I do."[3]

Coggeshall cited an example of Lincoln's humor which enraged the dour Secretary of War, Edwin M. Stanton. "On the night of Lincoln's second election, close friend Charles A. Dana was waiting to see the President who was talking with journalist Whitelaw Reid. Stanton came in. Lincoln was leaning back in his chair and laughing with Reid about something he had just read, written by Petroleum V. Nasby,[4] editor and humorist of the *Toledo Blade*."

Stanton exclaimed to Dana: "There sits a man around whom the heartstrings of the nation are wrapped tonight, being amused over a damned montebank."[5]

Lincoln overheard the remark and summoned Stanton into his office. "Mr. Secretary," Lincoln asked, "have you ever read anything written by Petroleum V. Nasby?"

"I haven't time for such buncombe," retorted the furious Stanton. Unperturbed, Lincoln replied: "Here is some buncombe that you will enjoy. Nasby says there are three kinds of fools. There is the natural fool and the educated fool and when you take a natural fool and try to educate him, you have a damphool."[6] Stanton stalked out of the President's office in rage.

CIVIL WAR ERUPTS

Soon after Lincoln's first inauguration, March 4, 1861, Colonel Coggeshall returned to Ohio where his responsibilities as Governor's Secretary and State Librarian pressed: Governor Dennison needed him to help cope with increased warnings of war.

The Southern states were of old-school Democrat politics. They deeply resented the prospect of having a Republican president, especially one dedicated to freeing the slaves. In October 1860, South Carolina announced that if Lincoln became president, it would secede from the Union. November 6, Lincoln was elected. In December, South Carolina seceded. In a domino reaction six more states had followed

---

[3]Ralph Coggeshall Busbey Papers, in the collection of the author.
[4]Pen name of David R. Locke.
[5]Ralph Coggeshall Busbey Papers, in the collection of the author.
[6]Ibid.

suit by February 1: Mississippi, Florida, Alabama, Georgia, Louisiana, and Texas. On February 4, 1861, at Montgomery, Alabama, they formed the Confederate States of America under President Jefferson Davis and Vice-President Alexander Stephens. Lincoln took office over a divided country with seven of the states in rebellion.

Upon secession, the South claimed government property in its territory. Through February 1861, secessionists took possession of arsenals in Georgia, Alabama, North Carolina, Florida, and Louisiana; forts in Alabama and Georgia; a navy yard at Pensacola, Florida; and Forts Jackson and St. Philip at the mouth of the Mississippi River. Total worth of the military assets was approximately $20,000,000.

On April 12, 1861, the South broke loose in fury. Confederates fired on Fort Sumter in the harbor of Charleston, South Carolina. Of the 140 guns in the parapet-pierced fort, only 48 were usable. The garrison numbered 128 effective fighting men including 40 workmen and a band. Between 3,000 and 4,000 Southern volunteers mounted 47 cannon and mortars. People came in buggies and gathered on rooftops, steeples, and wharves to watch the government troops inside the fort defend themselves in vain. The flag was shot away.

News that Old Glory had been fired upon traveled fast. From Maine to Oregon it electrified the North where the call spread: "The Union must be preserved! Away with compromise! Away with further attempts to conciliate traitors! To arms!"[7]

Colonel Coggeshall recorded the shocking event: "Fri., April 12. War news. Rumors of firing upon Ft. Sumter. General excitement. Sun., Apr. 14. City full of rumors of war. . . . Mass of people very decided that at whatever cost or sacrifice the Government must be sustained."[8]

Already, southern rebels were sending trainloads of weapons to their secessionist sympathizers in the north. Coggeshall noted in his Columbus diary: "Gov. [Dennison] determined to arrest transportation of arms through Ohio from points in rebel states."

April 15, President Lincoln issued a call for 75,000 volunteers. Each free state responded with twice its quota.

The first volunteer group to assemble was the Sixth Massachusetts Regiment. On April 19, it reached Baltimore. Eight railroad cars carrying soldiers journeyed safely across the city and on to Washington. But the next four railroad cars were attacked by hooting mobs of secessionists, determined that the Bay State troops should never reach

---

[7] E. Benjamin Andrews, *History of the United States,* Vol. III, Charles Scribner's Sons, New York, 1926, p. 335.

[8] William T. Coggeshall, Civil War Diary, as Military Secretary to Ohio Governor William Dennison, 1861–62, copy in the collection of the author.

the capital. The secessionists threw brickbats and stones, fired bullets from sidewalks and windows until police held back the rioters so that the distressed troops could join their comrades. The rioting rebels burned the bridges north of the city. No more troops could reach Washington by this route.

Meanwhile, the capital city had been expecting an attack from the South. As of April 13, only 15 companies of local militia and six of regulars were in the city. Pickets were posted continually on roads and bridges outside. On April 18, 400 Pennsylvania troops arrived, followed the next day by the Sixth Massachusetts Regiment.

Washington was rife with reports that groups in Maryland and Virginia were gathering to descend upon the capital. The nation's public buildings were barricaded and provided with guard sentinels. Lincoln's friend General Cassius Clay organized 300 volunteers to guard the White House and to patrol nearby streets. The Government seized the steamers on the Potomac and also all the flour within reach. Meanwhile, enemies in Baltimore cut off telegraphic communication between Washington and the North. President Lincoln and all Unionists agonized in suspense.

On April 22 the Massachusetts Eighth and New York City's Seventh Regiments arrived in Annapolis. But the railroad to Washington had been torn up and the engines damaged. Maryland Governor Thomas Hicks warned the forces not to stop on Maryland soil. With furious work, "repairs were promptly made, the track relaid, and about noon of the 25th the gallant New Yorkers landed in Washington amid shouts of joy. Up Pennsylvania Avenue the solid ranks swept, bands playing and colors flying, to gladden the heart of the weary President Lincoln who welcomed them at the White House. A sudden change came over the city. Secessionists slunk away, the faces of the loyal beamed with joy. The national capital was safe."[9]

MILITARY SECRETARY FOR OHIO

Eleven days after the attack on Fort Sumter, Governor Dennison appointed William Coggeshall Military Secretary for Ohio, in charge of communications. This included telegraphing and personally carrying messages and official communiques. On April 23, in the cracked blue leather journal that was to become his Civil War Diary, he penned: "Position confidential. Given charge of telegraphing for war dept's. and O.V.M. [Ohio Volunteer Militia]." It was both a heavy and delicate responsibility.

---

[9]E. Benjamin Andrews, *History of the United States,* Vol. III, Charles Scribner's Sons, New York, 1926, pp. 341–2.

There was extreme and widespread bitterness in the North during the Civil War. Northerners *against* slavery were bitter against the South. Northerners *for* slavery (secessionists) riled and plotted against their neighbors.

Coggeshall's diary gives insight into the times:

"June 9, 1861: Went to Bellair [sic] [Ohio] from Grafton. Lew Wallace's[10] Indiana Zouaves on the train. Women spit at soldiers on the way. Ohio boys guarding railroad. Visited camps of 15th and 16th near Grafton. Troops in good conditions wherever under discipline. 16th wretchedly demoralized."

On June 10, 1861, Colonel Coggeshall rode horseback with General Morris, dined with Colonel Steadman, attended military council at Dumont's headquarters, and later recorded in his diary "Steadman eager to advance. He simply detests Dumont."

COGGESHALL—AIDE TO LINCOLN

Soon after Coggeshall was appointed Military Secretary for Ohio, President Lincoln asked him to return to Washington as a military aide to the Commander-in-Chief. The alert Colonel would serve both as bodyguard and as secret agent on missions to assess the Confederate's military strength.

On horseback, Coggeshall carried vital messages from Lincoln to Union troops stationed in Virginia. The Colonel attended councils of war in the White House and on the battlefields. He maintained liaison with two Ohioans in the Cabinet, Secretary of War Edwin M. Stanton and Secretary of Treasury Salmon P. Chase. The Colonel recorded his eyewitness observations of Cabinet meetings and informal sessions.

On May 3, 1861, the call was issued for 42,000 troops to serve the Union for three years. On May 13, General B. F. Butler took Baltimore, putting it firmly in the Union camp. But Virginia seceded within a few days and the Confederacy moved its capital to Richmond. Washington was protected to the north but facing the enemy on its southern shores.

Anxiety arose again over the safety of the capital. If the city was attacked, the President and Cabinet were to take quarters in the Treasury Building. It was heaped all around with sandbags and well guarded with 500 soldiers.

---

[10]Lewis Wallace was a lawyer, novelist, and soldier who rose to Major General in the Union Army. He served as Governor of New Mexico and Indiana, and was Minister to Turkey. In 1880, Wallace wrote the popular novel *Ben Hur: A Tale of the Christ*.

Washington, D.C. Oct. 7. 1861

His Excellency
 Gov. Dennison
  My dear Sir:
   Mr. Gurley tells me there are Six Regiments now in service from Ohio, who have not been commissioned either by you or me — I shall be glad if you will commission the officers, as I understand they are very uncomfortably situated, not knowing where they belong, or whether they belong anywhere; and as I do not wish to commission them over your ~~hand~~ head.

Yours very truly
A. Lincoln

P.S. If you perceive no valid objection, let the commissions date, from the time they ought to have had them
A.L.

Letter from President Lincoln to Governor Dennison of Ohio dated October 7, 1861.

In late May, Colonel Elmer Ellsworth's New York Fire Zouaves crossed the Long Bridge over the Potomac from Washington at 2:00 a.m. and captured Alexandria, Virginia. In mid-June, Harper's Ferry in Virginia[11] fell to the Confederates some 50 miles northwest of Washington.

Sporadic skirmishes between North and South served as sparks lighting the fire of war. "Engagements at Aquia Creek: Skirmish at Fairfax Courthouse," headlines read. "Fight in Western Virginia; The Affair at Big Bethel—captures and seizures of vessels and men."[12]

CIVIL WAR WASHINGTON

When the war began, Washington was under construction. Now, scaffolding broke the horizon over the incomplete Capitol Dome. Building materials congested the area around it. Work on the Washington Monument halted at midway.

Throughout the war, Washington buzzed with the dense activity of military preparations and movement. It was not easy to move through the wartime traffic jams in the capital's dirt streets. Pennsylvania Avenue, the main dirt thoroughfare, was dusty as a desert in dry weather and a sea of mud when it rained.

"Guns large and small were hauled through the streets to defenses surrounding the Capitol."[13] On one occasion, Colonel Coggeshall paced his horse around a 15-inch, 25-ton Rodman gun pulled by 14 oxen.

Housing was in short supply for the army regiments. Early in the war, many of the volunteers for President Lincoln's friend, General Cassius Clay, had to be housed in the East Room of the White House.

Volunteers for the Union Army often blocked the road in front of the War Department while they awaited induction. Cattle grazed on the White Lot at the southern end of the White House grounds and meandered onto the streets. Covered wagons loaded and unloaded supplies beside the Corcoran Art Gallery which the Army was using as its clothing department.

The Treasury Building was converted into the mess hall for soldiers. At its courtyard, covered chow wagons made continual food deliveries in what seemed a frontier-style covered pioneer train.

---

[11]Harper's Ferry has been in West Virginia since June 20, 1863, when western Virginia seceded from Virginia and formed its own state.
[12]Stanley Kimmel, *Mr. Lincoln's Washington,* Bramhall House, New York, 1957, p. 56.
[13]Ibid.

FIRST UNION DEFEAT
JULY 21, 1861

Bull Run Creek was the first meeting on the battlefield. The Union soldiers in blue faced the gray Confederate Army on Virginia's rolling hills near Manassas Junction some 24 miles southwest of Washington. "On to Richmond! Take the Confederate Capitol!" the Blues cried as they marched into battle.

The battle surged back and forth for an entire day. General Irvin McDowell's Union forces had the edge until late afternoon when 3,000 Confederates arrived by rail. The rebel reinforcements broke Union ranks, frightening some Union soldiers into flight among the scores of Washingtonians in buggies and on horseback who had come out to view the anticipated Union victory. Finally, General McDowell ordered retreat. But chaos and confusion ensued. Dozens of wounded men and supplies were left behind. The debacle secured a Confederate hold close to Washington.

Military strategists later evaluated this initial battle by volunteers as "one of the best planned but one of the worst fought."

Heartbreaking as it was, this first Union defeat at Bull Run paid dividends; more men and money poured into Washington to avenge the Union's losses. The defeat spearheaded the erection of a chain of defenses around the 34-mile circuit of Washington City. Eventually, there were "68 forts and batteries with emplacements for 1,120 guns on which 807 canons and 98 mortars were mounted. There were also 93 manned batteries for field guns and 20 miles of rifle trenches connecting the main works."[14]

WAR SPREADS

By 1862, the war had spread into the Mississippi Valley and the southeastern states. The North conducted the Civil War in three arenas: 1) the western campaigns, to clear the Mississippi River and thus divide the Confederacy; 2) the campaigns in the center, to reach the sea at Mobile, Alabama, Savannah, Georgia, or Charleston, South Carolina, cutting the Confederacy a second time; and 3) the eastern campaigns, to take Richmond and capture or destroy the main Confederate Army, ending the Confederacy.

On many cold, dark nights, Colonel Coggeshall huddled beside flickering campfires with scantily clad, hungry, and weary soldiers trying to bolster their courage to continue the war against discouraging

---

[14]Stanley Kimmel, *Mr. Lincoln's Washington*, Bramhall House, New York, 1957, pp. 67, 68.

odds—despite losses of Union battles and comrades. He relayed instructions from Lincoln and exchanged secret messages with Union generals in Virginia at a time when the fate of the northern forces and the nation was unknown.

In March 1862, during an all-night war council held under a drenching rain on a mud-soaked battlefield, Coggeshall contracted pneumonia. He returned to Columbus and then moved to Springfield where, a year after pneumonia, the Colonel fought hard to avoid the smallpox epidemic in Central Ohio. At Camp Chase prison near Columbus, 2,000 rebel soldiers died. Coggeshall was stricken. His diary entry was brief: "Confined to house with smallpox. Suffered about six weeks . . . May 7, 1863."[15] The 38-year-old had to taper off his role as White House courier, but would remain in the Secret Service more than a year carrying out missions for President Lincoln.

LINCOLN'S TRUST

Coggeshall had a rare opportunity to work closely with the man whose life he had saved. The diaries kept throughout the time he worked with Lincoln present new insights into the man "upon whom more hopes hang than any other living," the man who led the United States through Civil War.

Lincoln showed implicit trust in Coggeshall. His feeling of being safe with the young man had first prompted him to ask him to go on the inaugural trip. Then, satisfied with Coggeshall's dexterity, intelligence, and trustworthiness during the early war years, Lincoln asked the Colonel to head an important agency. Mary's 1908 letter explained:

> "President Lincoln often referred to Mr. Coggeshall and recommend[ed] him as the best man to head the Secret Service of the Government."

Coggeshall declined the post but agreed to continue work in the Secret Service. He would commute among Washington, Columbus and Springfield, Ohio, on secret assignments for Lincoln for what Mary later called "three full and busy years."

FRICTION IN LINCOLN CABINET

As a new President, Lincoln first revealed untested political acumen in his appointments to the Cabinet. The President aimed at healing the wounds of the nation at the highest level while risking open dissension. Indeed, the new President named to the Cabinet four men

---

[15]William T. Coggeshall Papers, in the collection of the author.

he had defeated for the presidency: William H. Seward, Secretary of State; Salmon P. Chase, Secretary of the Treasury; Simon Cameron, Secretary of War; and Edward Bates, Attorney General. Lincoln regarded the four as best fitted for their roles even though as candidates they had bitterly opposed him. During the years around the Cabinet table, however, all four would take every opportunity to disagree with the President. Coggeshall noted many heated exchanges among Cabinet members in his diaries.

Seward, a New York Senator, was bitter that Lincoln had defeated him for the Republican nomination. When Lincoln was elected, the feisty senator headed south, presumably to accept an important post in the Confederacy with Jefferson Davis. Lincoln learned of Seward's intentions and dispatched Coggeshall to halt his defection by offering him the all-important post of Secretary of State. Coggeshall caught up with Seward at Cincinnati. After hearing the President's proposal, Seward haughtily accepted, then blurted out, "For God's sake, Coggeshall, keep your mouth shut"[16] . . . about his plan to join the enemy. Five years later Seward would be Coggeshall's superior.

Seward, a strong Republican force in the Northeast, had led the polling on the first ballot at the 1860 Republican Convention but he did not get enough votes for nomination. In successive ballots, his support gradually turned to Lincoln. Seward was to remain bitter for many years. Once he blurted out to Coggeshall: "Disappointment? You speak to me of disappointment—to me who was justly entitled to the Republican nomination for the Presidency and who had to stand aside and see it given to a little Illinois lawyer."[17]

Coggeshall's grandson, Ralph Coggeshall Busbey (1890-1959) would later give further insight into the hostility of Seward, Chase, and Edwin Stanton who early replaced Cameron as Secretary of War. In speeches, Busbey stated:

> "Salmon P. Chase . . . like Seward, was egotistical and a political opportunist. He openly regarded it as a dishonorable trick that any other candidate than himself should have been brought out for the presidency. . . . Chase of Ohio had organized the Free-Soil Party, predecessor of the Republican Party. Yet Lincoln fearlessly named him to a key Cabinet post, Secretary of the Treasury. . . . A third who hated Lincoln, yet whom Lincoln named to his Cabinet [to succeed Cameron as Secretary of War] was Ohioan Edwin M. Stanton. He also thought he should have been president."[18]

---

[16]Ralph Coggeshall Busbey Papers, in the collection of the author.
[17]Ibid.
[18]Ibid.

On October 11, 1861, Coggeshall commented in his diary: "Chase and Seward have indulged in a very plain disagreement." (It is not known whether this refers to a private or publicly known difference.) On November 25: "Gov. Dennison reported they [the Cabinet members] are little governments unto themselves" and that Lincoln had told him: "Now, if Confederate President Jeff Davis was to get me and I told him all I know, I couldn't give him much information that would be useful to him." On December 7, 1861: "Governor said management of war had slipped from Cabinet. Mrs. Dennison said Seward took too much wine at a dinner she took with him in Washington. Chase looked to separation [of the North and South] as a final result inevitable. [Postmaster] Blair says none of the Cabinet have sense. . . . Rumored in Washington that Mrs. Lincoln told state secrets."

This is the only reference in Coggeshall's diaries to Mary Todd Lincoln. She was bright and witty and highly educated in French. She was a Kentucky belle from a wealthy Lexington family. But despite her status, Mary Lincoln was an enigma in Washington, D.C. Along with her generosity, tenderness toward the President, devotion to her sons, and almost daily visits to hospitalized soldiers, Mrs. Lincoln also suffered from hallucinations and occasional unexplained rages. She insisted upon being addressed "Madame President," had preferred candidates for every government vacancy, and considered herself an astute politician. According to Governor James A. Rhodes of Ohio and Dean Jauchius, authors of The Trial of Mary Todd Lincoln,[19] she stopped a lot of corruption in the Civil War.

Mrs. Lincoln was by turns happy and outgoing, then in the depths of despair. Historians have since revealed that she suffered from a mental disease not diagnosed in the nineteenth century but in our day it would be "manic depressive" induced by severe sugar diabetes.

Excerpts from Coggeshall's diary eloquently reveal the friction in the Lincoln Cabinet and Lincoln's magnanimity in overcoming the petty rivalries with which he had to cope. On October 23, 1862, Coggeshall wrote:

> "The Cabinet, it strikes me, is like a collection of powerful chemicals—each positive, sharp, individual—but thrown together, they neutralize each other and the result is an insipid mess."

Three months later:

> "January 19, 1863: Dennison told me [Postmaster General] Blair and [Secretary of War] Stanton at sword's points . . . Blair

---

[19]James A. Rhodes and Dean Jauchius, The Trial of Mary Todd Lincoln, The Bobbs-Merrill Co., Indianapolis, Ind., 1959.

sneers at Chase." (Blair wanted military occupation of Texas. Chase did not.)

One undated entry records an incident when Secretary of War Stanton lost his temper over Lincoln's release of prisoners. At times, Lincoln had released prisoners after family pleadings or unusual circumstances. On November 4, 1864, he issued orders involved in Coles County riots: "Let these prisoners be sent back to Coles County, Illinois—those indicted to be surrendered to the sheriff of said county, and the others be discharged."[20] After one such instance, Stanton raged that "The only thing left for us to do is to get rid of that baboon in the White House."

When the matter came to Lincoln's attention he said: "Stanton said I was a baboon, but that is only a matter of opinion. The thing that concerns me is that Stanton said it and I find he is usually right."

Yet it was Secretary of War Stanton who, later, standing at Lincoln's bedside as he passed away, uttered: "He now belongs to the ages. There lies the mightiest man who ever ruled a nation."

LINCOLN AT GETTYSBURG

The turning point of the Civil War was fought in July 1863 at the devastating Battle of Gettysburg in Pennsylvania. On July 1, General Robert E. Lee's Confederate Army of 75,000 was routed by the 85,000-man Union Army under General George G. Meade. The battle had lasted three days. Both North and South suffered monumental casualties. It was the bloodiest battle in American history, with 51,000 soldiers wounded, dead, or missing. Union forces took heart from their victory and continued their momentum. The very next day, July 4, the Confederates were routed from Vicksburg, Mississippi, by General Ulysses S. Grant of the Union Army.

On November 19, four months after the Battle of Gettysburg, President Lincoln journeyed to the Pennsylvania battle site to dedicate Gettysburg as a National Cemetery. Coggeshall was there too.[21]

Seated on a flag-draped wooden platform were whiskered dignitaries, military personnel, and a few ladies in bonnets and shawls. Hundreds of persons stood on the blood-stained battlefield.

---

[20]Earl Schenck Miers, *Lincoln Day by Day, 1809-1865*, Vol. III, 1861-1865; C. Percy Powell, Lincoln Sesquicentennial Commission, Washington, 1960, p. 293.

[21]Coggeshall covered the historic event for the *Ohio State Journal,* for which he frequently wrote articles on the Civil War, and for the newspapers for which he was correspondent: *The New York Times, New York Tribune, Boston Commonwealth, St. Louis Republican,* and *Ohio Statesman.*

Haggard and hatless, Lincoln rose and began to speak. His surprisingly brief oration was a Gettysburg Address, reminding the torn nation of its democratic mission:

> ". . . The brave men, living and dead, who struggled here have consecrated (this ground) far above our power to add or detract. . . . The world will little note nor long remember what we say here, but it can never forget what they did here. . . . It is for us the living . . . to be here dedicated to the great task remaining before us . . . that we here highly resolve that the dead shall not have died in vain; that the nation under God have a new birth of freedom, and that government of the PEOPLE, by the PEOPLE, and for the PEOPLE, shall not perish from the earth."[22]

Men in the crowd clasped top hats and woolen caps to their chests in respect for the fallen dead.

The Gettysburg Address reflected the spirit of the United States and, throughout history, has been considered as a perfect piece of oratory.

Secretary of Treasury Chase's growing bitterness against Lincoln was evidenced on November 26, 1863, when Colonel Coggeshall recorded his impressions of a visit with him in Washington:

> "Cordially received. Talked about war. Chase despondent. Says it is no use for him to struggle with present administration. Mr. Lincoln purposeless. Firm only from his inertia. Generous, kind, in some regards, wise, but as a precocious child. Has no practical power. No Cabinet meetings for two years for counsel. Meetings for jokes. Unless people recover from infatuation of confidence in Lincoln, bankruptcy inevitable. Perhaps that to come because we deserve to suffer for participation in slavery. Must be a change at the White House."[23]

This was one week after Lincoln's speech at Gettysburg.

Chase and Lincoln differed on the deployment of troops and the second attempt, at Antietam, Maryland, to take Richmond. Also, for a time, seeing the appalling loss of lives and depletion of financial treasure, Chase and Secretary of State Seward challenged Lincoln to accept peace with the Confederates on the easiest terms. This, Lincoln refused to do.

---

[22]Coggeshall's record of the occasion stresses emphasis on the word PEOPLE, contrary to what every school child in the United States has learned—"OF the people, BY the people, and FOR the people."
[23]William T. Coggeshall Papers, in the collection of the author.

In June 1864, Chase resigned as Secretary of the Treasury but the man was too good to lose. Lincoln appointed him Chief Justice of the United States Supreme Court. The appointment later proved wise. At the impeachment trial of Lincoln's successor, President Andrew Johnson, Chief Justice Chase showed great wisdom in his conduct of the historic debate in the Senate. The eleven charges weighed against Johnson ranged from drunkenness to willful violation of the Tenure of Office Act.[24] Some of these charges had been brought by greedy northerners who wanted to have severe reconstruction rules so they would acquire vast acreage in Georgia and Alabama. On the charges listed, Chief Justice Chase showed there was no constitutional basis for impeaching Johnson. He was acquitted by one vote less than the two-thirds majority needed to impeach.

Lincoln was not only opposed by some of his Cabinet members. He was also victimized by some civilian leaders. Coggeshall's diary contains a complete and graphic account of the forging of Lincoln's name to a fictitious proclamation in 1864, as part of a plot of enemies of the Union. The forgery took place on May 17, 1864, and startled the United States, by calling forth 40,000 men for the army. The Coggeshall records tell of the arrest of officials of newspapers publishing the forged proclamation in New York.

CONTROVERSY OVER GENERAL McCLELLAN

As a professional journalist and a Secret Service agent, Coggeshall was conditioned to hunt for the truth in the lives and conduct of persons in powerful positions. He expressed his opinions forthrightly and widely, and had little patience with those seeking military or government positions who did not openly support the northern cause to preserve the Union and free all slaves. He remained a watcher of those in powerful posts.

Politics began creeping into the military shortly after the Civil War began and the North started mobilizing troops.

Coggeshall agonized in his diary that unworthy men gained office.

"May, 1861. Misfortune that in so many regiments, politicians are elected colonels. A great misfortune that Ohio has not in all departments, officers who command respect, who are responsible and competent in war as well as in peace."

---

[24]The major charge brought against Johnson by the House of Representatives was that he willfully violated the Tenure of Office Act when he removed Secretary of War Stanton from the Cabinet after the Senate refused to concur in his removal.

Capt. W. S. Rosecrantz —

"You will have Lt. B. Sitts go to Marietta & act as act. Commissary — until seated
& measures as that all the stores may be regular.
You will forward stores. The troops will go down
in the morning. Lumber is to rest their subsistence —
provisions enough to the morning —

G. B. McClellan
Maj. Genl. Comdg.

Directive to Captain W. S. Rosecrantz, from Major General George B. McClellan, Commander Ohio Militia, April–June, 1861.

Again on June 3, 1861, Coggeshall lamented the "suspicions on good grounds that . . . influences are at work at headquarters of the Department of Ohio to force men into permanent positions in the army who will use their prominence for political meanness."

One politician whom Coggeshall considered an opportunistic straddler was General George B. McClellan, formerly of the Virginia Militia. McClellan, who was living in Cincinnati, was appointed Major General of the Ohio Militia on April 23, 1861.

Concurrently, McClellan was sought by Pennsylvania to command its army, but on April 24 he replied:

> "General Curtis, Harrisburg: Your telegram to Chicago never reached me. Before I heard from you that you wanted me . . . I had accepted the command for the Ohio forces. They need my services and I am honor bound to stand by them. I regret that I cannot command the Pennsylvania troops and thank you for the offer. G. B. McClellan."[25]

Many considered the General a military genius, but Coggeshall had his doubts and wanted to know exactly where McClellan placed his political allegiance.

On June 14, 1861, Coggeshall wrote in his Civil War Diary:

> "I am compelled to entertain strong suspicions that the ultimate purpose of Democratic politicians who now manifest patriotism is not commendable, and . . . *McClellan is a sympathizer or a servant.*"

McClellan's military star, however, kept rising. After only two months in Ohio, he became Commander of the Abolition Army in Western Virginia and defeated the rebels in minor engagements at Phillippi, Richland Mountain, and Carrick's Ford. This enabled anti-slavery Western Virginia to secede from pro-slavery Virginia and eventually become West Virginia.

In mid-July 1861, McClellan's victory at Rich Mountain, West Virginia, captured bold-face type headlines in the Washington press: "EXTRA EXCITING WAR NEWS—GENERAL McCLELLAN'S VICTORY COMPLETE—PEGRAM'S ROUTE COMPLETE—HE IS OVERTAKEN AND SURRENDERED WITH THE REMNANT OF HIS TROOPS. McClellan has now 1,000 prisoners, with all their artillery, baggage, wagons, tents, etc., even to their tin cups."[26]

On Sunday, July 21, fighting broke out at Bull Run Creek near Manassas Junction, Virginia. This was the first attempt to take

---

[25]Ralph Coggeshall Busbey Papers, in the collection of the author.
[26]Stanley Kimmel, *Mr. Lincoln's Washington,* Bramhall House, New York, 1957, p. 62.

Richmond. Hearing the cannon's roar and gunfire, and confident of another win, hundreds of Washingtonians rode out to the battlefield in carriages and on horseback to witness Union General Irvin McDowell's victory. But by late afternoon the spectators realized the Union was getting its first defeat. War wasn't a sporting event. The spectators turned to flee, causing a disarray that only added to the chaos as the Union soldiers retreated in the same direction, leaving dozens of their wounded behind. This debacle left Washington City more vulnerable to a Confederate attack.

A week after the defeat at Bull Run, or Manassas, Lincoln appointed McClellan as Commander of the Army of the Potomac.

The General ordered all "untrained and undisciplined volunteers to a 'division drill by trumpet' at least once a week" answering "a criticism that the volunteers did not know a single call 'on the brazen instrument' and it was highly necessary that they be instructed on such military tactics."[27]

Four months later on November 1, Lincoln appointed McClellan Commander-in-Chief of the Union Armies. Washington celebrated with a huge parade and fireworks.

Meanwhile, reports of battles in Missouri (Wilson's Creek) and of fighting off the coast of North Carolina were ignored by Washingtonians. They feared rumors of another battle close by.

During the next few months, the President and the new Secretary of War, Edwin M. Stanton who replaced Cameron in January 1862, "were at loggerheads with McClellan . . . regarding the deployment of troops and the logistics of the next attempt to take Richmond."[28] General McClellan dared disagree with the President and the public was starting to clamor against him.

Lincoln had set a deadline of Washington's birthday, February 22, 1862, for McClellan to make his move in his Peninsular Campaign to take Richmond. Not until mid-March did the General advance. Fighting continued until early July. He repulsed seven attacks at Seven Pines by Confederate General Joe Johnston who, after being wounded, was replaced by General Robert E. Lee.

In the Seven Days' Battles from June 26 to July 2 with Lee, McClellan won a strong position near Richmond. But suddenly Stonewall Jackson's cavalry approached on McClellan's right flank and put him in a position of great danger. Lee expected McClellan to retreat all the way down the Peninsula and get cut to ribbons. But on

---

[27]Stanley Kimmel, *Mr. Lincoln's Washington,* Bramhall House, New York, 1957, p. 65.
[28]*Civil War: The Years Asunder,* by the Editors of *Country Beautiful,* Waukesha, Wisconsin, 1960, p. 56.

July 2, McClellan skillfully withdrew his whole army to Harrison's Landing far up the James River estuary, had the cooperation of gunboats, and was safe to try to take Richmond again. Lincoln had even visited him at Harrison's Landing and given the soldiers a big morale boost. But after 10 battles, McClellan's army retreated. Lee had won the Seven Days' Battles.

Throughout the campaign McClellan repeatedly asked Lincoln to release more divisions from the capital. Lincoln refused primarily because "the wily Stonewall Jackson and his cavalry were creating havoc in Virginia's Shenandoah Valley and the paranoia in Washington was turning into sheer panic. Lincoln refused to leave Washington in a position he considered as grossly exposed."[29]

An example of the Lincoln-McClellan disagreement is a letter Lincoln wrote to McClellan April 9, 1862, asking him to explain a discrepancy:

> "There is a curious mystery about the number of troops now with you. When I telegraphed you on the 6th, saying you had over 100,000 with you, I had just obtained from the Secretary of War a statement, taken, as he said, from your own returns, making 108,000 then with and en route to you. You now say you will have but 85,000 when all en route to you shall have reached you. How can the discrepancy of 23,000 be accounted for? I suppose the whole is with you by this time. And if so, I think it is the precise time for you to strike a blow."[30]

Later, McClellan explained the discrepancy in his book *McClellan's Own Story, the War for the Union*: ". . . at that time, instead of 100,000 men, I had—after deducting guards and working parties—much less than 40,000 for attack, and that the portion of the enemy's lines which he [Lincoln] thought I had better break through at once, was about the strongest of the whole, except, perhaps, the town [Yorktown, Virginia] itself."[31]

Colonel Coggeshall, for years suspicious of the General's judgment and ambition, capsuled public reaction to McClellan in a two-week period in March, 1862:

> "Distrust of McClellan's capacity openly expressed. March 2d."

> "People indignant over McClellan. Beginning to believe the man is known by the company he keeps. March 14." ". . . [Gov.]

---

[29]*Civil War: The Years Asunder,* by the Editors of *Country Beautiful,* Waukesha, Wisconsin, 1973, p. 65.
[30]Ibid., p. 66.
[31]Ibid.

Dennison went to Washington on account of McClellan. Lincoln and Dennison resisted clamor against him until McClellan got into the field. Dennison confident he will prove military skill but acknowledges great chagrin over Manassas (No. 2). March 17."[32]

Coggeshall's personal reaction to Lincoln's dilemma was sympathetic: "Administration still halting between two opinions. I have sometimes thought the President might be likened to a boy carrying a basket of eggs. Couldn't let go his basket to unbutton his breeches—was in great distress from a necessity to urinate—and stood crying 'What shall I do?'—Oct. 23d."[33]

Battles in the Civil War see-sawed between defeats and victories for both sides. Lincoln insisted on constantly adding fresh troops and supplies. Thus, the Union gradually wore down the Confederate forces. But the entire country was becoming weary. The public was impatient to end the war. There were conflicting reports about the Union successes, due, no doubt, to indecisive battles and communications lag. In one week early in 1862, for instance, Savannah was reported "taken," . . . "not taken," . . . then "taken!" . . . "Such conflicting reports should have warned . . . that the road to victory was to be long. But the people wanted an end to the war, and all exciting news" rekindled public "hysteria for conclusion."[34]

In 1862 Lincoln instructed McClellan to defend the capital city and the fortifications around it. The Confederates had already taken Harper's Ferry, Virginia,[35] some 50 miles northwest of Washington.

On September 17, fighting broke out south of Hagerstown at Antietam Creek near Sharpsburg, Maryland, 59 miles from the capital city. General Robert E. Lee, Commander of the Confederate Army, had made his first invasion of the North. McClellan's northern troops and Lee's southern soldiers fought across the Antietam Creek in the bloodiest day of the war. Nearly 24,000 men died. Lee's rebel forces were out of ammunition and provisions and were almost surrounded. Lee withdrew to Virginia.

Surprisingly, McClellan did not pursue General Lee into Virginia. Instead, he jubilantly wired Major General Henry Halleck in

---

[32]William T. Coggeshall Papers, in the collection of the author.
[33]Ibid.
[34]Stanley Kimmel, *Mr. Lincoln's Washington*, Bramhall House, New York, 1957, pp. 92, 93.
[35]Harper's Ferry is now in West Virginia. The western part of Virginia seceded from Virginia June 20, 1863, and formed its own state.

Washington: "We may safely claim a complete victory."[36] McClellan was premature in thinking he had a swift end to a good cause. He thought he was victorious but Lee had not yet been conquered.

McClellan had let the probable capture of Lee and thousands of Confederate soldiers slip out of his hands at Antietam. Of this failure, Lincoln said of McClellan, who had always been his friend, "He's got the slows."[37]

The public and the press sharply criticized McClellan for not pursuing Lee. Dissatisfaction mounted on all sides.

On November 8, 1862, Coggeshall recorded in his diary:

"[Gov.] Dennison finally admitted he thought McClellan was an instrument of intrigue."

Finally, early November 1862, Lincoln discharged McClellan from his command as Commander-in-Chief of the Union Armies and Coggeshall most gratefully recorded:

"McClellan dismissed. Loyal men rejoiced. (Nov.) 11th."

1864 ELECTION—LINCOLN DEFEATS McCLELLAN

After three years of battle and debacle, Coggeshall's early intuition about McClellan proved correct.

In 1864, McClellan became the Democratic candidate opposing Lincoln for the presidency. Lincoln defeated McClellan with 55% of the popular vote. The count was: Lincoln—2,206,938; and McClellan—1,803,787. The electoral vote: Lincoln—212; McClellan—21. It was a firm victory for Lincoln but the scars of distrust about McClellan would remain even though letters by the General to his wife and a book he wrote somewhat vindicated his position.

McCLELLAN'S OWN STORY

In two letters to his wife, Ellen, McClellan gave his version of Antietam.

On September 18, 1862, he wrote:

"We fought yesterday a terrible battle (Antietam) against the entire rebel army. The battle continued fourteen hours and was terrific; the fighting on both sides was superb...we gained a great deal of ground and held it. It was a success, but whether a decided victory depends upon what occurs to-day. I hope that God has

---

[36]Stanley Kimmel, *Mr. Lincoln's Washington*, Bramhall House, New York, 1957, p. 106.
[37]Ibid., p. 112.

given us a great success. It is all in His hands. . . . The spectacle yesterday was the grandest I could conceive of; nothing could be more sublime. Those in whose judgment I rely tell me that I fought splendidly and that it was a masterpiece of art. I am well-nigh tired out by anxiety and want of sleep. God has been good in sparing the lives of my staff."[38]

On September 20:

I am much better today . . . have been under the weather since the battle. The want of rest and anxiety, brought on my old disease [malaria]. The battle of Wednesday was a terrible one. I presume the loss will prove not less than 10,000 on each side. Our victory was complete, and the disorganized rebel army has rapidly returned to Virginia, its dreams of 'invading Pennsylvania' dissipated forever. I feel some little pride in having, with a beaten and demoralized army, defeated Lee so utterly and saved the North so completely. Well, one of these days history will, I trust, do me justice in deciding that it was not my fault that the campaign of the Peninsula [to take Richmond] was not successful. . . . Since I left Washington, [Secretary of War] Stanton has again asserted that I, not [General John] Pope, lost the battle of Manassas No. 2! . . . I am tired of fighting against such disadvantages, and feel that it is now time for the country to come to my help and remove these difficulties from my path. If my countrymen will not open their eyes and assist themselves, they must pardon me if I decline longer to pursue the thankless avocation of serving them."[39]

From *McClellan's Own Story, the War for the Union,* the Major General revealed reactions about his dismissal from the Union Army Command by Lincoln:

"The order depriving me of the command created an immense deal of deep feeling in the Army—so much so that many were in favor of my refusing to obey the order, and of marching upon Washington to take possession of the government. My chief purpose in remaining with the army as long as I did after being relieved was to calm this feeling, in which I succeeded.

"I will not attempt to describe my own feelings nor the scenes attending my farewell to the army. They are beyond my powers of description. What words, in truth, could convey to the mind such a scene—thousands of brave men, who under my very eye had changed from raw recruits to veterans of many fields, shedding tears like children in their ranks, as they bade good-bye to the

---

[38]*Civil War: The Years Asunder,* by the Editors of *Country Beautiful,* Waukesha, Wisconsin, 1973, p. 78.
[39]Ibid., p. 79.

general who had just led them to victory after the defeats they had seen under another leader? Could they have foreseen the future their feelings would not have been less intense!"[40]

SIDELIGHTS ON GARFIELD, GRANT, AND JOHNSON

Sidelights, both gossipy and speculative, in Coggeshall's diaries reveal personal insight into two Lincoln appointees: Generals James G. Garfield (Ohio) and Ulysses S. Grant.

"Feb' y. 28, 1862. On train for Baltimore met Miss Ranson, the Ohio artist, who is a great friend of Mrs. Gen. Garfield whom she thinks the General neglects because he does not appreciate her. A lady from New England, with whom he fell in love in college, holds his love and waits in single blessedness for something to turn up. A Miss Booth also holds his regard. Mrs. Garfield is very unhappy but quiet.

"March 2, 1865. Saw Chase and Garfield on Street. Garfield not cheerful or social to me.

"March 4, 1865. Inauguration day. [Vice-President] Johnson's speech gave me a violent chill. Was the most disgraceful exhibition I ever witnessed."[41]

"March 7, 1865. Dined at Dennison's[42] (in Washington). Remained in evening. Met. Gen. Garfield and wife. Played euchre with Mrs. Dennison, Garfield, and Mrs. G. Dennison and Garfield got into discussion on [General Ulysses S.] Grant. Dennison sustained Grant as first military man of nation. Says the whole Cabinet defers to him and that he will win. He is exhausting the Confederacy.

"March 8, 1865. Dennison says the place for him preferably is in the War Dept. Says it is not organized. [Secretary of War] Stanton has no method. His whole department is in confusion and he is in fact only a clerk for Gen. Grant."

"March 28, 1865. Granville Moody called at office. Told story of conversation with [Vice-President] Andy Johnson at Nashville when Buell commanded and the city was threatened. Andy said, 'I'll

---

[40]*Civil War: The Years Asunder*, by the Editors of *Country Beautiful*, Waukesha, Wisconsin, 1973, p. 79.

[41]This may have been an instance of Johnson's well-known drunkenness—one of the shortcomings which brought about the eventual impeachment proceedings against him.

[42]Dennison was the third Ohioan Lincoln chose for his Cabinet. Already, Edwin M. Stanton was Secretary of War and Salmon P. Chase was Secretary of the Treasury until June 1864 when Lincoln appointed him Chief Justice of the Supreme Court. Two weeks before the general election Dennison was appointed Postmaster General.

DAILY OHIO STATE JOURNAL

PUBLISHED BY
WM. T. COGGESHALL & CO.

Office No. 19, East State Street.

WEDNESDAY MORNING, MARCH 8, 1865.

TERMS OF SUBSCRIPTION.

Terms of the Daily Journal.
Single Subscribers, 1 year, by mail.................$9 00
Single Subscribers, 6 months, " 4 50
Single Subscribers, 3 months, " 2 25
Single Subscribers, 1 month, " 0 80
Single Subscribers, per month, delivered by carrier.. 90
Single Subscribers per week, delivered by carrier.. 20
To agents in clubs 15 cents per week each copy.

Terms of the Tri-Weekly Journal.
Single Subscribers, 1 year.............................$4 50
Single Subscribers, 6 months......................... 2 25
Single Subscribers, 3 months......................... 1 15
Single Subscribers, 1 month........................... 0 40

Terms of the Weekly Journal.
Single Subscribers, per year..........................$2 00

TERMS OF ADVERTISING.

DAILY—One Square, each insertion, ... 75 cents.
" Special Notices per Square, each insertion.................................$1.25
" Local and Business Notices, per line, each insertion................... 20 cents.
WEEKLY—One Square, each insertion........$1.50
" Local and Business Notices, per line, each insertion................... 30 cents.

☞ One square covers three-quarters of an inch of space in the columns of the JOURNAL.

☞ Marriage Notices will hereafter invariably be charged 50 cents when under five lines, and 50 cents per square when occupying more space.

Central is a road which has reputation for watchful management. What was the matter last week the public ought to know.

I have often been interested on a railway trip, in noticing the fragments of conversation which may be caught when the cars stop. Now-a-days three topics seem to engage the traveling public—coal-oil—the draft, and Sherman's movements. Vigorous efforts are being made in this State to fill quotas by recruiting, but a draft is anticipated in many localities.

Among the incidents of my journey, thus far, was one peculiar to the exigences of war. At Pittsburg I met a squad of soldiers belonging to Gen. Blair's Corps in Sherman's army. They had been left behind with baggage when Sherman moved from Dalton for the sea coast, and they were last week on their way to New York, where they expected to be shipped to their companions at some point on the sea coast—they supposed, Wilmington.

The weather was delightful on the day I left Ohio. The night I crossed the Alleghany Mountains, it was very cold. I am now in Central Pennsylvania. On last Saturday this town was merry with sleigh bells. For three months the sleighing has been excellent, and the snow now lies six or eight inches deep in the valleys and on the mountain sides. Old settlers call this the severest winter for many years.

This is one of the venerable towns of Pennsylvania, situated at the foot of a rich valley, on the Juniata river, near a range of grand mountains. Here my boyhood was spent. The town in general, public buildings, streets, familiar dwellings, appear to me insignificant compared with the recollections of youth; even the river disappointed me, but the mountains are grander and nobler—more imposing than ever memory presented them.

I go to-morrow to Harrisburg, thence to Washington, to witness the events preliminary, and attending Mr. Lincoln's second Inauguration. W. T. C.

Ohio State Journal, March 8, 1865. Published by Wm. T. Coggeshall & Co., Coggeshall—editor and publisher.

be damned if I give up the city.' Moody saw Andy in Washington who said he was not drunk on inaugural day and would be sober hereafter."

Two weeks later on April 9, 1865, Confederate General Robert E. Lee surrendered to General Ulysses S. Grant at Appomattox Court House, Virginia. The Civil War was over.

CIVIL WAR BULL SESSIONS

As a student of his time, Coggeshall followed the interpretation and analysis of the Civil War at home late into the night. Often he invited competent monitors of public opinion and statesmen for fireside talks. Fellow journalists, state legislators, bankers and businessmen, Ohio Gov. William Dennison, talked long past midnight and philosophized about the patterns of the war. The smoke from their stogies and corncob pipes swirled 'round their heads while the men would contemplate the turn and twist of events, debating which next step would be most valuable to the country.

CHAPTER 5
COGGESHALL'S EMANCIPATION PROCLAMATION

Lincoln fathered an Emancipation Proclamation; William Coggeshall sired an Emancipation Proclamation. Both came to term on September 20, 1862.

Many times, Coggeshall's grandson Ralph Busbey told the story about Coggeshall's Proclamation and left many notes about it.[1]

After Colonel Coggeshall left the strenuous Secret Service duty on battlefields in 1862, he returned to Ohio and for $5,000 bought the *Press Republic* newspaper in Springfield, Ohio, where he moved the family.

Sitting at his roll-top desk in the small *Republic* office he penned this diary note:

"September 20, 1862. Sixth child born: girl: King House, Main Street."

The ink had scarcely dried when he received a telegraphic dispatch from Washington from Treasury Secretary Salmon P. Chase. It stated that "President Lincoln [had] just read to some of his Cabinet, the final draft of his Emancipation Proclamation."[2]

Coggeshall knew at once what he wanted to name the baby, but vowed he would not name her until Richmond fell!

He closed his diary, left the *Republic* office and half-ran the two blocks home to Mary.

---

[1] Ralph Coggeshall Busbey Papers, in the collection of the author.
[2] Ibid.

Bursting into the house he blurted out, "I know what I want to name the baby. I know what I want to name her."

He confided the name to Mary. "That's strange," she said. "All right, I'll let you give her that name on one condition. That, when she grows up, if she doesn't like it, she can change it."

"If she does," retorted Coggeshall, "she'll have to change her other name too! And, I won't name her until Richmond falls!"[3]

Two days later, on September 22, Lincoln formally convened his Cabinet to hear his Proclamation.

Following Union General John Pope's disaster at Bull Run on August 30 and the catastrophic results of the Battle of Antietam on September 17—the war's bloodiest day when 24,000 soldiers on both sides were killed—Lincoln sought desperately to preserve the Union. His solution to the slavery problem was the Emancipation Proclamation.

> "Secretary of War Stanton later described the depressed atmosphere at the Cabinet meeting. Lincoln began reading from a book by Artemus Ward and burst out laughing. Not one of his Cabinet officers joined him. Finally he said, 'Gentlemen, why don't you laugh? With the fearful strain that is upon me night and day, if I did not laugh I should die, and you need this medicine as much as I do.' With that, Lincoln put his hand in his tall hat that sat upon the table, pulled out a piece of paper,"[4] and read the famous document. It declared: "All Persons held as slaves within states at that time in rebellion against the Federal government, shall then, thence forward and forever be free."

The Cabinet approved Lincoln's preliminary Emancipation Proclamation issued September 22, 1862. On January 1, 1863, Lincoln signed the Proclamation into law.

REACTION TO LINCOLN'S PROCLAMATION

A testament to guarantee the equality which spawned the founding of America, the Emancipation Proclamation nonetheless aroused hatred and dismay in a nation accustomed to slavery.

Coggeshall chronicled in his diary the passage of the document, and the reaction it brought across the nation, from his perspective in Ohio:

> "Jan'y. 1, 1863. Proclamation of freedom generally anticipated. Could not help regret that Mr. Lincoln had not seen proper to

---

[3]Ralph Coggeshall Busbey Papers, in the collection of the author.
[4]Ibid.

adopt the policy inaugurated by [General] Fremont[5] and given his generals to understand that it [the Proclamation] was right and should be supported.

"Jan'y. 2, 1863. Proclamation published in *Republic*. Colored people rejoiced. Reports that Cabinet did not approve proclamation no doubt correct. The Administration as a civil power is necessarily held responsible, and that complicates politics in the future. Demagogues will make capital out of it by means of ignorance and prejudice.

"Jan'y. 11, 1863. Believe nation has more to fear from demagogues and traitors who call themselves Democrats than from poor rebels.

"Jan'y. 13, 1863. Richard Smith (*Cincinnati Gazette*) says the only way out of our national difficulties is for Lincoln to resign.

"Jan'y. 18, 1863. [Secretary of Treasury] Chase and [Secretary of State] Seward at first against Proclamation. Chase consented. [Postmaster General] Blair for military occupation of Texas.

"Jan'y. 19, 1863. [Governor] Dennison told me Blair and [Secretary of War] Stanton at sword's points. Blair sneers at Chase."[6]

In some areas hatred toward Lincoln increased.

BABY FINALLY NAMED

Coggeshall's determination not to name the baby girl until Richmond, the Capital of the Confederacy, fell, seems strange. But, understanding the turbulent times, he was motivated more by the chaotic political situation to choose a baby's name than by sentiment or family tradition. He lived in a nation where unprecedented history was being made and the birthright name of his sixth child would forever indicate the spirit of the time which kept men enacting laws to help their less fortunate fellowmen. And correcting society's inequities had long been Coggeshall's theme.

But, it would be two-and-a-half years after the baby was born before Richmond fell to the Union Army on April 3, 1865.

By that date, the Coggeshall family and baby had moved back to Columbus where Coggeshall, now publisher of the *Ohio State Journal*, lay ill in bed. Late in the evening, five-year-old Hattie rushed to her father's bedside and breathlessly announced, "Pa, they're putting up

---

[5]General John Charles Fremont was Commander of the western division of the Union Army at St. Louis.
[6]William T. Coggeshall Papers, in the collection of the author.

flags downtown." "You know what it means?" Coggeshall rejoiced, "Grant has whipped Lee!"

Perspiration broke out all over him. "I am too weak to halloo but not to appreciate the situation. Now, Richmond is ours. Down goes gold and other things."[7]

"In less than an hour, Coggeshall called the family to his bedside and announced the formal name for his two-and-a-half-year-old daughter. . . . He had named her . . . 'Emancipation Proclamation Coggeshall.'"[8]

---

[7]William T. Coggeshall Papers and Ralph Coggeshall Busbey Papers, in the collection of the author.
[8]Ibid.

CHAPTER 6
FIRST ABSENTEE BALLOTS

Because of Colonel Coggeshall and Mary, the Clark County, Ohio, Regiment fighting in Tennessee got to vote in the presidential election of 1864—the first year of absentee ballots.

1864 PRESIDENTIAL ELECTION

The 1864 campaign was potentially explosive. There were sizzling issues at stake. Would Lincoln be re-elected? He had fired General George McClellan as Union Army Commander; now McClellan was his Democratic opponent for the presidency.

Congress had passed legislation that, for the first time in U.S. history, voting would be allowed away from home . . . via absentee ballots. Each state had then to approve or disapprove. Ohio approved, as did all other states—except Indiana.

The worrisome question was: would ballots get to the battlefields safely? Would conspirators try to destroy them?

Ohio was important to Lincoln in the 1864 election because Ohio was a Republican stronghold; it had the largest number of volunteers in the Union Army; Indiana's vote would be lost; and McClellan's Democratic running mate as vice-president was an Ohioan, George W. Pendleton.

The Ralph Busbey Papers describe how his grandparents, William and Mary Coggeshall, were crucial in getting ballots to one battlefield.

It was October 1864. Coggeshall was publisher and editor of the *Springfield Press Republic*. Lincoln instructed him to print ballots for the Clark County soldiers. He stopped all work to do so. Hastily, he and some patriotic Springfield citizens (Ohio Legislator Samuel

Shellabarger, Judge White, E. M. Doty, Dr. John R. Rodgers, and others) met to decide how to carry out the presidential wishes.

They decided that Coggeshall should print the ballots on his presses and devised a plan of action to get them to the Clark County Regiment in Tennessee. On that autumn night, Coggeshall went to work at once with a trusted assistant. They did not finish until dawn.

Secrecy was of the utmost importance. But, somehow, the story leaked out. The morning that they finished printing the ballots, Mr. Shellabarger, who lived several miles out of town on the Dayton Pike, was walking to the *Press Republic* office. He overtook two men whom he spotted at once as Secessionist sympathizers from a nearby hamlet. He surmised their sympathies by their dress and gestures. Cautiously listening, Shellabarger overheard their conversation.

With a start, he realized the guarded secret had leaked out. They knew that a messenger from the *Republic* office (the trusted young Mr. Brown) would secretly take the ballots by rail to Cincinnati and thence, by guarded boat, to the battlefields themselves.

Shellabarger followed closely, listened carefully, and overheard the zealous sympathizers reveal a dastardly plot. They would intercept the messenger, grab the ballots, and destroy them all.

Confident of the detail of the plan, Shellabarger hurried off, barged into the *Republic* office, and disclosed the scheme to Coggeshall. The men devised a counterplot. High drama was in its developing stages. This is how it was enacted:

Brown, as scheduled, left the *Republic* office carrying a package, the exact size as prescribed. It contained blank paper, no ballots. Brown left the building and the plotters, monitoring his movements, deviously followed him to the railroad depot where he boarded the Cincinnati train. They followed. Arriving in Cincinnati, Brown registered at the nearby Burnett House hotel. His two shadowers, still following closely, entered the same hotel, and placed their names on the register beneath his.

Soon after Brown left the Springfield office, Shellabarger hurried out of the *Republic's* building for his country home, carrying the first American absentee ballots under his arm. His haste was to visit a son who was home on a furlough and was to report back for duty that day. After a short exchange between father and son, Shellabarger, Jr. was sent to Dayton on horseback to spend the day with friends.

An hour later Coggeshall and Mary, as was their custom, started out in the buggy for their usual evening drive. They were to hasten to Shellabarger's house, get the ballots, and drive on.

However, upon arrival at Shellabarger's, Coggeshall became violently ill and had to be helped into the house and abandon the trip.

Left alone, Mary announced *she* would make the trip. She was determined and Coggeshall convinced the Shellabargers to let her try. Taking the precious bundle of ballots and a hand-made revolver, Mary grabbed the reins, whipped up the horse, and started the perilous journey.

She had to drive through a Secesh[1] hamlet but, because of the darkness, escaped recognition. On, on Mary compelled her horse, its neck lathered where the reins rubbed. The night grew darker and seemed to engulf the wheels of the buggy and swallow its very occupant. Suddenly, the bright light of a lantern burst out of the darkness in front of the horse, a hand grabbed the reins, and Mary was surrounded by Secesh men, including the very ones who had helped devise the plot to destroy the ballots.

Quick-thinking Mary rose to the emergency: "My husband is sick and I am hurrying for a doctor. Please tell me where I can find one, quick," Mary pled.

Unsuspecting, the men released the reins, gave directions, and the 38-year-old woman breathlessly sped on, her heart pounding with the anxiety of near discovery.

She drove the horse, never easing the pace until, a mile east of Dayton, she caught sight of the blinking lights of the toll gate.

She slowed the exhausted horse to a walk and continued until she saw a man on horseback come from the side of the road. Swiftly, he approached the buggy, leaned low, and saluted with his right hand using the pre-arranged signal. Mary thrust the package of ballots into his arm and he dashed off in the opposite direction. From appearances, the rider was an old man; in reality, he was Shellabarger, Jr., disguised in beard and faded topcoat.

Shellabarger lashed his horse into a gallop, tore through the toll gates of Dayton, passed the frightened guards, and rushed for the depot. The train was pulling out and gaining speed. Tearing along with reins loose and clinging to the horse's neck, young Shellabarger brought the horse alongside the gray wooden cars and overtook one. Then, crouching cautiously on his knees, he leaped onto the last platform, and landed just in time to regain his balance.

With the ballots safe in his knapsack, Shellabarger called a final command to his horse, "Go home, Rex." The overworked animal turned and slowly trotted back alone to his master's stable three miles away.

But these few scenes were by no means the only fruitful scheme of the day.

---

[1]Slang term used at that time for Secessionist, Southern sympathizer.

Arriving in Cincinnati, Shellabarger went to the Burnett House and registered his name beneath that of Brown and the two conspirators.

The next morning, Brown, knowing his every movement was being watched, started down the road to the boat landing. The conspirators followed and, when he was halfway to the river, pounced from behind. It was a lonely spot and Brown, unarmed, had no protection. But he was young and strong. He resisted the assaulters.

Meanwhile, in the midst of the scrimmage, a feeble old man hobbled along with the aid of a cane and passed the three. He stopped, expressed sympathy for Brown, and pointing to his feeble limbs and hunched back, explained he could not help. Finally, he hobbled on, boarded the boat, and removed his disguise.

Brown, resisting the two assaulters until he saw Shellabarger safely on board the boat, at last allowed the conspirators to search him. They tore open his coat, grasped the package, and flung its wrappings to the ground. As they opened the package, blank slips of paper fell to the ground. Realizing their plot had been thwarted by a counter-plot, they rushed frantically to the boat landing. But the boat had started and, as they reached the landing, Shellabarger waved triumphantly to shore. Their plot had been outwitted. Dejectedly, the interceptors turned toward the hotel.

Shellabarger proceeded safely to the Tennessee battleground, delivered the ballots to the commanding officer of the Springfield Regiment, and reported back for duty.

Election day arrived. Soldiers in the Springfield Regiment were given a chance to vote. Where ballots had been filtered to other battlegrounds, for the first time in American history, political choice was penned on a field of battle.

Lincoln was re-elected President over General McClellan by 55% of the popular vote (2,206,938 for Lincoln to 1,803,787 for McClellan), and received 212 electoral votes out of 233, a mountainslide.

In Ohio alone, the President had a majority of 60,055. The tally was: Lincoln—home vote, 224,008; soldier vote, 41,646; total, 265,654. McClellan—home vote, 195,811; soldier vote, 9,788; total, 205,599.

The absentee voters helped roll up a big victory for Lincoln. William and Mary Coggeshall contributed to that victory.

CHAPTER 7
TWENTY DAYS

It was Monday, April 3, 1865. Union General Ulysses S. Grant drove Confederate General Robert E. Lee out of Richmond. The capital of the Confederacy had fallen. The Civil War was over.

This started a series of celebrations in Washington amid shouts of "Glory Hallelujah! Hail Columbia! Richmond Ours!" While soldiers were yelling "No more hardtack."

On the first night of celebrating, Washington was flooded with light. The 110 windows of the Treasury Department facing Pennsylvania Avenue sparkled with twelve lights each, and gas lights, shaped in large letters forming the word UNION, flared at one side of the Patent Office Building. Fireworks filled the sky, bands played on every downtown street, and crowds shouted and sang patriotic songs.

On April 9, Lee formally surrendered to Grant at Appomattox Court House, Virginia. The next day all government offices in Washington closed, people swarmed through the streets and to the White House, navy yard men and a band paraded down Pennsylvania Avenue with two howitzer guns in tow and, at the White House, amid cheering thousands, boomed a salute for the President. Lincoln appeared and made a brief speech.

Most government buildings and residences continued to be brightly lighted at night until April 13 when everybody prepared for a "General Illumination" presenting "an unbroken wall of flame."

Yet in the shadows of this brilliant celebration lurked an ominous character with a diabolical plot which foreshadowed tragedy for the nation.

William Coggeshall was in and out of Washington around the edges of that tragedy.

Meanwhile, President Lincoln, wearied by four years of nation-splitting war, set to the task of reconstruction and reunification.

COGGESHALL WITH LINCOLN BEFORE ASSASSINATION

On Good Friday, April 14, 1865, President Lincoln summoned Colonel Coggeshall to the White House. Why, is unknown. After a private meeting, Coggeshall bade President and Mrs. Lincoln goodbye and left the White House to take the 6:45 p.m. B & O express back to Columbus while the Lincolns prepared to attend a stage play, "Our American Cousin," at the Ford Theatre.

When Coggeshall arrived in Columbus the next morning on Saturday, April 15, he learned the shocking news that Lincoln had been shot at the theatre by actor John Wilkes Booth and died at 7:22 a.m.

Years later, based upon her February 25, 1908, letter,[1] Mary Coggeshall relayed the sad information:

> "Mr. C. was in the East until the evening of April (14) when he bade the President and wife goodbye . . . [for the last time]. . . . Reaching Columbus in the early morning he [learned] news of his [Lincoln's] assassination."[2]

Memories of the first assassination attempt on Lincoln rushed back to Coggeshall. He had thwarted the heinous act four years earlier on Lincoln's inaugural trip to Washington. Now, he had been with the President only hours before the Great Emancipator's murder.

Coggeshall could have easily speculated, "if only *I* had been his bodyguard last night . . ."

The nation writhed in pain. Black flags were pulled to the tops of buildings. Hundreds gathered on the White House lawn on Easter, many chanting "Black Sunday, Black Sunday."

The hunt for the assassin was unrelenting. John Wilkes Booth was a Southern sympathizer, and had previously tried to assassinate Lincoln, had planned to poison him, and schemed to abduct him. But all his earlier plans had failed. A newspaper notice of Lincoln's appearance at Ford's Theatre on the 14th provided the right opportunity.

Lincoln's bodyguard for the evening, John Parker, was three hours late to accompany Lincoln and left the theatre to go to a nearby

---

[1]Mary Coggeshall Papers, in the collection of the author.
[2]Ibid.

bar.[3] Booth readily entered the presidential box. With a single pistol shot he inflicted the mortal wound in the back of the President's head. Booth then jumped to the stage and made his getaway on a horse at the rear of the theatre. Simultaneously, fellow conspirators tried to kill Vice-President Andrew Johnson and Secretary of State Seward but bungled their attempts.

The Sixteenth New York Cavalry tracked Booth to the farm of Richard H. Garrett in Virginia twelve days later. The actor-assassin was either shot or committed suicide at 7:03 p.m. on April 26 after the Cavalrymen set fire to the barn in which he was hiding. His body was returned to Washington and secretly buried under the stones of a cell in the Old Penitentiary adjoining the Arsenal grounds.

Not all persons, however, shared grief over Lincoln's death. In Sistersville, West Virginia, lived one Moses Peregoy, a hard-headed, old-time rebel from Baltimore. When Lincoln was assassinated, all the citizens of Sistersville hung crepe on their doors. All, that is, except Moses, and his neighbors set out to lynch him. Finally, his wife found a piece of black cloth and hung it on the doorknob. Moses was saved.[4]

LINCOLN FUNERAL TRIP

For three weeks the nation mourned while the martyred President made his last journey—from Washington back home to Springfield, Illinois.

WASHINGTON
Tuesday-Friday
April 18, 19, 20, 21, 1865

On April 18, 25,000 persons paid homage to the fallen President at the White House where his body lay in state from 9:30 a.m.

On April 19, services were held in the East Room of the White House at 12:10 p.m., conducted by Rev. Dr. Gurley of New York Avenue Presbyterian Church. At 2:00 p.m. the funeral procession started from the White House to the Capitol Building.

The President's remains were conveyed in a bronze casket on a carriage draped in black. Lincoln's gray horse, saddled with the martyred President's boots reversed in the stirrups, was led by a groom. Mottoes such as "TREASON HAS DONE ITS WORST" hung in public places. An estimated 30,000 took part in the procession. The

---

[3]"The Lincoln Conspiracy," NBC-TV, May 16, 1978.
[4]Moses Peregoy was the great-grandfather of Suzanne Katz Morris who lives in Columbus, Ohio.

Sons of Temperance was the largest civic group represented; 44 persons could walk abreast and five carriages drove side by side in the line of march. The body was placed in the Rotunda of the Capitol to lie in state.

Like the country, Coggeshall agonized at the nation's loss. On April 15 he published a special edition of the *Ohio State Journal,* which he had bought three months earlier, and penned in his diary, "Feel as if a dear family friend is gone."

According to Coggeshall's grandson, Ralph Busbey, the Colonel returned to Washington for the funeral of his slain friend and President. He was on the funeral train as a member of the Honor Guard of the State of Ohio and also was reporting the twelve funerals.

In the *Columbus Dispatch Magazine,* November 30, 1958, Busbey wrote:

> "Countless authors have let their thoughts run rampant as they have chronicled, largely from hearsay, the events of the funeral trip from Washington, D.C. to Springfield, Ill., with Lincoln's body. But there is at least one factual account of the entire funeral cortege—a day-to-day on-the-spot reporting of the events of the funeral trip as they happened. . . . Serving as he did as correspondent for many newspapers, including the *New York Times* and *Herald Tribune,* the author [Coggeshall] frequently quoted himself as such representative instead of using his own name."

Of the Washington ceremonies Coggeshall quoted the *New York Times*:

> "In point of sad sublimity and moral grandeur, the spectacle was the most impressive ever witnessed in the national capital. The unanimity and depth of feeling, the decorum, good order, and the complete success of all arrangements and the solemn dignity which pervaded all classes, will make the obsequies of Abraham Lincoln the greatest pageant ever tendered to the honored dead on this continent."[5]

The President's coffin was put aboard the Funeral Train for Lincoln's last trip. Stifling emotion, Colonel Coggeshall boarded that train and took a seat close to the funeral car. Filled with the painful memory of the earlier triumphal Inaugural Train in 1861, he described the draped iron horse hearse of mourning.

> "The Funeral Train consisted of nine cars, eight of them furnished in succession by the chief railways over which the

---

[5]William T. Coggeshall, *Lincoln Memorial,* Ohio State Journal, Columbus, Ohio, 1865, pp. 133, 134.

remains were transported. The ninth car, containing the body, was the 'President's car,' originally designed for both convenience and relaxation for the President and other government officers in traveling over the United States Military Railroads. [Its design included] a parlor, sitting room, and sleeping apartment. It had been thickly draped in mourning within and without, the heavy black drapery being relieved with white and black rosettes, and silver fringes and tassels.

"The windows were draped with black curtains, and the entire furniture shrouded in black. A plain stand covered with black cloth, was placed in the car at one end, and on this the remains of the President rested. On a similar stand, at the other end of the car, was the coffin holding the remains of Willie Lincoln. [Willie, 12, died in the White House of typhoid fever on February 20, 1862, and his body had been placed in a vault at Oak Hill Cemetery.]

"The other cars of the train were new and elegant, and tastefully draped in mourning. The locomotive was also heavily draped. . . .

"A pilot engine, furnished by the several railway companies on the route, preceded the train over each line of the roads traversed."[6]

Lincoln's remains would travel back across nearly the same route he'd taken four years previously to become president. Only Pittsburgh and Cincinnati were omitted and Chicago added.

Over 1600 miles, the Funeral Train would stop in twelve cities: from Washington to Baltimore, Harrisburg, Philadelphia, New York, Albany, Buffalo, Cleveland, Columbus, Indianapolis, Chicago, and home at last to Springfield. In each of the twelve cities the remains would be viewed in an open casket. Impressive processions would follow brief services of eulogy. In effect, Lincoln had twelve funerals, Coggeshall reported.

En route on the funeral trip, Coggeshall conceived the idea of preserving a memorial to Lincoln—a record of his ironic double journey—the Eastern trip to Washington to be inaugurated the 16th president of the United States in 1861 and the Western trip from Washington back to a cemetery in Springfield, Illinois, a scant four years later. An eyewitness on both trips, Coggeshall had been bodyguard on the first and reporter and member of Ohio's Honor Guard on the second.

Coggeshall's one last tribute to his beloved President and friend would be a memorial book and the newspaper he owned, *The Ohio*

---

[6]William T. Coggeshall, *Lincoln Memorial,* Ohio State Journal, Columbus, Ohio, 1865, p. 142.

LINCOLN MEMORIAL.

THE

JOURNEYS

OF

ABRAHAM LINCOLN:

FROM SPRINGFIELD TO WASHINGTON, 1861,
AS PRESIDENT ELECT;

AND

FROM WASHINGTON TO SPRINGFIELD, 1865,
AS PRESIDENT MARTYRED;

COMPRISING AN ACCOUNT OF PUBLIC CEREMONIES ON THE ENTIRE ROUTE, AND FULL DETAILS OF BOTH JOURNEYS.

BY WILLIAM T. COGGESHALL.

PUBLISHED FOR THE BENEFIT OF THE OHIO SOLDIERS' MONUMENT FUND, BY THE OHIO STATE JOURNAL, COLUMBUS.

Frontispiece and title page of *Lincoln Memorial* highlighting Lincoln's inaugural and funeral trips.

State Journal, would publish it in 1865. From the book sales, he planned to erect a monument to Lincoln and the Ohio Soldiers.

Throughout the funeral journey, Colonel Coggeshall observed a sorrowing nation come to gaze and pay a last farewell to the slain leader "not [for] the gratification of a morbid curiosity but [with] an earnest, loving desire to gaze for the last time on the features of a great and good man, to whom they were gratefully and doubly endeared by the atrocious act which destroyed his life."[7]

> "Grief stricken mothers of sons who had fallen in the Civil War, tenderly strewing flowers upon the President's casket and many kneeling to kiss it as they filed by . . . the crew of the train on the run of the inaugural trip from Erie to Cleveland on the same locomotive that had taken the inaugural train over the same route . . . a 'Miss Field' of Wilson Street in Cleveland, erecting an arch of evergreens on the bank of Lake Erie near the tracks which bore the funeral train from Buffalo to Cleveland, and kneeling in the arch as the Goddess of Liberty in mourning as the engineer slowed his train as a salute to her . . . an aged woman, standing in the heavy rain, her hands outstretched, one holding out a piece of sable and the other a bouquet of wild flowers, as tears coursed down her cheeks . . . a farmer and his wife and children standing for hours in the rain on their farm, through which the train was to pass near St. Paris, Ohio, and kneeling on the damp ground as the Funeral Coach passed."[8]

At stop after stop, 34 girls, stars or insignia, one for each of the states in the reunited union, appeared in processions and decorations.

BALTIMORE
Saturday, April 22

The Funeral Train from Washington arrived at Baltimore at 10:00 a.m., under heavy rain. The coffin was transported in a glass hearse to the Exchange Building. At 2:30 p.m. the train left for Harrisburg.

HARRISBURG
Saturday, April 22

The train arrived in Harrisburg at 8:00 p.m. on April 22 where the grieving faithful filtered mutely past the casket until midnight. The next morning, the casket was opened at 7:00 a.m. for two hours.

---

[7]Ralph C. Busbey, "When America Mourned," *Columbus Dispatch Magazine*, Nov. 30, 1958, p. 34.
[8]Ibid.

PHILADELPHIA
Sunday, April 23

In Philadelphia, eight black horses with silver-mounted harnesses drew the hearse, taking the coffin to Independence Hall.

> "The lid of the coffin was removed far enough to expose the face and breast of the deceased. . . . On the old Independence bell and near the head of the coffin, rested a large and beautifully made floral anchor. . . . The public was admitted until midnight. . . . Hundreds of people remained around Independence Hall all night waiting anxiously for the doors to open again. . . . From six o'clock on Sunday until one o'clock on Monday morning, the public was admitted."[9]

FROM PHILADELPHIA TO NEW YORK
Monday, April 24

As the train passed through Newark, New Jersey, the "trees and housetops, door-steps and car-trucks were occupied by thousands of mourners. The United States Hospital was suitably decorated. In front were a large number of soldiers, some of them on crutches."[10]

NEW YORK CITY
Monday and Tuesday, April 24, 25

From Jersey City the coffin was taken across the Hudson River by ferry boat. Within a few hundred yards of the dock "the German singing societies of Hoboken commenced a funeral ode from the first book of Horace . . . from nearly 100 voices . . . as far as the eye could see there was a dense mass of heads protruding from every window in the street."[11]

"The sides and back of the hearse were of plate glass and on the top were eight large plumes of black and white feathers."[12] It was received in City Hall Park a few minutes past 11:30 a.m. An average of eighty persons passed the coffin a minute—forty on either side.

"The steamboat Granite State, from Hartford [Connecticut] brought down over 300 passengers, who marched from the boat to City Hall to view the body. The doors closed at 11:30 a.m."[13]

---

[9]William T. Coggeshall, *Lincoln Memorial*, Ohio State Journal, Columbus, Ohio, 1865, pp. 152–155.
[10]Ibid., p. 157.
[11]Ibid., pp. 160–161.
[12]Ibid., p. 162.
[13]Ibid., p. 169.

As on the trip four years earlier, Coggeshall noted that the New York procession "was the grandest—the most imposing ever organized in the United States. It marched in eight divisions, which embraced military and civic associations representing all the lines of martial service, and all the various walks of official and business life."[14]

Ceremonies held in New York's Union Square on Tuesday, April 25 included a hymn William C. Bryant had composed only a few hours earlier:

ODE—ABRAHAM LINCOLN

"O, slow to smite and swift to spare,
    Gentle and merciful and just,
Who in the fear of God did'st bear
    The sword of power, the nation's trust.

"In sorrow by thy bier we stand
    Amid the woe that hushes all,
And speak the anguish of a land
    That shook with horror at thy fall.

"Thy task is done, the bond are free—
    We bear thee to an honored grave,
Whose noblest monument shall be
    The broken fetters of the slave.

"Pure was thy life—bloody close
    Hath placed thee with the sons of light,
Among the noblest host of those
    Who perished in the cause of right."[15]

The procession escorting the hearse to the railroad station "must have contained full 60,000 men."[16]

The two lead locomotives used for the trip from New York to Albany, the "Constitution" and the "Union," were the same that had conveyed Lincoln from Albany to New York on his inaugural journey.

"At Hastings, the home of Commodore Farragut," Coggeshall described, "a huge arch erected near the depot bore the following inscription: 'We will cherish the memory of Abraham Lincoln by supporting the principles of free government, for which he suffered martyrdom.' . . . At West Point, the Cadets were drawn up in line . . . half minute guns were fired."[17]

---

[14]William T. Coggeshall, *Lincoln Memorial,* Ohio State Journal, Columbus, Ohio, 1865, p. 171.
[15]Ibid., pp. 195, 196.
[16]Ibid., p . 197.
[17]Ibid., p. 201.

ALBANY
Wednesday, April 26

The train arrived in Albany Tuesday night at 11:00 p.m. At one o'clock the next morning on April 26, the coffin was opened in the Assembly Chamber of the Capitol. Viewing continued until 2:00 p.m. Then there was a procession.

BUFFALO
Thursday, April 27

The train left Albany at 4:00 p.m., journeyed through Schenectady and Syracuse, and arrived in Buffalo April 27 at 7:00 a.m. The sorrowful public filtered into St. James Hall until long after sundown. "Buffalo omitted an extensive display of the military and civilians since it had had a funeral procession on the day the obsequies took place at Washington."[18]

From Erie to Cleveland, "as far as possible, everything connected with the train was the same as on the occasion of Mr. Lincoln's journey over that road in 1861," Coggeshall observed. "The locomotive, the William Case, was the same."[19] The original engineer had died but the fireman, the conductor, and the superintendent were the same.

CLEVELAND
Friday, April 28

A 24' x 36' building, 14 feet high, with a pagoda roof, was erected in the Park on the downtown Square to house the presidential coffin. "The building was well lit with gas at night."[20]

Unexplainable behavior ensued when the train arrived in Cleveland at 7:00 a.m. "When the coffin was brought from the car, so great was the anxiety of the people to see it, that numbers of them, most of them women, got under the train and remained there until warned by the police to save their lives...."[21]

> "Over 6,000 [marched] in the procession of organized societies.... Among viewers were invalid soldiers from the military hospital ... and many a bronzed veteran's eyes were wet as he gazed upon him who had laid down his life for his country.... [The

---

[18]William T. Coggeshall, *Lincoln Memorial,* Ohio State Journal, Columbus, Ohio, 1865, p. 207.
[19]Ibid., p. 209.
[20]Ibid., p. 215.
[21]Ibid., p. 219.

martyred President's] features were but slightly changed from the appearance they bore when exposed in the Capitol at Washington."[22]

Shortly after 10:00 p.m. the coffin was closed again and at midnight the train left for Columbus.

COLUMBUS
Saturday, April 29

Awesome solemnity pervaded the Rotunda of the State House in Columbus where four years earlier great conviviality and adulation were poured out to the visiting President-elect. "The Rotunda was transformed into a gorgeous tomb [with] a column of light streaming down from the lofty dome."[23] Now, a saddened 50,000 men, women, and children silently streamed past the funeral bier from 9:30 a.m. to 4:00 p.m. Men clasped bowler hats or woolen caps to their chests, women wept into their shawls and neckerchiefs, and boys and girls reverently paid their youthful respects to the great man whom they adored.

The eloquently silent tribute echoed the jubilation and cheering of four years earlier.

Until the time of Mr. Lincoln's burial in Illinois, Central Ohioans revisited the catafalque in their Ohio State House and placed fresh flowers daily around the dais where the President's coffin had rested.

The crewmen on the train which left Columbus at 8:00 p.m. for Indianapolis noted "bonfires lit up the country for miles" and that "hundreds of people assembled around them, waved flags and handkerchiefs slowly."[24] At two o'clock in the morning on Sunday, April 30, at Richmond, Indiana, "A committee of ladies brought wreaths. One, for Abraham Lincoln, bore the words 'The nation mourns.' The other, for Willie, had written upon a card, 'Like the early morning flower he was taken from our midst.'"[25]

INDIANAPOLIS
Sunday, April 30

The State House Square was enclosed at Indianapolis. A bust of Lincoln, by T. D. Jones of Cincinnati, stood at the head of the coffin.

---

[22]William T. Coggeshall, *Lincoln Memorial,* Ohio State Journal, Columbus, Ohio, 1865, pp. 225, 226.
[23]Ibid., p. 244.
[24]Ibid., p. 254.
[25]Ibid., p. 258.

"The colored Masons, in regalia, and colored citizens generally, visited the remains in a body" and formed a "very respectable procession, at the head of which was carried the Emancipation Proclamation, and at intervals, banners bearing the following inscriptions: 'Colored Men, Always Loyal;' 'Lincoln, Martyr of Liberty;' . . . and 'Slavery is Dead.'"[26] The rain was so heavy that the funeral pageant had to be cancelled.

CHICAGO
Monday and Tuesday, May 1, 2

As the Funeral Train neared Chicago, Coggeshall noted, "40 maimed heroes of the war and a large representation from the troops on duty at Camp Douglas, gave the soldiers' salute and stood reverently."[27] In the city itself, the coffin was taken to the Court House. Between Lake Michigan and Michigan Avenue, Lake Park was "filled with military and lay people including 10,000 school children."[28]

The wonderful thing about Chicago, Coggeshall wrote, was that "excepting that of New York City, the procession was the grandest and most impressive"[29] . . . "37,000 persons joined in the procession and not far from 120,000 souls participated in and witnessed the sad ceremonies . . . people of all walks of life, ages, ethnic, and religious groups, marched for four long hours. . . . In the procession with the Chicago Board of Trade was Mr. Daniel Brooks, of New Hampshire, who, when a boy of sixteen, marched in the funeral procession of George Washington."[30]

SPRINGFIELD, ILLINOIS
Wednesday, May 3

A similar scene occurred in Springfield where hundreds walked the streets, unable to find accommodations.

The Funeral Train reached Springfield on May 2 at 9:00 p.m. The coffin reposed in the Representatives Hall in the State House. On the dais where the catafalque was laid, two mottoes stood out: "Washington the Father" and "Lincoln the Saviour." The viewing lasted 24 hours, with lines of mourners filling the hall throughout the night—75,000 persons paid their last respects to their slain statesman and leader.

---

[26]William T. Coggeshall, *Lincoln Memorial,* Ohio State Journal, Columbus, Ohio, 1865, p. 265
[27]Ibid., p. 268.
[28]Ibid., p. 269.
[29]Ibid., p. 274.
[30]Ibid., p. 280.

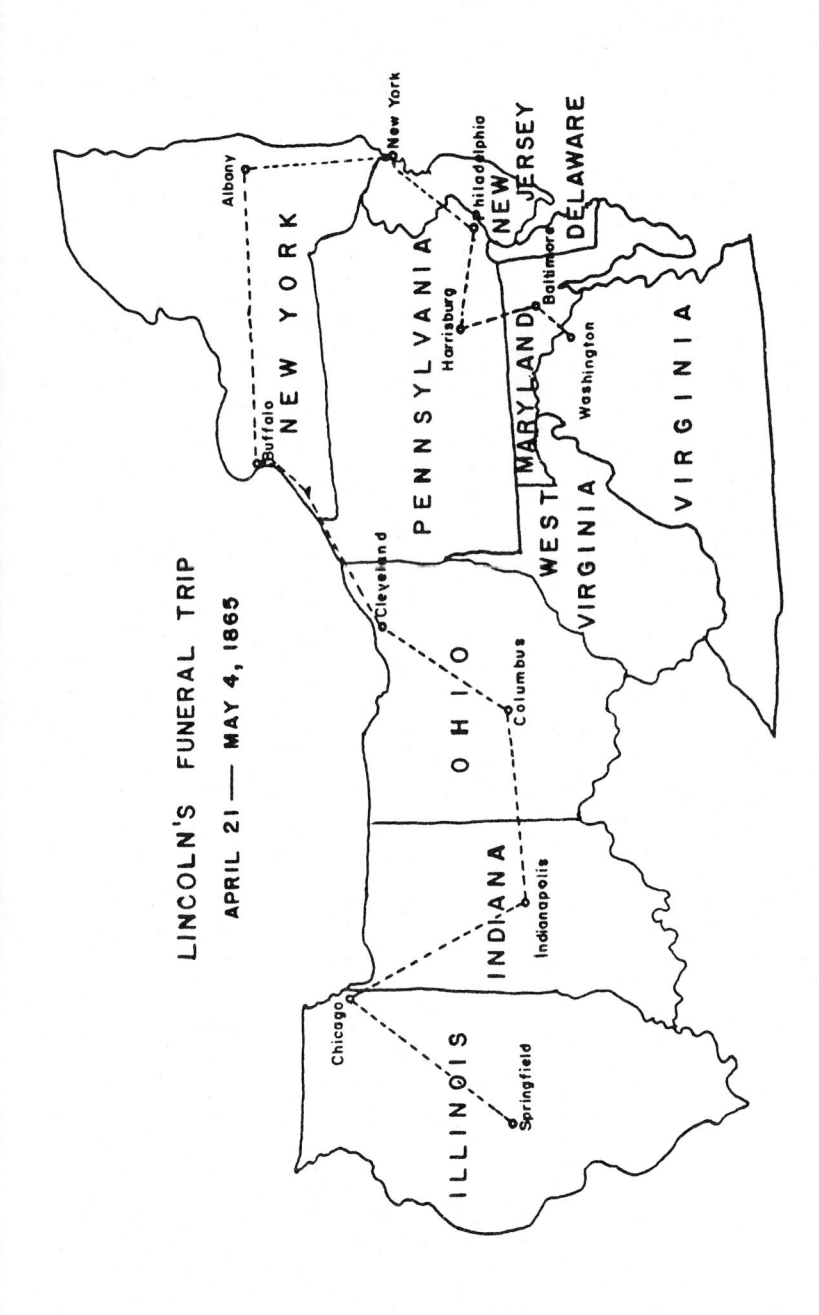

The Journey from Washington to Springfield as President Martyred, 1865.

BURIAL—THURSDAY, MAY 4, 1865
Springfield, Illinois

At 11:30 a.m. the funeral cortege with military escort began to move from the Illinois state Capitol while a band played "Lincoln's Funeral March." The route went by Mr. Lincoln's former house, on the corner of Eighth and Jefferson Streets, to Oak Ridge Cemetery.

The coffin was lifted into the tomb by the Veteran Reserve Guard in the presence of the Guard of Honor, Lincoln's sons Robert and Thaddeus [Tad], and other relatives. The remains of little Willie were deposited in the same tomb. Mrs. Lincoln did not attend. She wept five weeks in the White House.

Two ministers read selections from the first chapter of John and extracts from the writings of Paul. Another minister read the last inaugural address of Mr. Lincoln which was followed by a dirge. A choir sang, accompanied by a band.

Bishop Simpson [first name unknown] then delivered a lengthy funeral address. He said:

> "There have been mournings in the kingdoms of the earth, when kings and princes have fallen, but never was there in the history of man such mourning as has accompanied this funeral procession. . . .
>
> "The admiration was for the man himself. . . . Men of all religious creeds have united in paying this mournful tribute. The Archbishop of the Catholic Church in New York and a Protestant minister walked side by side in the sad procession, and a Jewish Rabbi performed a part of the solemn services. . . . I believe that by the hand of God he was especially singled out to guide our Government in these troubled times. . . .
>
> "Far more eyes have gazed upon the face of the departed than ever looked upon the face of any other departed man. . . .
>
> "He had a mind which could follow step by step with logical power the points he desired to illustrate. He gained this power by the close study of geometry, a determination to perceive the truth, and when perceived, to utter it. . . . His moral power gave him pre-eminence. . . . Men saw in him a man whom they believed would do what was right, regardless of all consequences. . . ."

Then Coggeshall continued: "During the hours of the services, by order of President Andrew Johnson, all public buildings at Washington were closed; the courts adjourned, all municipal offices closed. Citizens closed their stores and half-hour guns were fired all the latter part of the day, closing with a national salute at sunset."[31]

---

[31]William T. Coggeshall, *Lincoln Memorial*, Ohio State Journal, Columbus, Ohio, 1865, pp. 302–322.

In Springfield, Illinois, Coggeshall wrote his eulogy to the man he had worked with and loved:

"Thursday, May 4, 1865. Memorable day—Thursday, May Fourth, Eighteen Hundred and Sixty-Five; at his home where the major part of an active life, singularly pure, had been spent, Abraham Lincoln was buried; Abraham Lincoln, the assassinated President, without a personal enemy—remarkably kind-hearted—of genial disposition, but brave and solemn-minded—forebearing, because far-seeing—uneducated in the management of public affairs, but successful because patient and honest, possessing native tact and practical shrewdness.

"Alone in history stand the journey of Abraham Lincoln, President elect, from Springfield to Washington, 1861; and that of Abraham Lincoln, President assassinated, from Washington to Springfield, 1865.

"Twenty days after the terrible night on which the assassin's bullet destroyed the most precious life in the American nation, the body which that great and good life animated is deposited in the humble cemetery where lie the remains of neighbors, relatives, and personal friends in private life; and friends, neighbors, and relatives in public life, join the surviving, in ceremonies which are some of the saddest that may ever be performed on the American soil.

"What do those twenty days mean? Twenty days of National mourning; twenty days of flags at half-mast; twenty days with emblems of sorrow on the peoples' dwellings, with sable drapery and solemn mottoes on all public buildings; twenty days of tokens of love, of tributes of respect such as never before were paid to mortal man?

"Do not those twenty days suggest something more solemn, more searching than tribute to personal worth, or acknowledgement of public service, however much it is worth—however valuable that service?

"Those twenty days embody and will develop clear purpose—earnest determination—purpose and determination born in sorrow—vowed in affliction, before which oppression may tremble, and by which justice shall rule.

"Wherever cannon announced today that Abraham Lincoln's grave was open at Springfield—wherever church bells tolled in harmony with the historic services at that grave—in thousands of homes—in places of business, heads were bowed and hearts were sad as if it were the grave of one by whose death an intimate family circle had been broken. Indeed it is scarcely a figure of speech to say, that by the open grave of Abraham Lincoln stood this day the American people.

"What a tribute! How solemn! A nation in habiliments of mourning looking into the open grave of a President—assassinated in the hour of jubilation over a great victory for justice, because he was true to the whole country—because he directed the crushing of an atrocious rebellion which the sum of villainies had instigated.

"Oh, People of the United States—Friends of Freedom—Defenders of Right—Protectors of Intelligence—Promoters of Morals and Religion—do not forget that open grave, nor the unparalleled crime which caused it to be dug.

"Never did any people possess holier ground on which to register solemn pledges than that which surrounds the grave of the martyr, Abraham Lincoln. Placing him among the men whose lives have been sacrificed that the Nation might live, may not every true American citizen repeat, and for himself adopt, and, to this memorable day, adapt those pregnant words spoken by Abraham Lincoln in the Soldiers' Cemetery at Gettysburg: . . .

"'We cannot consecrate, we cannot hallow this ground. The brave men, living and dead, who struggled here have consecrated it far above our power to add or detract.

"'The world will little note nor long remember what we say here; but it can never forget what they did here. It is for us, the living, rather to be dedicated here to the finished work that they have thus so far nobly carried on.

"'It is rather for us to be here dedicated to the great task remaining before us, that from these honored dead we take increased devotion to that cause for which they here gave the last full measure of devotion; that we here highly resolve that the dead shall not have died in vain; that the nation shall under God have a new birth of freedom, and that government of the people, by the people, and for the people, shall not perish from the earth.'"[32]

Smallest Known Lincoln Book—Size of a Penny.

---

[32]William T. Coggeshall, *Lincoln Memorial,* Ohio State Journal, Columbus, Ohio, 1865, pp. 325–327.

PART II
THE DIPLOMATIC YEARS

William T. Coggeshall, U.S. Minister to Ecuador, 1866.

CHAPTER 8
U.S. MINISTER TO ECUADOR

After Lincoln died, Coggeshall began reconstructing his life. A new baby helped. Little Martha Turner had arrived March 4, 1865, the day her father, "especially invited," was in Washington witnessing Lincoln's second inauguration. On April 13, the Colonel made a second trip to the Capital, summoned by the President on some secret mission. When Coggeshall returned to Columbus April 15, he was distraught at the assassination of Lincoln. Baby Martha's chirps and gurgles brightened his day.

After Lincoln's death, Coggeshall compiled *Lincoln Memorial,* his account of Lincoln's trip from Springfield, Illinois, for the first inauguration, and his funeral trip from Washington back to Springfield for burial. A huge undertaking, the 327-page book was off the presses before the end of 1865.

On November 8, 1865, Coggeshall sold his daily morning newspaper, *The Ohio State Journal,* to become, for the third time, Private Secretary to an Ohio governor, newly elected Governor Jacob D. Cox.

The publication of *Lincoln Memorial* brought Coggeshall back into the public and political eye. His homage to Lincoln would prove a boost to his career, one which would also address a growing personal concern. Ever since he had contracted pneumonia the rainy night of the battlefront war council in 1862, the Colonel's respiratory system had troubled him. He finished *Lincoln Memorial* conscious of his worsening condition, now tuberculosis.

A professional opportunity arose which seemed suited to address his health concerns. In late 1865, the post of U.S. Minister to Ecuador became vacant when Ohioan Friedrich Houssarek, former editor of the

Cincinnati Gazette, resigned the position. Talk started that William Coggeshall might be a likely successor.

Ohio public figures rallied for the Coggeshall appointment. Postmaster General William Dennison and Governor Jacob D. Cox submitted Coggeshall's name for the vacancy to President Andrew Johnson. Opposition came from some who questioned Coggeshall's health and who believed that an emissary from the considerably anti-Catholic Ohio to a devout Catholic country was questionable. But eminent Ohioans Chief Justice Salmon P. Chase and U.S. Senator John Sherman strongly supported the nomination.

These prominent Ohioans, for three of whom Coggeshall had been secretary when they were governors—Chase, Dennison, and Cox—knew Coggeshall's devotion to the Republican Party, his statesmanlike conduct, and his fame as a journalist. They doubtless wanted to help his efforts to regain good health. The Colonel awaited only the formal announcement.

U.S. INTEREST IN SOUTH AMERICA

The United States had an affinity for South American countries in their 19th century struggle to free themselves from Spain. The U.S. had achieved its freedom and independence from Great Britain and "naturally sympathizes with those who aspire to . . . like ideals. In the United States there has always been a prompt and cordial response to the appeals of those who would be free, even as we are free. Our sympathy with oppressed people found expression in behalf of the South American republics in their effort to sever the bond that held them to Spain."[1]

Ohio, a Republican stronghold, had also held key positions in countries newly free from Spain in the 1800s. From 1852 to 1865 five Ohio governors and one newspaperman were U.S. Ministers to Central and South America.[2] The newspaperman, Friedrich Houssarek, was the one Coggeshall hoped to succeed.

DREAMS OF ECUADOR

William Coggeshall began to dream about seeing another country, serving his nation abroad, and becoming Minister to Ecuador. While

---

[1]Charles B. Galbreath, *History of Ohio,* Vol. II, American Historical Society, Chicago and New York, 1925, p. 546.
[2]Gov. Ethan Allen Brown was Minister to Brazil; Gov. Reuben Wood to Chile; Gov. Wilson Shannon to Mexico; Gov. Thomas Corwin also to Mexico; and Gov. David Tod to Brazil. The newspaperman was Friedrich Houssarek, former editor, *Cincinnati Gazette;* he resigned as U.S. Minister to Ecuador in 1865.

"the equator country" was far away and would entail a long journey, the location of Quito, its capital, appealed to the Colonel. Situated in the Andes Mountains, at an elevation of 9,350 feet, Quito would have the climate, Coggeshall thought, that could help cure his worsening tuberculosis.

Much history abounded at Quito. From 1633 when the Spanish conquered the Inca Indians in their rich northern empire, Quito had been the seat of Spanish headquarters in the northern part of South America. Pillaging Spanish soldiers had brought great Inca Indian art treasures to the city, creating a cultural as well as governmental center. Liberal Ecuadorian forces defeated the Spanish near Quito on May 24, 1822, and Ecuador became part of the great Colombian Republic but seceded May 13, 1830, to establish its own republic.

Coggeshall could write about the enchanting country and his experiences. He even planned to write a novel. But mostly, he anticipated that the mountain air above the equatorial jungle would be good for his lungs. He could get well in Ecuador, earn $7,500 a year, return with a tidy sum in the bank, then pursue his writing career unabatedly.

Oh, there would be adjustments to make. He would have to leave Mary and four of the children at home so their schooling could continue. He could take 14-year-old Jessie with him. She would be his link with family. And she would serve the U.S. Legation beautifully as hostess and secretary.[3] The sacrifice would be worth it. He hoped for the assignment.

While preparing for the formal announcement of his appointment, William bought a house for Mary. It was on the well-to-do east side of Columbus and befit the status of a diplomat. He wrote in his diary:

> "March 12, 1866. Wife 40 years old today. Her birthday present will be the house on 7th St. which I have bot [sic] for the residence of the family during my absence in Ecuador. Brick house—1st from S. side Broadway [Broad St. was also called Broadway] on W. side 7th. $3,600."[4]

On May 4, 1866, President Andrew Johnson appointed William Coggeshall U.S. Minister to Ecuador. Congress approved the appointment on May 11.

The new Minister wrote scores of letters to political associates expressing his gratitude and, to friends, sharing his anxiety about making the move and leaving his family.

---
[3]A two-person U.S. Legation was common in the mid-nineteenth century, especially in a small country.
[4]William T. Coggeshall Papers, Ohio Historical Society.

SAD DELAY

Coggeshall and Jessie were scheduled to sail from New York on June 30, 1866, but on June 11, he was forced to request a stay of departure. "On June 4th, our little baby girl joined the angelic force. Might my departure date for South America be delayed." The sailing date was changed to July 11.

The interlude following Lincoln's death, when baby Martha had brought such happiness in spite of grief, ended all too quickly. Martha died of marasmus[5] at age 15 months.

After the funeral, the grieving father wrote: "Baby buried today at Greenlawn—lies near the center of Greenlawn on the eastern slope. Her little feet toward the rising sun. Wife much cast down. Talks about Equador. Would to God she could go, but I dare not harbor the thought of breaking up my home and risking the children, Mamie, Hattie, and Prockie in a foreign land—a tropical land—'terra incognito.' June 6, 1866."[6]

Aware of his impaired health, on June 15, 1866, Coggeshall appended to the piles of paper and books in his library this note: "Should I never return from South America, I desire to have published for the benefit of my family these volumes containing my historical and biographical sketches, miscellanies, and lectures and addresses."[7] Mary found the request in her husband's desk drawer after he and Jessie sailed.

FUNDS FOR MARY

The day that Coggeshall left for New York to set sail, he provided for Mary's finances: "July 6th, 1866. Arranged this day with 1st National Bank for Columbus for banking business. *Wife to draw on 1st Nat. Bank* as necessities require, $1,000 per year. Penrose Jones to act for Mrs. Coggeshall in business matters. Leave for New York tonight with Father, wife, and Jessie."[8]

Penrose Jones was to look after the family's business affairs but trusted family friend, 26-year-old William Harrison Busbey, would prove to be the family's mainstay during Coggeshall's absence. Busbey had served three years in the Civil War, had been city editor of the *Ohio*

---

[5]"Marasmus—gradual loss of flesh and strength from no apparent cause, occurring chiefly in infants," *Random House Dictionary.*
[6]William T. Coggeshall Papers, Ohio Historical Society.
[7]Ibid.
[8]Ibid.

State Journal when Coggeshall owned it, and was loved by the entire Coggeshall family.

SAILS FOR ECUADOR

Mary and Coggeshall's father went to New York to see the Colonel and Jessie off on a steamer to South America on July 11, 1866.

To Mary, New York City was a frightening place—and the sight of a huge ocean liner about to take two of her most precious people away from her wrenched her heart.

The farewell at the New York dock was fraught with emotion. Mary was used to saying goodbye to William and conditioned to weeks without a husband. He had frequently been away as a newsman or member of the Secret Service. But this time he would be gone at least two years. Saying goodbye to 14-year-old Jessie was heartbreaking. A period overseas would be a marvelous experience for the teenager but what awaited her in a backward foreign land her mother could not imagine. Perhaps one or both could come home on holiday after a year. Or, if William renewed his ministership in two years, perhaps Mary and the children could join him.

The steamer's whistle blew a shrill blast and the ship's purser gave the final call for visitors to leave the deck. Mary and William's father tearfully hugged and kissed the voyagers goodbye. Coggeshall was going to new shores to serve his country and to regain his health. He might also get material for a novel. Mary's and the children's welfare would be in the good hands of Mr. Jones and Mr. Busbey. And housekeeper Mollie would carry the heaviest household chores. But, it was anguishing for William to share with his wife the last kisses and caresses for years to come.

Once again, Mary was left to manage the family, this time with the quadruple responsibility for children Willie, 17; Mamie, 10; Hattie, six; and Emancipation Proclamation (Prockie), only three.

U.S. PREPARATION FOR DIPLOMATS

"In the mid-nineteenth century there was very little foreign travel and few people had first-hand facts about other nations. Diplomats were sent into foreign service with hardly any preparation" by the U.S. State Department, according to Milton Gustafson, Chief, Diplomatic Branch, National Archives, Washington, D.C.[9] Diplomats received only "probably a copy of regulations . . . they were supplied with internal law

---

[9]Telephone conversation June 24, 1981.

procedures and diplomatic protocol of the United States. The relevant laws of the U.S. were kept in the office of the foreign post." At that time, "common sense and good judgment were the attributes most needed for the work of foreign diplomacy." Mr. Gustafson also said that in that day diplomatic missions did not have large staffs of trained people.

William Coggeshall went to Ecuador with little knowledge of the country except what he read in geographies and might have briefly learned from the State Department or gleaned from reports of previous Ohioans who had been U.S. Ministers to South American countries. He only had two months in which to prepare and brief orientation with President Andrew Johnson and Secretary of State William H. Seward commencing June 24.

VOYAGE TO SOUTH AMERICA

The voyage to South America was restful and uneventful. Coggeshall used the time to sleep, sun his ailing chest, play checkers, plan the operations of his new post, study U.S. regulations and protocol, plan ways to pay his bills, and prepare paper and ribbon ties for his diaries. He would send diaries home to Mary and the children so that they too could experience the journey. "We were given seats at the Captain's table, Jessie having the seat of honor at his right," Coggeshall wrote. . . . "She was seasick two days"[10] . . . but recovered.

On the Caribbean side of Panama, the travelers disembarked then went by train to Panama City on the Pacific Coast. After six days of sightseeing in the city, they boarded a sailing vessel for the northwest coast of South America and enchanting Ecuador.

Only 25 passengers were aboard the cutter sailing the Pacific Ocean.

> "Jessie is the only lady on board and, of course, monopolizes the beaux. Among them is an old Bachelor, 60-year-old Mr. Rittenhouse, Paymaster in the Navy, whom she likes very much because he quotes pretty verses to her,"[11] her admiring father wrote.

When they crossed the equator, the new diplomat noted: "I was not conscious of any change in earth or sea or sky."[12]

---

[10] William T. Coggeshall Papers, Ohio Historical Society.
[11] Ibid.
[12] Ibid.

"... At Payta [Paita], Peru I leave this Cutter ... then we take a small steamer, go up the coast again to Quayaquil river and then to Quayaquil city. It is about 60 miles from the coast.

"... My health is good. I cough some, but eat and sleep well."[13]

At Paita, Coggeshall sent a business directive home: "I hope Willie has sold the Printing Office clear. If the Cord Press is not sold, Mr. Jones had better advertise it in the *Cincinnati Commercial*."[14]

SOUTH AMERICAN SITUATION

When Coggeshall was assigned to Ecuador, South American countries were in the first phases of independence from Spain. Earlier in the century, in 1808, Napoleon had conquered Spain and put his brother Joseph on the Spanish throne. This triggered a reaction among the Spaniards against rule by a Frenchman. The discontent rippled to the Spanish territories which also proclaimed their allegiance to the deposed king, Ferdinand VII. Restored in 1814, Ferdinand was an absolute ruler whose return to the throne unleashed much internal strife and political chaos throughout the Spanish empire.

Wars of Independence in South America followed from 1809 to 1825. Over two decades, South American countries won their independence: Chile in 1818; Brazil, 1822; Peru, 1824; and Bolivia, 1825. Ecuador, Venezuela and what was then New Granada (Colombia) won their independence as the unified state of Great Colombia in 1819-1822 but this broke up into the present day states in 1830-1831. Ecuador gained independence in 1830. When Spain was forced to concede the loss of most of its American territory, Madrid refused to recognize the independence of Chile and Peru.

ECUADOR, THE REPUBLIC

The first president of Ecuador had been the conservative General Juan Flores. Serving from independence on May 13, 1830, to 1835, and 1839 to 1845, "Flores achieved social reforms and material progress"[15] but in 1845 he was overthrown by liberals.

In 1861, Gabriel Garcia Moreno, an arch conservative, had become president of Ecuador. Under him, only Catholics could be "classified."[16]

---

[13]William T. Coggeshall Papers, Ohio Historical Society.
[14]Ibid.
[15]William L. Langer, *Encyclopedia of World History,* Houghton Mifflin Co., Boston, 1940 and 1948, p. 814.
[16]Had rights and privileges.

Moreno governed with absolute authority under the constitution of April 1861 which granted wide powers to the president. "He believed the Roman Church was supreme over all earthly powers" and in 1862 concluded a concordat with the papacy which "accorded the church great authority, influence and wide privileges."[17]

In 1863 President Mosquera of Colombia had urged Ecuadorians to overthrow Moreno, but Moreno was elected president of Ecuador on three different occasions. Geronimo Carrion, who had succeeded him as president in September 1865, was President of Ecuador when Coggeshall arrived in August 1866. In 1865 and 1866, Ecuador joined Peru and Chile in an alliance against Spain. Also, Chile, Ecuador, Peru and Bolivia had formed an Anti-Spanish League. There were reports that Venezuala would soon join the League.

The Anti-Spanish League was a political alliance against Spain's efforts to reoccupy Lima, Peru, and Valparaiso, Chile. Spain had never recognized their independence gained earlier in the century and was at war with them from 1863-1866. In 1865 the Spanish started a brief encounter with Peru. Part of Peru's wealthy resources Spain wanted were the Bird Islands, uninhabitable, but the site of rich fertilizer from pelican and other big bird droppings (guano). The fertilizer was mined in the caves of the isles off Peru's Pacific coast. Chile and Peru had formed the Anti-Spanish League which Ecuador and Bolivia joined, Bolivia at that time having had territory on the Pacific coast.

ARRIVAL IN ECUADOR

On August 1, 1866, American Diplomat William T. Coggeshall and daughter Jessie arrived at Guayaquil, Ecuador's largest city and chief port. They were the guests of U.S. Consul L. V. Prevost. Before the strenuous days ahead, they managed to attend the theatre and two operas after which Coggeshall wrote to Mary, "it would amuse you to see the women here embrace."

During their first month, the two Americans prepared for the trip on horseback and mule over the Andes Mountains from Guayaquil to the Ecuadorian capital, Quito. The route over narrow mountain passes and deep valleys would be an adventure for two Ohioans. The prospect of seeing the 20,561 foot "Giant of the Andes," Mt. Chimborazo, and other scenic marvels, fascinated them. Who knew what wonderous beauties lay beyond?

The end of August, on Sunday the 26th, they left Guayaquil for a weekend boat trip on the "Virees," boat of the American Steamship

---

[17]William L. Langer, *Encyclopedia of World History,* Houghton Mifflin Co., Boston, 1940 and 1948, p. 814.

*Diary of Journey
from Guayaquil to Quito.*

Bodegas, Aug. 27th/66

The American Steamship Company through Capt. Lee, put the Steamer Ireneo at my disposal, under Capt. Brogdon & accompanied by Mr Prevost & wife & children, also by Mr Ponlowigne & several friends, also Mr Goin, his partner in Quito, also Col. Aguerre who is deputed by the government to escort us. We left Guayaquil at 2 o'clock on the afternoon of Aug. 26th. I had made my calls of farewell the night previous to a number of friends. Came to bid us goodbye, among them Mr Medina, Mr Smith, Señor

Sample: Coggeshall diary from Guayaquil to Quito, Ecuador, 1866.

Company, to the small town of Bodegas (now called Babahoyo), 40 miles upstream. There they would purchase supplies for their journey to Quito. They would need at least a month's worth of provisions.

Accompanying them on the boat trip were U.S. Consul at Guayaquil L. V. Prevost, his wife and children; Colonel (Commandante) Aguerre, Coggeshall's Ecuadorian government escort who addressed the American as "Senor Ministro;" Senor Gouin,[18] Quito's leading merchant who would lead them over the Andes Mountains, and his servant, Pedro; a Senor Pondavigne; and the Coggeshall's servant, Modesto.

Coggeshall's diary gave reactions to his impressions of life in the equatorial country. He was captivated by the striking beauty:

> "The tropical scenery relieved by waving palms and feathery bamboo . . . a sunset which, tinged with purple, a high hill which had a foreground of vivid green plain decorated with cocoa palm, mangrove, banana, bamboo and fruit."[19]

> "My guns are a great curiosity here. The Henry and Wesson are the first in this country. . . . I had my rifles and an English shotgun. We amused ourselves shooting at alligators with indifferent luck. The day was too cool for them. . . . Mr. P. (Pondavigne) had with him a liberal supply of brandy and wine and a portion of the company was very gay . . . the company amused themselves with cards and wine," while I "swung in a hammock or lounged in the Captain's office."[20]

The boat arrived at Bodegas at 10 o'clock at night and the curious travelers took a short walk.

The new diplomat was struck by the first sight of the natives.

> ". . . the original Indian on his native soil: a coppered colored, stout built, roundheaded, square faced, black eyed, straight black-haired, homely meek man. . . . They come on foot many miles with heavy burdens to sell a few vegetables or coarse fabrics, or as carriers. They are scantily clothed and *are not cleanly* in appearance."[21]

Noticing no unfamiliar native products except "the seed corn covering for hats," Coggeshall bought one for Jessie for three dimes. "The market people pay a reale [10 cents] a day to use the market and squat on the ground around their property.

---

[18]Throughout the William and Jessie Coggeshall diaries and letters from South America, Quito's leading merchant and storekeeper was always referred to as "Mr. Gouin." No first name for him was ever mentioned.

[19]William T. Coggeshall, Diary of Journey from Guayaquil to Quito, 1866, in the collection of the author.

[20]Ibid.

[21]Ibid.

> "In the market place were asses, horses, mules, oxen and sheep as beasts of burden. The Llama, too, is often brought here."[22]

The next day during a Monday morning canoe ride, the visiting foreigners saw plantations, orange groves, cotton and coffee fields.

Jessie visited "The plantation of Mr. Flores" (son of Ecuador's first president, General Juan Flores) where she received "a huge bouquet of jasmine, oleanders, roses and immortelles."

Col. and Senora Aguerre hosted them that evening. Neither the Aguerres nor Modesto, the Coggeshall's servant, spoke any English, so the new diplomat and Jessie "attempted to learn Spanish," making, in their own opinion, "a little progress."

That evening, after the steamer left to return to Guayaquil, the Americans stayed overnight in the Government House at Bodegas and made last-minute preparations for their trip. Coggeshall wrote:

> "We take with us beds, provisions, table furniture, etc. . . . I spent $500 at Bodegas, more than expected, part of which goes *into clothing for* Jessie the customs here requiring things which she did not bring. Great mistake she did not get a supply of shoes in Columbus. . . . Yesterday Madame Prevost said, 'Senor, you must have a pot!' 'A flower pot?' said I. 'No, no, Senor.' 'A pot to cook our dinners in?' 'Oh, no Senor, a pot for private use!' You may suppose I was amused, and you may be, because the incident illustrates the customs of the country. We take our 'water closets' as we journey to Quito. . . ."[23]

On Monday morning "we marked our packages and saw them loaded on mules: 21 packages—9 mules. We have *two* more mules for *baggage* and one for each of us and one for [each] servant. The Colonel [Aguerre] has *two* mules." They had a 17-mule train; horses for Gouin, Aguerre and Coggeshall; and a mule for Jessie. "This afternoon Jessie's mule was brought and saddled. It is an old white mule as docile as a sheep. She makes a magnificent appearance on it."

Explaining their Government House accommodations, Coggeshall complained, "our servant put our beds last night in hammocks, and we would have slept well, but for the noise the soldiers keep up. . . . The Government House is guarded. Orderlies are at the chief entrance, and a guard, who shoulders arms as we pass. In the court the soldiers drill. At night they sing (horribly). A trumpeter announces change of the

---

[22] William T. Coggeshall, Diary of Journey from Guayaquil to Quito, 1866, in the collection of the author.
[23] Ibid.

Minister Coggeshall's route to Quito.

guard every 4 hours and consequently we are kept alive to the power and *grandeur of Ecuador.*"[24]

TO QUITO

At 8:00 a.m. on Tuesday, August 28, the Coggeshalls left Bodegas accompanied by Commandante Aguerre, Senor Gouin, his servant Pedro, and their own servant Modesto. "Our preparations on the Plaza attracted a large number of wondering natives, who for a long time will talk about the 'Senorita Americana y blanca mula,'" the proud father wrote.

"Mr. Gouin led the procession out of Bodegas. Jessie followed, then the Commandante, then 'Senor Ministro' and after him the servants and baggage," Coggeshall wrote. "We passed over a winding, level road for several hours . . . our way led along a stream and mud holes were frequent. I had some fear as to Jessie's equestrianism, but she got along well. . . . I soon found that I had a poor horse. . . . I carried my Henry rifle and the servant a shotgun. I had opportunity to shoot at a pheasant—a handsome bird—also at some water birds and at a pigeon, all of which I missed. I begin to think the shotgun a failure. For the Henry rifle there was no use,"[25] the diplomat observed.

After about three hours the travelers stopped at Savanata—a small river town of "bamboo houses, dirty people, donkeys, and miserable cans,"—to eat breakfast. "The servants procured meat and eggs. We had sardines, pates and eggs, english [sic] crackers, wine and coffee. Dirt was obvious, but we shut our eyes. . . . After a heavy prescription of cognac (brandy)[26] I lay on the porch for half an hour. I was very conscious that a ride of 20 miles before breakfast is no joke."

After nourishment the travelers rode past the first plantations of oranges and bamboo—some of the canes were 40 feet high. "Bamboo is invaluable here," Coggeshall observed, "for houses, in the walls, in the floors, ladders, oars, spouts and posts."

They also saw two groups of "natives bearing pianos on their shoulders to Quito. They carry the piano on a bamboo frame held on the natives' shoulders—10 or 12 of them. They do not walk but go on a short trot, frequently stopping to rest. Their only clothing is short

---

[24]William T. Coggeshall, Diary of Journey from Guayaquil to Quito, 1866, in the collection of the author.
[25]Ibid.
[26]This is the first reference the former strong advocate of temperance made to his own use of an alcoholic beverage. It is not clear whether he used the word "prescription" in its medical sense.

breeches or a breech cloth and poncho. . . . The natives are very homely but very polite. They take off their hats to us and say 'Good day (Buenas Dias).'"[27]

ROUGH RIDING

Riding through a thicket of bamboo, large trees and dense vines, a vine caught Jessie in the neck and pulled her to the ground but "she was not hurt."

"Generally," Coggeshall noted, "the road was horrible: rocky, narrow, steep and slippery; a mere rocky path in many places. Several times we crossed rapid streams in one of which my horse fell down on his knees. I'm determined to replace him with a mule." They saw a squirrel, "very much like the grey one of Ohio." Coggeshall shot "a large bird—a Toucan, and a burrowing animal, a Huachusett." But his hunting was short-lived. The servant's mule, to which Coggeshall's shotgun was attached, frightened, threw Modesto, and the spring holding the barrel to the stock was broken. "So I was compelled to give up shooting."[28]

At night the adventurers hung their hammocks to sleep. The first night's stop was in a rum "manufactory" in which the second floor was used as lodgings for family, servants, chickens and travelers.

On the second day, Wednesday, as they began to climb Mt. Cordillera, "Senor el Ministro" replaced his horse with a mule. "The road was precipitous, narrow and rough, sometimes not two feet from the edge of fearful precipices." The group gathered orange blossoms and admired the rare flowers. Orchids grew wild.

After a noon breakfast, for which their table and chairs were boxes, the group found, for the first time, luzenne (a tropical plant yielding a kind of banana) to feed to their mules. They also saw sheep, goats and turkey. "A huge gobbler for breakfast was $1.25." Also seen were plaintain[29] and orange groves, and many droves of mules and donkeys laden with potatoes, corn, chickens, sonsa perilla,[30] wool, lard and luzenne. For the first time, the Americans also saw llamas . . . "several of them bearing burdens, their intelligent heads high in the air,

---

[27]William T. Coggeshall, Diary of Journey from Guayaquil to Quito, 1866, in the collection of the author.
[28]Ibid.
[29]A kind of banana with fruit larger, less sweet, and more starchy than the ordinary banana.
[30]Pear-shaped Peruvian tall grass.

their pleasant eyes apparently watching you . . . their ambling gait, graceful, if peculiar . . . a very pretty picture."[31]

Approaching the town of Maranda, at the foot of Mt. Chimborazo, "whose peaks are generally lost in the clouds," the scenery was very beautiful but the road "difficult. The track is worn into deep gullies and often I could ride or walk at the same time, the belly of my mule being below the tops of the gully banks."[32]

At sunset the travelers sighted Mt. Chimborazo's tall white peak, 20,561 feet—"the most celebrated volcano in the world—now quiet." This was a sight they had been waiting for: Coggeshall took off his hat in respect to its breathtaking beauty.

SAN MIGUEL TO GUARANDA

That night they stayed at San Miguel in "horrible quarters. Our room, on the ground floor, is used as a granny (granary) . . . unmentionable stenches." The U.S. Minister got into a hammock, was exhausted and "Jessie made me a brandy punch, under the influence of which I went to sleep in my hammock. She slept on a table. I passed a feverish night and was glad when day broke."

The next morning, Thursday, they witnessed a funeral procession of "30 or 40 Indians, men and women, and several priests . . . in canonical robes, and boys carrying lanterns and lighted candles. The corpse was borne on a bamboo litter by four men. When the bell rang, the procession moved; when it stopped, the bell was quiet. The stoppages were indulged about every 10 yards."[33]

That day, Coggeshall managed to ride for several hours in a fever. The mountain views were splendid and at one stretch they rode half a mile between lines of rosebushes, but the road was treacherous and they stopped. The new diplomat determined to rest one day—"changed my clothes for thicker and, after taking several grains of quinine, feel able to go forward tomorrow."

En route they "descended a narrow, rocky path several hundred feet—and then crossed a remarkable natural bridge, an arch, rising 100 feet above the rocky bed of the river." The group stayed overnight at Guaranda, a town "built chiefly of adobe—3 or 4,000 inhabitants—several times suffered earthquakes."[34]

---

[31] William T. Coggeshall, Diary of Journey from Guayaquil to Quito, 1866, in the collection of the author.
[32] Ibid.
[33] Ibid.
[34] Ibid.

JESSIE IN DANGER ON MT. CHIMBORAZO

Their route went over Mt. Chimborazo, more than 100 miles on the road to Quito. Climbing the "giant of the Andes" was a thrilling, chilling, frightening experience.

On Saturday, September 1, 1866, the Coggeshalls were roused at 3:00 a.m. from their couches at Guaranda and advised to dress in extra shawls, ponchos and mufflers to ascend the great mountain. Fresh horses awaited Coggeshall and Commandante Aguerre while Jessie would continue on her white mule.

"We rode out of Guaranda in single file, Mr. Gouin in the lead, Jessie next." The group started the ascent of the mountain at 4 a.m. and soon had "magnificent moonlight views. As the sun rose, it created a breathtaking rainbow upon the mists of the valley." Along the trail Coggeshall recognized "the whortleberry.[35] . . . I plucked the fruit as I rode along. It tastes precisely like the whortleberry of Ohio tho not quite so sweet."

At 9:00 a.m. the group stopped at a "tambo" (tavern), mountain hut, for eggs to eat with their cold chicken. The servants prepared coffee "and on the ground floor of the hut, spread first some lye, then a rubber poncho, then some napkins . . . squatting down, we ate breakfast."[36]

At the snowline of Mt. Chimborazo, about 18,000 feet, "the wind blew violently and it was very cold." But the climbers continued their ascent into the bitter wind of the high equator. At the highest point of the road—a narrow plain called the arsenal—"the wind struck us like a swift current of water; cold, cutting and bringing with it dense snow. Above and around us was a dense cloud of snow. We could not see in any direction. The sharp wind cut through our clothing and the sand and snow hurt our faces.

"Our Mt. Chimborazo costume would amuse you. Jessie wore a mask and a rubber poncho. I had my thickest clothing with extra drawers, extra woolen shirt, a huge poncho and a big muffler around my face, yet I suffered intensely. I was never more muffled for a long sleigh ride in the severest weather of Ohio.

"Jessie was in danger of being blown from her mule . . . it staggered once or twice. Crying out, she held on for dear life. I rode

---

[35]Blackberry.
[36]William T. Coggeshall, Diary of Journey from Guayaquil to Quito, 1866, in the collection of the author.

as near her as I could."³⁷ The strong teenager managed to stay astride her mount.

Finally the riders came down and their path wound around Chimborazo to a hut where they arrived about 3:00 p.m. From this point they saw 20 or 30 condors battling with wild dogs over a dead mule at the bottom of a deep ravine.³⁸ "Mr. Gouin fired his pistol among them and several condors took wing."

Cold, fatigued and hungry, Coggeshall "offered five dollars for a fire, but if I had offered a hundred, it had been in vain." After a cold supper the father, daughter, two servants, a dog and "countless hordes of fleas went to bed in that miserable hut" in all their layers of clothing. "Jessie slept in full Chimborazo costume and was a rare beauty emerging from her resting place on the morning of Sept. 2nd," her caring father observed.

> "I cannot even conjecture how high we were, but at the highest point, we saw no animal life whatever. The Tambo where we slept is more than 12,000 feet—above the region of trees—surrounded by no vegetation but a kind of brown heath which bears a blue flower."³⁹

ROBBERY AT MOCHE

The countryside from Chimborazo to the village of Moche was dotted with plains, snowy mountain peaks "in every direction, deep ravines, beautiful haciendas and smoke-emitting huts—the fuel probably being straw and dried cactus branches—of which there are vast amounts here."⁴⁰

Moche was located at the top of a steep hill. In the marketplace Coggeshall was buying two gratnias, a small Ecuadorian coin, when "a big Indian snatched" his "two reale pieces and fled." Commandante Aguerre chased the robber, choked him nearly to death, and retrieved the coin.

---

[37] William T. Coggeshall, Diary of Journey from Guayaquil to Quito, 1866, in the collection of the author.
[38] The condor is the national bird of Ecuador. It and a snow-covered volcano appear on Ecuador's national seal.
[39] William T. Coggeshall, Diary of Journey from Guayaquil to Quito, 1866, in the collection of the author.
[40] Ibid.

AMBATO—AND LICE

On Sunday, September 2, Ambato was the next stopping point on their journey, after "fields of potatoes, luzenne, corn, wheat, barley . . . and also cherry trees precisely like the wild cherry of Ohio."

Nestled deep in a valley, Ambato was a pleasant change from the poor, isolated mountain villages. The tile-roofed large low houses, regular streets, gardens, churches, and plaza filled with people in gaily colored ponchos, inspired Coggeshall to note, "a lovelier scene I never saw." Its cultivated hillsides displayed peach trees in bloom, orange trees, and "sweet and sour fruit trees peculiar to the tropics."

Ambato was the Capital of a province, had "5 to 6,000 population," a beautiful fountain in its plaza, and was celebrated for its "dulees" (preserves) and its workers in leather. Its streets were "paved in the Spanish fashion. . . . If it were peopled with Yankees it would be a paradise."

For a reale they bought nearly a gallon of large, delicious strawberries. "Peaches, apples, papayas, blackberries, cherries and all tropical fruits also grow here. The climate is delightful—the soil rich—and the numerous gardens, beautiful."[41]

But the diplomat's first impression of the people of Ambato paled when he saw women in the marketplace picking lice from their children's heads and eating them. "To one I said 'Malissimo' (very bad). She laughed and continued to reap her family harvest."

The party obtained new horses at Ambato and Jessie exchanged her white mule for a white horse. The group now traveled the National Road, "the Government Camino," for the 75 miles from Ambato to Quito. "But a small portion [of the road] is here built, however. Two miles from Ambato we take again the old Inca track. I have seen nothing yet but a want of enterprise which prevents the construction of a superior road from Guayaquil to Ambato. The National Road will pass from Ambato to Riobamba, hence to Quito."[42]

They passed over barren tracts of iron ore, thick growth of whortleberry, and cactus hedges with the blossoms of heliotrope.

COTOPAXI VOLCANO

That afternoon, a few miles from Latacunga, "we enjoyed our first view of a volcano—the famous Cotopaxi. It was belching a huge column

---

[41]William T. Coggeshall, Diary of Journey from Guayaquil to Quito, 1866, in the collection of the author.
[42]Ibid.

of black smoke." Cotopaxi is the highest active volcano in the world, 19,498 feet. Coggeshall estimated they came within 200 to 300 feet of Cotopaxi's 15,646 foot snowline.

LATACUNGA

> "About a mile from Latacunga we struck again the National road and crossed two or three bridges most admirably constructed."

In Latacunga they walked about the town. "It is built chiefly of lava from Cotopaxi and has had several earthquakes. There are five or six churches, a Cathedral and a College. It houses a Museum, mineralogical and geological Cabinets, five or six professors and about 100 students. . . . Lava lies about the streets everywhere—huge blocks of it I could easily lift."[43]

In the street, the Americans passed a procession of Indians carrying a dead man, "who had been accidently killed," on a bamboo litter. The foreigners heard "a great noise over him in one of the churches."

To the Americans, Cotopaxi was probably the most beautiful mountain in the world. "It rises like a cone from the plain . . . evidences of the violence of the crater were around us all day. . . . And the cold wind, direct from Cotopaxi, blew violently on our backs all day." At night they expected Cotopaxi to belch fire and smoke—"but the giant disappointed us."

> "Near our road in the vicinity of Cotopaxi is a remarkable hill called Loma de las Incas. It rises from the plain like a dome and is said to have been heaped up by order of the Incas."[44]

MYCHACHE

On Tuesday, September 4, the party arrived at the town of "Mychache" (Machachi), 30 miles from Quito "in the center of a very rich plain. . . . We enjoyed the National road from Latacunga to this place, except at two points where the work is not yet complete. It is a wide, well constructed highway with water courses on each side of it and admirable bridges. It leads through a rich plain covered with cattle, sheltered on both sides with mountains."

---

[43]William T. Coggeshall, Diary of Journey from Guayaquil to Quito, 1866, in the collection of the author.
[44]Ibid.

The people "of Mychache are skilled in native manufactures such as mats, carpets, saddle cloths, etc. A mat or cloth, which requires 10 or 12 days' labor, costs three or four pesos" (thirty or forty cents).

> "After dinner Mr. Gouin and the Commandante remained in our room and we had wine and toasts to continued good acquaintance and good luck."[45]

On the morrow, they would reach Quito . . . they thought.

FARM REST STOP

On Wednesday, September 5, "a cavalcade of gentlemen met us, all superbly mounted [on horseback]," who invited the Coggeshalls to breakfast and an overnight stay at the farm of an American citizen, Antonio Salvador, 24 miles from Quito. Included in the "cavalcade" were Salvador's brother-in-law, Antonio Flores, son of Ecuador's late ex-president, brother of the Flores whose hacienda Jessie had visited at Bodegas; Antonio's brother-in-law, Rio Firio; and Mr. Gouin's brother. "At the commodious farm house, sumptuously furnished," the Americans met Senor Flores' sisters—Mrs. Salvador and Mrs. Stagg, wife of a general. As a leading Ecuadorian family, the Floreses would figure prominently in the Coggeshall's stay in Ecuador.

After breakfast, Senor Gouin and Commandante Aguerre rode on to Quito "to see that rooms were prepared for us at the American Hotel" while the Coggeshalls decided to stay at the hacienda overnight.

In the farm fields, the new ambassador witnessed "40 or 50 Indian men and women harvesting wheat in the same manner as in the time of the Incas. They cut the grain with sickles, throw it in piles . . . sing as they work, are slow and wasteful . . . the grain is stacked on the field and is thrashed with oxen which tramp it out to be winnowed, as was the Inca custom . . . it is a wasteful culture."[46] The laborers were paid three cents a day.

The new diplomat watched and described in detail the Ecuadorian manner of breaking a colt. . . . "At Columbus, it was thought a great feat for the horse tamer to ride without a headstall. Here, that is the common way. A noose around the lower jaw forms bridle and bit, and donkeys, mules and horses are usually ridden that way by the common people."[47]

---

[45]William T. Coggeshall, Diary of Journey from Guayaquil to Quito, 1866, in the collection of the author.
[46]Ibid.
[47]Ibid.

BIRTHDAY PRESENT

The following morning, still at the Salvador hacienda, a long-hoped-for sight finally greeted Coggeshall's eyes. He wrote: "September 6, 1866. This is my 42nd birthday, and I suppose it was in honor thereof that Cotopaxi gave a splendid exhibition. Suddenly, a huge column of white smoke was projected from its crater and stood above its snows for two hours, unbroken by the wind . . . a beauty and a wonder." As though by some mystical magic, the great volcano knew this was Coggeshall's birthday and, for him, launched a giant candle in the sky.

QUITO AT LAST

On September 7, 1866, Antonio Flores accompanied the travelers on the last leg of their journey to Quito. After the "wretched hamlet of Tambillo, . . . the scenery is green and indescribably beautiful. After about an hour and a half we had our first clear view of Pichincha, the Volcano, at the foot of which Quito is situated. Quito has white steeples and tile roofs, in a beautiful plain dotted with cattle. . . . Beyond is a high hill, said to be artificial . . . to its left, are the peaks of Pichincha, portions of which were lost in the clouds . . . and in the distance, other mountain peaks. . . . We reached our Hotel, found our baggage and took possession of our rooms about 3 o'clock, glad that our journey was ended. . . ."

> "In the States, the distance from Guayaquil to Quito was reported at 150 miles. Here, it is disclosed to be 240 miles from Bodegas [near Guayaquil] to Quito."[48]

It had been a journey of 13 days.

---

[48]William T. Coggeshall, Diary of Journey from Guayaquil to Quito, 1866, in the collection of the author.

U.S. Minister to Ecuador William T. Coggeshall, age 42, and daughter Jessie, age 15. (Ohio Historical Society)

CHAPTER 9
DIPLOMATIC DUTIES

William and Jessie Coggeshall were relieved to be in Quito at last. Indians unloaded their 17-mule train of trunks of clothing, dishes, furniture, books and U.S. government records at the American Hotel. Their hotel suite would serve as home and office, the U.S. Legation. Later, they hoped to lease a house.

FIRST DIPLOMATIC SPEECH
AT PRESIDENTIAL PALACE

The Coggeshalls' first month in Quito was happy. The U.S. Minister organized his office, met Quito officials and the diplomats from other countries and wrote dispatches to Secretary of State Seward in Washington—William H. Seward to whom Coggeshall had first offered that same cabinet post for Lincoln in 1860. Coggeshall began dispatches with "Hon. W. H. Seward," and closed them with "Very Respectfully, Your obedient servant, W. T. Coggeshall."

Jessie acted as her father's secretary. She would take dictation or copy communications from the Ecuadorian government or other diplomatic missions. All their writings were in longhand. Jessie was also the Legation hostess, responsible for Modesto, the servant, and a cook. She organized her beautiful china and linens, marked with their name, and studied the booklet on U.S. protocol.

The new Americans were quickly welcomed into Quito's diplomatic life. On September 15, Ecuador's Minister of Foreign Affairs Manuel Bristamente, wrote a letter to Coggeshall himself, congratulating the United States for sending to Ecuador such an "illustrious and competent" representative.

Three days later the U.S. Minister gave his first diplomatic speech to Ecuadorian officials, the diplomatic corps resident in Quito, and "persons of note" at a "grand banquet" at the Presidential Palace honoring the anniversary of Chile's independence from Spain. Referring to Ecuador, Peru and Bolivia, allies against Spain's efforts to regain Peru and Chile, Coggeshall said:

> "I appreciate the emotions of South American Republicans because it brings home to my heart the sacred memories of 1776 and the glorious results of the struggle for independence then begun in North America. . . . I represent the people of my nation when I trust that the prosperity of the South American Republics may be so marked that when a new century is ushered in, they will be independent not only of Spain, but of any power disposed to interfere with the advance of Republicanism upon this Continent."[1]

After the banquet, bull fights were held in Quito's Plaza Santo Domingo. During one intermission, the Ecuadorians gustily cheered "Olee! Ministre Coggeshall! Olee! Olee!" Coggeshall acknowledged their loud shouts with a friendly wave while Jessie smiled happily. The bull fights continued eight days.

On September 20 the new diplomat presented his credentials from U.S. President Andrew Johnson to Ecuadorian President Geronimo Carrion at the Presidential Palace. As reported in the official national newspaper, *La America Latina*, Coggeshall stated that his country's recent Civil War had "enhanced patriotism" and devotion to the Republican form of government. "The U.S.," he said, "could sympathise politically with South American countries" in their struggle for freedom from Spain. His mission, he stated, was to "strengthen the friendly political intercourse now existing" with Ecuador and "to interchange industrial and commercial information to promote the interests of both Republics."[2]

In his response, President Carrion noted that "The unhappy Civil War . . . gives additional evidence of the inseparable adhesion to liberty of the (U.S.) government and the people . . . which is shown wherever their voice is heard."[3]

The father and daughter were impressed by their warm welcome to Ecuador: the greetings from the government; the invitations to other legations; the guidance by Mr. Gouin who had led them over the Andes Mountains and was Quito's leading merchant; and the smiles and waves of the Ecuadorians. Representing a rich and powerful nation, they were

---

[1]William T. Coggeshall Papers, Ohio Historical Society.
[2]William T. Coggeshall Dispatches from Ecuador, 1866-67, U.S. Department of State.
[3]Ibid.

northern neighbors in the hemisphere . . . and were dignified and brilliant.

But the Coggeshalls would come to realize they were Protestant in a devoutly orthodox Catholic country.

THE DARLING OF QUITO

On September 22, two weeks after arriving in Quito, Jessie turned 15. Tall and thin, unlike the Ecuadorians, she was an object of great curiosity. Her long black hair framed a creamy-white Dresden-doll face. Her brown eyes were snappy. She was a spunky independent girl who spoke her mind crisply yet with the grace of a lady of manners.

Jessie dressed beautifully. When she walked, swarthy native Indian women moved their baskets of fruits and handmade leather items so she could pass easily on the roughly paved streets. Scrubby little Indian boys tagged at her heels to touch her sweeping skirts. She could see townspeople peeking at her from behind curtains and over balconies. Some called out greetings to her. She would reply with a word or two in broken Spanish.

Everywhere Jessie went she was called "La Francaise Senorita Norte Americana" . . . the French Miss of North America, a clear compliment to her grace.

The youngest diplomatic hostess at 15, Jessie assumed her social duties with ease. Helping out with five younger brothers and sisters at home and being the daughter of a famous author had prepared her.

LIFE IN THE U.S. LEGATION;
JESSIE, SECRETARY AND HOSTESS

Life in the U.S. Legation was varied. Its door was open to rich and poor alike. Coggeshall sponsored discussions with other diplomats. He held open house once a week. Secretary Jessie kept notes. Dinners, parties, and receptions were an essential part of the diplomatic life.

Jessie maintained diplomatic decorum. Her table was sought after for the finesse of its mistress and its elegant china and table linens, rare in Quito.

As some of Jessie's letters reveal, however, the young American deplored the demeanor and naivete of the average Ecuadorian and she would criticize the natives quaintly but frankly in letters to her mother: . . . "people here think they can ride to the U.S. on a mule; the Vice-President put his knife in his mouth; sloppy women catching fleas and lice and eating them . . . men and women performing their natural necessities in the street. . . . I almost vomit as I write."

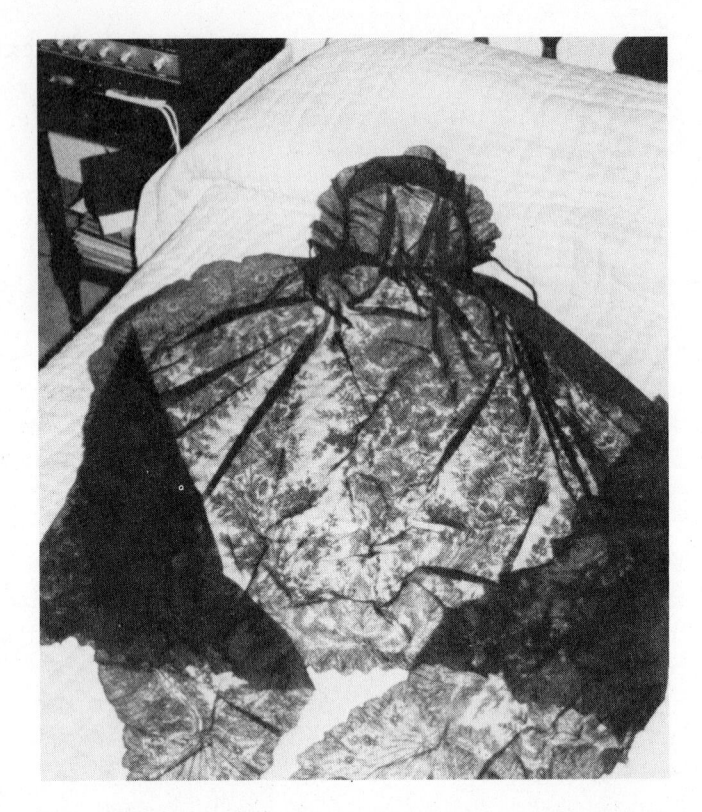

Jessie Coggeshall's mantilla—black lace with hood tied with black velvet ribbons. (Dr. Mary Harbage)

Evenings when there were no social engagements or local celebrations the father and daughter would read or write letters.

For recreation, the two would ride horseback in the countryside. They loved the tropical scenery, rich lush foliage, plentiful produce and mountainous landscapes which yielded new breathtaking pictures on every excursion. The climate, they wrote, was "Septemberish in December."

On their outings the Coggeshalls would observe Ecuadorians weaving straw mats and blankets or cutting designs in leather with simple tools. "For women, toil is probably the severest," Coggeshall wrote. Indian women, he noted, had to trot across fields with sticks as they herded cattle.

Most of Minister Coggeshall's attention focused on problems affecting Americans and on the political stability of the new Latin American region.

AMERICAN PROBLEMS

Gold Seekers

Approximately 20 United States citizens resided in the Quito area. Intermittently, other American adventurers from the States passed through the capital in the 1860s searching for gold and silver in Central and South America.

Reports of huge reserves of gold in the Andes Mountains were part of the lure. When the Spaniards had invaded South America in the 1500s, they killed and looted sacred strongholds of the Inca Indians, considered inconsequential heathens in the way of the Christianity the Spanish were trying to spread. When the Spaniards captured the last Inca King of Peru, Atahualpa, the Incas retreated and hid legendary caches of gold in the mountains.

By mid-October, ten Californians had visited Quito and the U.S. Legation. They had been miners in Barbados, New Granada.[4] Three of them, George O. Mason, G. W. Mosure and David B. Horton, left Quito with an Ecuadorian company for the region of Canelos southeast of Quito between the Cordillera (mountain range) and the Amazon River, "which is reported rich in gold," Coggeshall wrote in a dispatch. "Some of the others will probably make an expedition to Cuenco where ancient gold mines are known to exist."[5]

At that time, gold and silver exploration was for the taking, but in the middle 1870s the Ecuadorian government claimed such reserves as government property.

Kentuckian in Despair

Among the few American residents in Ecuador was William Bryant of Kentucky who had been in the South American Country since 1858. A farmer and "licensed merchant" in the province of Esmeralda on Ecuador's northwest Pacific coast, Bryant supplied wood, fruits, tobacco and other goods to captains of whaling boats. Shortly after Coggeshall arrived, in September 1866, Bryant was accused of smuggling eight sacks of flour into Esmeralda and, after a legal bout with the Governor, was fined 118 pesos. Bryant refused to pay.

In an eloquent 12-page letter to American Minister Coggeshall, Bryant sought help as "an American and a Republican." The smuggling charge, he maintained, had been concocted by his competitor, a

---

[4]Colombia.
[5]William T. Coggeshall Dispatches from Ecuador, 1866–67, U.S. Department of State.

Portuguese farmer named Bos who also sold produce to whalers. Bos was supported by an unscrupulous Collector (of taxes) and the Governor of Esmeralda. "The sacks of flour have never been seen or purchased except by them," Bryant wrote. He had been tried and acquitted but the Governor had torn up the papers confirming his innocence.

Instead, the Governor had levied the fine against the American. When Bryant refused to pay, he was thrown into "the lowest level" of a broken down jail. But Bryant escaped and in October made his way to Quito to make a personal appeal to the U.S. Minister.

"I would rather abandon my property and see the gathering of my tobacco and cotton crops stopped," Bryant told Coggeshall, "than pay a fine which was imposed wrongly and illegally in the crime of smuggling imputed to me which is entirely false."[6] He asserted that the provincial government authorities were united in a "plot to injure and oppress the majority of the merchants and leading men" of Esmeralda.

Coggeshall wrote Ecuador's Foreign Affairs Minister Manuel Bristamente about the case. Bristamente replied that Bryant had previously been fined for smuggling and that, as a resident of Ecuador, he was subject to the same laws, punishments and fair treatment as an Ecuadorian citizen.

For more than a month while Bryant dodged the authorities, Coggeshall pursued the farmer's problem. Finally, in early December he wrote to Secretary of State Seward for guidance, recommending that the case be "settled by judicial and not diplomatic action."

Seward's reply is unknown. So is the fate of William Bryant.

Questionable Citizenship

After several months in Quito, Coggeshall queried Washington about changing U.S. citizenship laws. He stated he knew of "several native Ecuadorians" who had gone to the States, resided there less than five years, spoke "not one word" of English, received U.S. citizenship and returned to lucrative farming and merchant businesses for which they paid no income taxes to the United States. He estimated the U.S. treasury was losing $10,000 annually by this type citizenship and asked, "why should not permanent residence in a foreign land make null and void certificates of naturalization?"[7]

---

[6]William T. Coggeshall Dispatches from Ecuador, 1866–67, U.S. Department of State.
[7]Ibid.

LATIN AMERICAN PROBLEMS

Amazon River Dispute

On November 1, Senor Luis Fuiz, an envoy from New Granada (Colombia), visited Quito to request that Ecuador join a Granadian protest against Peruvian and Brazilian regulations governing navigation of the Amazon River, which ended in Peru southeast of Ecuador. Ecuador declined the request, Coggeshall wrote, because it would contradict its alliance with Peru. "The free navigation of the Amazon to its mouth," Coggeshall concluded his report, "is of so great importance to all the South American Republics that sooner or later a surrender of the monopoly by Brazil must be insisted upon. November 3, 1866."[8]

Peace Efforts

Coggeshall also informed Washington of impending political problems. The diplomatic representatives of Chile and Peru, he reported, had heard rumors that Spain was planning to reorder her fleet to the Pacific to bombard Chilean and Peruvian seaports and to seize and occupy their capital cities of Lima and Valparaiso. Coggeshall informed that Ecuador's envoy to Chile, Garcia Moreno, had just returned and declared, "There is no immediate prospect of peace between Spain and the Allied Republics."

Ship Burning

In mid-November, the U.S. Minister wrote Secretary of State Seward that Ecuador's official paper, *Nacional,* reported that Ecuador's Supreme Court of Justice decided "there is no cause for prosecuting judicially Samuel Montenegro, Fernando Cesares and Elvira Vernaza as in any way responsible for the burning of the [American] steamer *Washington.*"[9]

Galapagos Islands

Six hundred miles off Ecuador's Pacific coast were the Galapagos Islands, Ecuador's prize possession. The islands had been formed by the residue of volcanoes erupting from the ocean's floor and were the unique site of nature's mutations and adaptations of life. Plants and

---

[8]William T. Coggeshall Dispatches from Ecuador, 1866–67, U.S. Department of State.
[9]Ibid.

animals found nowhere else on earth inhabited the Galapagos or "turtle" chain. Each of the 13 islands had its own variety of tortoise: some were large enough for man to ride. The only known penguins in a tropical environment and finches whose beaks could crack nuts and berries also roamed the islands. Although located near the Equator, the cold Humboldt Current flowing north from the coasts of Chile and Peru enabled the arctic penguin to flourish in what Coggeshall described as "nature's isolated laboratory."

In the autumn of 1865, British holders of Ecuadorian bonds were negotiating to buy the Galapagos Islands, although such a sale was "forbidden by the Constitution of Ecuador and by treaty stipulations," Coggeshall informed the State Department on October 28. The Ecuadorian government was considering an arrangement which would transfer ownership of the Galapagos to British bondholders yet retain Ecuadorian political jurisdiction over the archipelago. The deal, however, came to naught. Today, the Galapagos Islands are Ecuadorian territory.

CHAPTER 10
LETTERS FROM QUITO

The Coggeshall's first preserved letters from Ecuador were dated August 1866, sent from Guayaquil. They briefly concerned business matters and a hunting trip. Then letters galore flowed from Quito to Columbus. Gay letters, glad letters, sad letters, mad letters. They went by steamer to Panama, across Panama by rail to the Atlantic Ocean, then again by large steamer to New York. With 10¢ postage, they took four or five weeks to reach the United States and home. Boxes took longer.

Coggeshall's letters were usually brief notes, dwelling on family business and gold transfer drafts to Mary. In a few, especially for the children, the diplomat depicted long rides and hunts in the country.

Coggeshall signed nearly all his letters to Mary with his initials "W.T.C." A few times, he penned "William."

Jessie's missives spilled out subtle thoughts, emotions, and weekly happenings in Quito culture in exquisite detail. She made no pretense of loving the Ecuadorians.

One of Jessie's letters threatened, "Mother, if you don't write, Father and I shall get married."

After settling in Quito, Jessie described the bull fights, the way women dressed, her fifteenth birthday presents, curiosity about her clothes, their hotel room, "some very curious members" of the diplomatic corps, protocol for her walking in the street, incidents about her hats, parties at the Floreses, and "the dullness of the place."

BULL FIGHTS; BIZARRE DRESS OF WOMEN

"Quito, October 3rd, 1866

"Dear Mother,

"There has been a great deal of excitement for some time in Quito which served to change the monotony of our lives—the bull fighting. . . . It lasted for one week and I think I never saw more brutal sport in my life. The bull pen, as it is called here, was in the Plasa Santo Domingo and the Government had erected on the four sides of the Plasa boxes of polcos, one above the other, which were rented for the season by the aristocrasy of the place, the common people were in the ring teasing the bull. I was invited to sit in the box of Mr. Flores with his sisters, Father was in the Chilian Minister's box. The sport began about 3 o'clock in the afternoon when a bull was let into the ring, and immediately the people began to tease the poor animal by throwing their ponchos before its eyes, pulling his tail, and torturing him in every manner possible, and it was not at all unusual for the bull to turn suddenly and catch some person and give them a toss in the air.

"The first day one man was crippled for life; the bull caught him and threw him up and when he fell he broke his leg—another man was teasing the animal when he put his horn through the man's bowels. The second day several persons were very severely hurt but not killed. The third day two men were terribly hurt—one of them had his leg broken, the bull took him by the seat of his pantaloons, and the man turned a somersault hitting his leg against the iron fountain in the middle of the ring, one horse was killed also, the bull thrusting its horn in the horse's stomach. The last day of the bull fighting it was something unusual, the bulls being decorated with very handsome saddles, made of velvet or some other rich material and very beautifully trimmed with beads and silver. This caused great excitement and their[1] was a great deal of quarreling, for the person who could snatch the colchon as it is called, on the saddle, was considered a hero. The last day one bull was sent into the ring, which had a very beautiful saddle and which was filled with powder and contrived in such a manner that when the bull would run, rockets would shoot out from the saddle in every direction which frightened the poor animal so that it would rush headlong against whatever attracted its attention and in this way several men were injured. After the man was knocked down, sometimes the bull would turn around and tramp on him and punch him with his horns. Last Sunday their was no bull fighting but their was a parade of soldiers in the plasa.

---

[1] Jessie nearly always spelled "there" as "their". Jessie's original spelling has often been retained without additional comment.

"In the evening I went to Mr. Flores house to a reception and enjoyed myself very much, as I always do at his house because his sisters and brothers, as well as himself, are very agreeable and kind to us. During the bull fighting I was with them most all the time. . . .

"The ladies have a very strange way of dressing in Quito. During the week they never wear stockings, a very few have waists to their dresses but wear dirty white linen waists unbuttoned from the neck down to the waist, most always have dirty hands and a pound of rice powder and paint on their faces. Last Monday night I went to a small dance given by a cousin of Mr. Flores, it was very small indeed, not over twenty persons were there. One lady, a cousin of the lady of the house, was dressed in very bad taste indeed, she had on a splendid white brocade silk, made bare armed and low necked, a yellow crepe shawl around her shoulders, white flowers in her hair and a beautiful pearl necklace, her hoops were very large and did not set well, her dress was very narrow and very crooked, and altogether she was very dowdy and very inappropriately dressed for the occasion, and the worst of it was she had worn that dress to the bull fight that afternoon. We had dancing and a very fine supper but I left before the supper.

"The last day of the bull fighting it began to rain before we had left our boxes and consequently we were obliged to stay in them until long after dark, and it was thundering and lightning most fearfully all the time but about seven o'clock we left the box and went into the house of a friend of Mr. Flores where I met the wife of the President and Mr. Bristamente, the Minister of Exterior Relations. . . .

"The last day of feast the young men of Quito were to dress in fancy dresses with masks. There were four companies and eight gentlemen in each company, one company had black horses and were dressed to represent Peru, another had sorrel horses and represented Chile, another had white horses and represented Ecuador, another had grey horses and represented Bolivia. After going through with their performance in the ring they unmasked, and their was brought into the ring a post with a beam projecting from it in the end of which was a hole, and through the hole was hung a ribbon with a small iron ring in one end. The young men then rode at full speed and tried to take the ribbon on the point of the lance, but only two or three were successful. The ones that were the victors accompanied by their companions, rode to the boxes of their separate lady loves and presented the ribbon which they had taken to the lady.

"In the evening we went to Mr. Flores house where we met five or six ladies, the Chilian Minister, the Bolivian Minister, the Peruvian Minister, the English Minister and his son, the French

Minister, and the American Minister was their also with his daughter, the other Ministers had their secretarys. About nine o'clock the young men who had performed in the afternoon came to Mr. Flores with their fancy dresses and a band of music, and we had dancing and refreshments. It was one o'clock when we left. A young man went off with father's hat and we were obliged to wait until a servant could be sent for it.

"The ladies were dressed in very singular taste. Their hoops were very large and ugly, and one lady had on a thin organdy dress with white ground [background] and a small bouquet of flowers, the dress was very long, and her skirt was very short and when she walked their was a black line around her and you could see her legs through her dress. Another young lady had on a white tarletan dress trimmed with pink tarletan, made bare armed and low necked, and she had a wreath of ivy leaves in her hair, she was very pretty indeed but her dress was horrible. While she was dancing she had the good sense to faint but she fell on the floor so hard that it shook the room. . . .

"Yesterday we went to Mr. Gouin's to dinner. Mr. Gouin is the gentleman who came with us from Guayaquil, dinner was very good indeed and we enjoyed it very much. In the evening we went to Mr. Flores house and . . . we had a great deal of fun playing pass the ring. We also had much sport with Henry Neale, the son of the English Minister. He is a perfect laughing stock for everyone—he was trying to dance the polka and as he does not know anything about it you may imagine what a strange looking object he was, and I, just to make fun of him, asked him to dance with me, and then there was some laughing for I can not dance the polka any too well. And then to cap the climax, when we went home, he offered me his arm and when we got to his father's house, he turned round and very cooly said good night.

"A week ago Saturday was my fifteenth birthday and I received some very beautiful presents. Father gave me a very beautiful vase for my wax flowers, Mr. Antonio Flores gave me a small emerald, his brother gave me a purse of white and red velvet, Mr. Hurtado gave me a beautiful card with 'My hearty congratulations' printed on it, and Mr. Gouin gave me a lovely purple velvet work box, furnished with gold thimble, sissers, needle case, and a small looking glass, and Kersu gave me a very pretty purse with pearl sides. . . . Father's health is much better and I think that the air of Quito is very good for him. These pictures which I enclose are of the Q [Quito] mountains and are very much like. I wish you to send me three or four pairs of kid gloves not light, but some pretty colors. . . . We have not received any papers yet nor the Godey[2] nor

---

[2]*Godey's Lady's Book*. First women's magazine in the U.S. founded in 1830 by the Frenchman Louis Antoine Godey.

any magazines, please get them and send them to us for we are almost starved for something to read, but be sure to send the back numbers of the Godey. Tell Mr. Busbey that I should like very much to receive a letter from him and I would answer it with much pleasure . . . I hope you enjoyed your visit to Springfield and Willie his to Akron.

"Mother you cannot immagine [sic] how I long for some fried potatoes, some good pies, and some home made bread. The bread in Quito is perfectly horrible, it is baked in rolls about a foot long and about two inches around it, so it is nearly all crust. Give my best best respects to Mr. Busbey and tell him that I wish I was in Columbus to go to the Theatre. Present my compliments to my gentlemen friends and love to the ladies and girls . . .

"From your very loving daughter,
Jessie Coggeshall."[3]

ECCENTRICS IN DIPLOMATIC CORPS

"Quito, October 19th, 1866

"Dear Brother Willie,

". . . You have no idea how dull Quito is. I do not know what to do with myself, I have no ladies society at all except the Misses Flores, but a great many gentlemen friends. There is nothing at all to do but to ride, walk, read, and study Spanish, and I am almost a prisoner in the hotel for I can not go anywhere unless Father goes with me, or I must have a maid servant walking behind me. Several times I have gone to Mr. Flores house alone and the people could not have stared more if I had been one of the Siamese Twins.

"My hats are the greatest curiosities in Ecuador, and my parasol and dresses. On Saturday night I went with Father and another gentleman to see the Church of Santo Domingo, when I went in of course I did not take off my hat, presently an old monk walked up to the gentleman whom I was with and asked him to tell me to take off my hat, but as he spoke in Spanish I did not understand him but when it was explained I very deliberately turned and walked out of the Church.

"The other day Father and I were in a store and were talking about it when a gentleman told me that the monk had been asked what he was going to do with me for wearing my hat in church, the monk answered that it must be the custom in my country or I would not do it. When Father was told about it he said 'Such a damn country' which occasioned quite a laugh.

---

[3]William T. Coggeshall Papers, Ohio Historical Society.

"Tomorrow is Sunday and the day for calling, and I must submit to be laced and greased and sit on a straight backed chair in the parlor to receive the gentlemen who will honor me with a visit. It is quite amusing when they call here because there are only one or two who can speak English, and as I speak very little Spanish and Father much less than I do, and with our mistakes in Spanish and theirs in English there is a great deal of fun. They usually begin to call about 11 o'clock and woe to the lady who is not dressed.

"They say here that I belong to the Diplomatic Corps because I copy all the dispatches of the Legation.

"The gentlemen in Quito put on as much style as if they were in London, Paris, or New York. When they call they wear white kid gloves, high hats, patent leather boots, and dress coats, and look as if they had just stepped out of band boxes. One in particular always wears white kid gloves no matter what kind of coat he has on or where he is going, and Father says that it gives him the colic when he sees the Chilian Minister coming in his white kid gloves.

"There are some very curious characters among the Diplomatic Corps. First their is Mr. Songrobear the French Minister who is the most eccentric man in Quito and he takes pride in being odd, he rides different from anybody else, dresses different, dances, talks, walks, eats, and drinks different from anyone else; when he rides he wears a brown velvet coat, light pants, white gloves, and a white straw hat with a piece of thin white muslin drawn over the crown, wrapped around it three or four times and hanging down behind in one wide streamer with fringe on the edge. Father calls it 'Songrobear's nightgown.' His horse is the only one of the kind in Ecuador and when he rides he goes on a fast gallop or a trot, and he says that their is not a person in Quito who can ride with him. I tried it one day but when I got home I was so tired that I could hardly walk up stairs and the next day I could not walk, for my leg was swollen under the knee, where it rubbed on the horn of the saddle, as large as a hen's egg. His whole house is trimmed with curtains which he made himself, but enough of Songrobear.

"Next is the English Minister Mr. Neal and son. Neal senior is a perfect gentleman, and has one hobby, and that is he is always talking about Japan and he has a very beautiful collection of Japanese curiosities. He is very quiet and a favorite with the ladies but as he is a married man and fifty-three years old, their is no use for any of them to try to catch him. His son is what Father calls in Spanish a 'burro' which when translated means 'ass.' He is about 19 years old, has a few very light eye winkers on his upper lip, and is decidedly green; he thinks that he can dance the polka beautifully and at Mr. Flores receptions it is my perfect delight to dance with him for the amusement of the spectators.

"One night at Mr. Flores . . . Henry Neale had a very conspicuous part. General Stagg, a very nice old gentleman and the husband of one of the Miss Flores, is in the habit of taking snuff and also is very deaf. Henry, who thinks he can play the piano splendidly, called the old general to him while he was playing and said, 'Now General, I will play something sentimental.' 'Oh,' said the General taking out his snuff box and tapping it with his fingers. 'You want some snuff do you?' You can imagine that young Neal felt rather green.

"Next their is Mr. Flores who has traveled in Europe, England, and in the States and speaks English very well. I think that he is the most conceited man that ever lived, he is very handsome and smart and he knows it, and he thinks that anything that belongs to the Flores family or in any way connected with them, must be perfection. According to what he says, a person would think that he was the richest man in Ecuador, and that they have the best coffee, the best chocolate, tea, and the best piano, and the handsomest house and the largest in Ecuador, also his emeralds, their are more to be found equal to them, and he has also been very careful to tell me three times that he always changes his stockings twice a day; but for all his faults he is very pleasant and has been very kind to me. I will finish my description [of Quito gentlemen] in my next letter. . . .

"Last week a gentleman promised to come on Wednesday morning with a horse for me at eleven o'clock, so fully expecting him I went to work and made me a riding dress, and worked so hard for three days and took no exercise that I was almost sick. When Wednesday morning came I was dressed half an hour before the time, Father's horse was saddled and two other gentlemen, Mr. Flores and Songrobear were waiting for us. Half past eleven came, and no horse or gentleman, twelve not come yet, one and not yet, and finally I told Father to go and leave me at home for I would not go if he did come so Father left me alone in my glory, and pretty soon I got so angry that I could not stay in the house any longer so I put on my hat and went up to Mr. Flores and there I met Mr. Songrobear who was so excited when he was informed why I did not go to ride that he shook his fists and said that all the people in Ecuador were just the same, they never were punctual, and that he always waited for the women just ten minutes and the men just five, and he talked French, Spanish, and English all at the same time.

"Mother says in her letter that you were going to have a party on my birthday. I only wish I could be there to enjoy it with you. . . .

"Last Sunday, about two o'clock in the afternoon we went to Mr. Gouin's house to have our photographs taken two of which we send you, we are going again next Sunday for more because these *are not very good. . . . In the box which we will send home for Christmas we will try and send you an emerald ring. I must close now, give my love to all the girls and boys and present my best best compliments to Mr. Busbey and his sisters. Kiss all the children for Jessie.*

> *"From your loving sister,*
> *Jessie Coggeshall."*[4]

---

[4]William T. Coggeshall Papers, Ohio Historical Society.

Paris Nov. 3rd 1866.

Dear Mother.

.... How diagnosable it is for one to go on the stall. I am a perfect anomaly, and it is not considered proper for a lady to go to the circus with a gentleman unless that gentleman is her father, brother, husband or one of her near relations, but she must never be seen without a gentleman even on a errand, but I have not regarded this condition at all, I go where I please and with whom I please ....

Your own loving daughter
Jessie Coggshall

Sample of Jessie's handwriting.

(Ohio Historical Society)

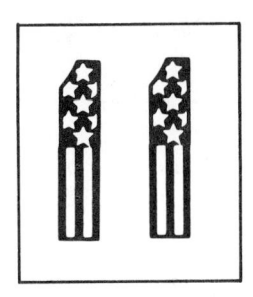

CHAPTER 11
PREJUDICE BEGINS

DISASTER IN DECEMBER

In December 1866, two funerals in Quito were held in contrasting manner. The funeral of Ecuador's ex-President, Juan Flores, took place with public pomp and eulogy. The funeral of Britain's Consul General, Colonel Edward St. John Neale—a heathen in Ecuadorian eyes—was held in guarded privacy in the midst of a religious fracas which spilled into political and diplomatic dispute. Coggeshall's furious intervention prevented an incident, but the event made international headlines.

For the Coggeshalls, the happy days of August, September, October and November began to give way to the dark days of December.

Colonel Edward Neale, the British Consul, was Coggeshall's best friend in the diplomatic corps. He visited them often, exchanged governmental philosophies and was Coggeshall's confidante. Colonel Neale was highly respected by all members of the diplomatic circle, Catholic and Protestant alike.

On Sunday, December 9, Colonel Neale entertained the Coggeshalls, Antonio Flores and General Stagg (who were brothers-in-law) at dinner. After eating, the group took coffee in the salon.

During the coffee hour, Colonel Neale became violently ill, "complaining of pain in his side." The doctor was summoned and, after assurance that their host felt better, the guests left. However, Coggeshall was apprehensive that the illness might be serious.

On Tuesday, the Coggeshalls sent their servant Modesto to inquire about Mr. Neale's condition. With news that he was decidedly improved, they left for a horseback ride to Guapulo in a valley three miles below Quito.

Coggeshall related in a December 21, 1866, letter to Mary what happened after that:

>"We gathered huge boquets [sic], gave our guides each a reale and started back to Quito. On the way we met our servant Modesto, on a mule. I was much surprised and cried out Porque Modesto—What for—He answered 'Senor Neale Muerto.' Mr. Neale [the English Minister] is dead. I was never more shocked in my life and we galloped over the plain, back to Quito, as rapidly as it was possible for Jessie to ride.
>
>"We took dinner with Mr. Neale on Sunday, December 9. About eight o'clock he complained of a pain in his side. It grew worse; we advised him to go to bed. He did so and sent for a Doctor. He continued to grow worse and died at 3 o'clock on Tuesday. We would not have gone to Guapulo on Tuesday, but his son sent us word, at ten o'clock, that his father was better—at eleven he began to sink. His disease was internal inflammation. The funeral was attended on Thursday—that is, there were funeral services over the body, it having been embalmed that it might be sent home to England. I was that day a Minister in two senses—U.S. Minister and Episcopal Minister. There are no clergymen, not Catholic, in Equador and I read the burial service. It was a hard task. Mr. Neale was a good man and I had learned to love him very much. He was the only friend here with whom I confidentially took counsel. He was 53 years old."[1]

When the Coggeshalls "rode back to Quito as fast as possible" the British Minister had been dead for more than an hour. They found him already dressed and placed upon a table in the salon. His 21-year-old, irresponsible son, Henry, an habitual drinker, walked about in a daze asserting that his father was sleeping.

CRISIS AT BRITISH CONSUL NEALE'S FUNERAL

The afternoon that Col. Neale died the Papal Nuncio declared that he could not be buried in Ecuador because he was "a Protestant," thus "a heretic," and could not be placed in consecrated ground. Ecuadorian soil was reserved for Catholics.

Coggeshall was "infuriated." As Jessie wrote to her mother, "Father for four days has been in a state of perpetual excitement and anger. He hates the Catholics anyhow, and the Nuncio in particular."

When Coggeshall learned of the Nuncio's restriction, from Senor Flores, he bristled with anger and retorted, "If Mr. Neale's son wants his father buried here it should be done in spite of the Nuncio. AND, if the

---

[1]William T. Coggeshall Papers, Ohio Historical Society.

government refuses to permit it, I SHALL DEMAND MY PAPERS AND RETURN TO THE UNITED STATES BY THE NEXT STEAMER!"

There are three long accounts of the resolution of the conflict: Coggeshall's dispatch to the State Department; the Ecuadorian government's report; and Jessie's letter. Her letter of December 15, 1866, to her mother most vividly records the agonizing dissension.

JESSIE DESCRIBES HASSLE OVER BURIAL; COGGESHALL FUMES

"Quito, December 15th, 1866

"Dear Mother,

"Why have we not received any letters from you? We received letters and papers from Mr. Busbey, but not a letter from home. It has been nearly two months since your last.

"This letter must be very short, because it is late, and I have been copying father's dispatches and, also, I am very tired, because I was at Mr. Neale's house all day packing his clothes and things to send to England.

"Last Sunday, Father, Mr. Flores, General Stagg and I took dinner with Mr. Neale and his son. Soon after we had gone to the saloon [salon][2] and taken coffee, Mr. Neale complained of a pain in his side, and was obliged to lay down on the bed; soon after, I went to Mr. Flores house with him, leaving Father with Mr. Neale.

"When Mr. Flores and I returned to Mr. Neale's house about 10 o'clock, Father told us that Mr. Neale had sent for the Doctor and he was afraid it was something serious.

"The next day we sent the servant to inquire how he was, and he returned and said he was better; the next day we received the same account of his health, and so Father and I went to Guapulo (a small place near Quito) on horseback to see a house. We staid [sic] there about 2 hours and were just climbing the hill when we met our servant on a mule who told us to ride back to town as soon as possible as Mr. Neale was dead. You can imagine how astonished and horrified we were with such sorrowful news.

"We rode back as fast as possible but when Father got to the house he had been dead for more than an hour, and was already dressed and placed upon a table in the saloon.

---

[2] Throughout her letter Jessie keeps spelling "salon" with an extra "o" which was the accepted spelling of that day, but which turns it into "saloon." It was the reception room of the house.

"He died without expressing any wishes, without making a will and without telling any one about his business or affairs. His son Henry seemed to be perfectly indifferent and dazed, and he would not believe that his Father was dead. When the Misses Flores went to the house, they told him that his Father was dead but he said 'no he was a little worse but now he was only asleep.' He does not seem to realize it yet.

"Mother, I am completely disgusted with Ecuador and every one in it, and I am sure that you will not wonder at it when I tell you what I have seen in the last week.

"Father for the last four days has been in a perpetual state of excitement and anger. The first thing which excited him was a remark made by the Representative of the Pope.

"The afternoon that Mr. Neale died, the Nuncio (as he is called) told Mr. Flores that he would not allow Mr. Neale to be buried because he was a Protestant. When it was repeated to Father you may be sure it made him furious for he hates the Catholics anyhow and the Nuncio in particular. He told Mr. Flores that if Henry Neale wanted his Father to be buried here it should be done in spite of the Nuncio, and if the Government refused to permit it he would demand his papers and return to the United States by the next steamer.

"Tuesday afternoon after Mr. Neale died Isabel Flores and I went to the house and got a bouquet to put on the street door as we do in the states, but as there are no door knobs in Ecuador we were obliged, with the help of Mr. Gouin, to nail it on the door.

"In the evening Mr. Gouin came to our house and told us that he had seen a man go to the door and steal the black corsage, put it under his coat or poncho, but before he had escaped Mr. Gouin took a cane, walked up to the man and made him put it back again. Such a thing as stealing the crepe from a dead man's door was something I had never expected to hear about, as bad as I knew the people of Ecuador to be. Mr. Gouin told us of another thing which happened here; a Frenchman died in Quito about 2 years ago but being a Catholic he was put in the church. The next morning when his friends went to the church to the funeral they discovered that some wretch had stolen the dead man's boots.

"The difficulty about Mr. Neale's being buried was soon overcome, as everybody supposed, by his son's disclosing that he would have his Father embalmed as he wished to have him sent to Europe. Finally it was decided that the body should be embalmed and that Father should read the burial services in the saloon of the house, on Thursday morning at 11 o'clock. Tuesday afternoon Mr. Saint Robert, Mr. Hurtado the Chilian Minister, and Father went to Mr. Bristamente, the Minister of Foreign Affairs, to see what part the Government would take in the ceremonies. Mr.

Bristamente said that they would have the soldiers out with the band, that he would attend the funeral, and as the Doctors said that it was not safe to keep the body in the house even after it was embalmed, as Henry had at first intended to do until it could be sent to Europe, that he would prepare a place for the safe deposit of the body.

"Accordingly, the next morning at 10 o'clock all the Diplomatic Corps, a guard of soldiers, several officers connected with the Government and a large number of citizens assembled in Mr. Neale's house. Everything passed off well and in good order. The corpse was borne upon the shoulders of six soldiers into the Plaza where it was saluted by a discharge of artillery, and followed by the friends and soldiers with the band, went to the church called Tejar.

"When the procession got to the gate of the church, it was met by the Bishop of Quito and the Nuncio who declared that the body should not enter the gate of the church. Then Mr. Bristamente ordered the soldiers to carry the corpse around to the back of the wall and break down the wall and go in that way, but Father made a grand fuss and shook his fist in Mr. Bristamente's face, declared it was a shame and an outrage and a disgrace to Ecuador and it would be talked about and discussed all over the world, until they gave that up and were going to put it over a fence and then carry it to the vault; but Father interfered in that and said that it was an insult to the memory of the deceased and to the country which he represented, and that the body should be taken into the church by the proper entrance or give it to the friends and they would return the corpse to the house.

"But the Minister of Ecuador declared that the will of the Government should be executed, and when he found that the whole Diplomatic Corps supported Father, he ordered that the body should be taken through the proper door, to the vault, which was done without further trouble.

"But instead of finding a room prepared for the body, as they had expected, they found nothing but a bare room without even a table to put the coffin on, and a horrible smell. The gentlemen returned to Mr. Neale's house, but on their way they were met by an aide-de-camp of the President who said that if it was necessary, to employ force to execute the order of the Government.

"When they got to Mr. Neale's house they looked as though they had had a day's work, many were so indignant that they could hardly stand still, and all of them looked as though they had been rolling in the dust, their boots looked as though they had never seen blacking and their faces were scarlet from the effects of their exertions.

"But their point was gained and the Nuncio was outwitted. The Nuncio is the most false and deceitful man that I ever heard of.

When he was invited to go to Mr. Neale's to eat a good dinner he did not think about his being a Protestant and when he could go to his house every Thursday night to the reception and drink his brandy and tea and smoke 5 or 6 of his cigars and slip five or six more in his pocket as did each of his secretaries, he did not think there was any sin in robbing and eating and drinking with a Protestant, but when that Protestant was dead, he would stand and declare that he could not be buried in Ecuadorian soil, and he would not permit the corpse to enter one of their horrible churches, because it was the corpse of a Protestant.

"And only a week before Mr. Neale died, on Sunday the Nuncio with his two Secretaries were at his house to dinner. Last Sunday we had the honor of a call from him and now Father declares that he will never return his call, and that he shall never enter our door again or ever eat a morsel in our house. There is another little incident about the Nuncio. When I went to church with my hat on everybody made a fuss, when it is a civilized custom all over the world. The Nuncio went to Mr. Neale's house to a reception and asked permission to keep his hat on which hat is about five yards around the rim and two or three broad. He could go into a house to spend the evening with gentlemen of society and have the impoliteness to ask permission to keep his hat on.

"Yesterday the Misses Flores and I were in Mr. Neale's house all day packing his clothes and Japanese curiosities of which he has a great many. He has a set of chess men which were made in Japan, they are valued in England, at least, a hundred dollars. He also has a great number of porcelain cups and saucers with beautiful letters and figures in Chinese on them in different gay colors. He also has all kinds of little articles made of wood: there are five teapots made of wood in the shapes of a swan, a duck and various other things. Everything he had was in horrible confusion, his private papers and official documents were all mixed together and it was most difficult to separate them.

"His son Henry has no more sense than a monkey. He never was told anything about his Father's affairs, he does not know whether he has property or not, he knows nothing about the table service. Since his Father died he has been staying at Mr. Flores and the servant has not made his bed since last Tuesday and for three days that we have been there at work, his dirty shirt was on the floor. When Father came there today he was very angry with him and told the servant to clean up the room, but nothing was done when we left at four o'clock, and I suppose it will be in the same condition tomorrow.

"The next mail I will write you more particulars and tell you something which has helped to stir the life of Quito but which is a little more lively in character. You must control your curiosity until next mail.

"Tell Mr. Busbey that I write to him by the next mail and that we are very much obliged indeed for the picture, and I think it is splendid. It is pronounced by every one to be 'muy bueno mozo' which means very good looking. I am very glad that you have gone visiting and had a pleasant time. What is the matter with Em? Mr. Busbey said that she was sick and that you had gone to Illinois to see her. Is she still crying for Charlie Dunlap or has she recovered from that fit of insanity? I sincerely hope so.

"As I have said several times before, the people are determined to have me married. Every place I go some one begins to talk about the rich and handsome young men of Quito, and ask me which one I would like to have, and as I do not speak Spanish very well it is the more embarrassing.

"It is very irregular that we have heard nothing from you concerning the box which we sent soon after we arrived in Quayaquil. If we do not receive some letters I will begin to think that the house is burned down and the whole of you are going crazy.

"That ring which George Blynn sent me has occasioned a great deal of remark, several gentlemen have asked me if I was engaged to be married because I wore a plain gold ring. I can not write any more because it is one o'clock and Father is going to bed.

"I hope that you will enjoy your Christmas box and think of us way down in South America without any Christmas. Give my love to all, and take a good share for yourselves and the children.

"Your Daughter,
Jessie Coggeshall"[3]

With Jessie's letter Coggeshall enclosed a brief note stating he had "so much official work" concerning the Neale death that he would write later; he was well; was sending photographs to give to friends; and would soon send a draft for $500 gold to Mary.

The day after Col. Neale's funeral the diplomatic corps met at the Chilean Legation and held "an animated discussion" about how to express dissatisfaction with the suppressive actions of the Bishop of Quito and the Delegado of the Pope. The diplomats adopted a series of resolutions in a letter to the Ecuadorian government. First they thanked the government for its part in the ceremony, then registered their "painful impressions" produced by the intolerance of the ecclesiastical authorities. Dated December 14, 1866, the letter was signed by J. Nicholas Hurtado of Chile, Casimo Corral of Bolivia, Luis Ruiz of Colombia, W. T. Coggeshall of the United States, Charles de Saint Robert of France and Jose Manuel Suares of Peru.

---

[3] William T. Coggeshall Papers, Ohio Historical Society.

AMERICAN PROTESTANT TO BE THROWN TO BUZZARDS

On December 15 Coggeshall wrote a long dispatch about the "Neale Incident" to Secretary of State Seward. While composing the dispatch, he received word that an American citizen named Cashmore was dying in a Quito hospital.

In a December 20 dispatch Coggeshall described the pressure put upon the dying man by the Superintendent of the hospital. The Superintendent declared he would "throw the man's corpse into a ravine for the buzzards" if the man kept refusing to be baptised by a Catholic priest.

As soon as possible the diplomat had a conference with Ecuador's Foreign Affairs Minister Manuel Bristamente as to "whether Christian burial according to Protestant forms would be permitted" for Mr. Cashmore.

Bristamente responded promptly that the "government of Ecuador had determined to set apart a place near Quito as a cemetery for the dead who do not die in the Catholic faith."

COGGESHALL DEMANDS CEMETERY FOR PROTESTANTS

In his dispatch of December 20 Coggeshall continued: "A treaty stipulation with the United States requires the right of burial for its Protestant citizens who may die in Ecuador." Coggeshall had not been aware of this because he could find no copy of the treaty in the U.S. Legation. He requested one of the State Department.

He ended his dispatch with: "Should not the citizen of the U.S. recover I will take good care that Ecuador shall execute its declared intentions. They represent a wide advance over the prejudice and intolerance, hitherto previously unrebuked by official orders, prevailing at this Capital. I have the honor to be, Very Respectfully, Your Obdt. Serv't., William T. Coggeshall."[4]

ECUADOR PROMISES A PROTESTANT PANTHEON

Coggeshall relayed the good news to Mary. Ecuador would establish a cemetery for non-Catholics.

---

[4]William T. Coggeshall Dispatches from Ecuador, 1866-67, U.S. Department of State.

"Quito, December 20, 1866

"Dear Mary:

"I wrote you a brief note on the 15th. I have since been so much occupied in the settlements of Mr. Neale's affair with his son who is—muy joven (very young)—that I have no opportunity to write. Today I am compelled to prepare dispatches for the Govt. exploring the circumstances succeeding Col. Neale's funeral.

"On Saturday I was informed that an American Citizen, named Cashmore, was dying in the hospital. I was determined he should have Christian burial. On Sunday I saw the Minister of Foreign Affairs and asked him what was to be done, telling him the Superintendent of the hospital had threatened to throw out the corpse to the buzzards—if the man persisted in refusing to confess.[5]

"The Minister answered that the Govt. had determined to appoint a place, to be dedicated to the burial of strangers. On Monday the Minister addressed a note to the diplomatic corps informing that body that it would set apart a burial place for strangers.

"This is a great point gained. But for my determined protest against the proceedings at the funeral of Mr. Neale it would not have been gained now or perhaps for many years to come. It is a conquest over priestcraft [the priesthood] which is signol [significant]. Treaties exist but they have been hitherto disregarded in this benighted Republic. If Mr. Busbey made an article on this question you might give him these facts.

"I have determined to send you two pounds of gold dust. I am satisfied it will be better than to send a draft on England. I will either send direct to you and you can sell it, in the best market possible after careful inquiry, or, as I may deem best on reflection send it to Jay Cooke c/o New York, for sale, the proceeds to be at your order. I will pay here 704 pesos, about $500, American gold for 2 pounds. It ought to be worth more in the States and net you 47 percent beside which will give you about $800 in greenbacks. The gold will go to Quayaquil next week and by the next steamer after this to Panama, where it will be delivered to Wells and Fargo's Express. You ought to get it about Jan. 20th.

"We are very anxious to hear whether you yet have our Quayaquil box and also hope the Christmas box will reach you before the appointed day.

---

[5]Go to confession—a baptised Protestant in danger of death could receive the sacrament of confession on the deathbed, if he requested it, and could be buried in consecrated ground.

"We intend to have a Christmas dinner about which Jessie will write you. You must give a full account of yours.

"This morning we rode out on horseback. The sky was clear, the sun warm, the fields green with grass, young corn, wheat and potatoes, in every direction—flowers beautiful and fragrant all around us, birds singing—beautiful vistas of snow clad mountains—air boiling as mid summer in the States—all on Dec. 20th. I take it you are enjoying bright fires and perhaps snow much nearer than on the peaks of high mountains.

"I am writing a letter to Mamie, Hat and Prock about a visit we made a few days ago to a garden which contained flowers, fruits, etc.

"My health is improved. You will see by the photographs sent that I am getting what they call here 'muy gordo'—Very fat.

"OCCASIONAL STREAKS OF HOMESICKNESS COME OVER ME, BUT I FIGHT THEM AS VALIANTLY AS JOHN BUNYON DID THE ADVERSARY. Sometimes I become so heartily disgusted with this people—however, that I am prone to indulge in very indignant words.

"You must be gay and lively and keep good heart in all things. I hope and pray the children are all well, and we want them very much to write us. Willie should write regularly. Where is father and how gets he along. Mr. Busbey wrote that he had gone to Washington. How about the patent.

"We have not for two months had any magazines. Our papers come very irregularly.

"When you don't want to send letters to Washington—put on a 10 cent stamp and direct to me care of U.S. Consul Panama.

"Bear my regards and Happy New Year—to all the friends especially to the Gov's. folks and Mrs. and Dr. Ide. I have letters under way for them.

"The Lord bless and preserve you all is the sincere prayer of

"As of old
W.T.C."[6]

FUROR REPORTED INTERNATIONALLY

Coggeshall's prediction was correct . . . the Neale Incident would create a furor. In five weeks after the news reached the U.S. State Department, *The New York Times* of January 25, 1867, reported the crisis as "Bigotry in Ecuador."

The *Times* article stated that the reason the Papal Nuncio refused burial for the Protestant Mr. Neale was because "the consecrated ground of the cemeteries could not be polluted by the burial of a

---
[6]William T. Coggeshall Papers, Ohio Historical Society.

heretic." That, after Minister Coggeshall, supported by the entire diplomatic corps, strongly protested using any but the customary front entry (and not by tearing down a rear wall) for conveying the body into the church, "the Ecuadorian Minister announced that the will of the Government should be enforced. . . . He directed the troops to clear the way for the procession. . . . The church authorities offered no resistance and the body was placed in the vault. [Returning from the church, the corps was] met by an aide-de-camp from the President, promising a military force sufficient to have proper respect shown to the remains of the deceased."

The incident was also reported in newspapers in Europe.

Rancor over Mr. Neale's burial was just the beginning of months of hassle over the establishment of a cemetery for non-Catholics. Sometimes when Jessie walked the dirt streets, little boys would taunt "Protestante, Protestante."

Coggeshall would write many more dispatches about the Neale Incident to Secretary of State Seward. In Ecuador he would find a creeping opposition to the thought of a cemetery for Protestants. Not only children in the streets but also small community officials and the Bishop from the home province of Ecuador's President would mock the America's Protestant Minister.

QUITO CUSTOMS

"Quito, November 3rd, 1866

"Dear Mother,

"I suppose that by the time you receive this you will be laughing over our photographs, but let me assure you that I am very elegant in the photograph as compared with my appearance when we crossed Chimborazo, at which time I had on that dark calico dress, my little grey sack, no collar, my water proof cloak, two pairs of gloves, a pair of father's wollen stockings drawn over my garters, my large straw hat, with a red india rubber cover, a green vail and a red silk mask, which was drawn over my head and came down on shoulders, completed my costume. Father said that I looked like a bundle of second hand clothing put on top of a mule. But the photograph shows exactly how I looked without my wrappings.

"My friends say, in Quito, that I am losing color but that I must be a great deal better looking than when I left home. I am not as fleshy but I have grown taller, and I have had worse health in Quito than I have had for three or four years, but it is owing to my eating very heartily and taking no exercise, sometimes I do not go onto the street from one week end to another. But you can not

immagine how disagreable it is for me to go on to the street. I am a perfect curiosity and it is not considered proper for a lady to go on to the street with a gentleman unless than gentleman is her father, brother, husband or one of her near relations, but she must never be seen without a gentleman or a servant, but I have not regarded this custom at all, I go when I please and with whom I please. In this country every man is considered to be a villain untill [sic] he is proven to be a gentleman, and very few are able to give any such evidence.

"You would be horribly shocked to see the way in which we have our room arranged, in the first place it is very long and wide, it has a very handsome carpet and handsome sofas, chairs, mirrors, and lamps, the doors are rough wood without paint and constructed in the roughest manner possible. Here it is the custom to invite all your friends to drink when they call in evening or on Sunday, consequently we have been obliged to buy bottles filled with cologne to put the wine in and we have bought enough cologne to last us for two or three years in order to get the bottles. On a table in one corner of the room we have two bottles of wine and a bottle of Cognac with three or four glasses sitting on a plated silver waiter. Such a show of liquor in the States would be a sure sign of drunkeness, but here it is not so. We are still living in the hotel because we can not find a house for less than $50 or $60 a month, which Father says he can not afford to pay, and which is all together too much for Quito. . . .

"Last night, Henry Neale, son of the English Minister, was here and we were trying to devise some plan for passing the evenings, we talking of forming a club to read aloud, each person reading by turn, but after several vain endeavors to fix upon some plan gave it up in despair.

"In my last letter I told you to send me a hat of the latest style, but instead of sending that, send me a small black riding hat, with a long green or grey feather, felt would be more becoming than any other shape, but I will leave you to consult your own taste, only be sure that it is small, black, and has a long feather. You might also send me a few new ribbons for bows. . . . I told you in my last letter about an emerald which a gentleman gave me for a birthday present. I have had it set in a plain gold ring, and it is now very beautiful. It is not very clear, but is large and has a splendid color.

"I have worn my white alpaca dress, once in Ecuador, and their is no prospect of my having it on again until I go home, and then I will have it new to wear to parties. I have not had on my grenadine dress in Quito because it is to cold, although I wore it a great deal in Guayaquil. My silk dress and my robe dress, and my black alpaca, with the changes which I can make by wearing a white waist or a silk jacket which I bought in Guayaquil, are all the dresses which I have to wear out, but as I do not go anywhere except on Sunday evening to Mr. Flores house, or when I take a walk, I have all that I need.

"Father and I are so horribly oppressed with the dullness of the place, that we sit for hours and talk about the parties we have been to, the dinners we have been to, the rides we have taken, the games we have played with the children, and about the good things that we have eaten in our own home, and prepared by your loving hands, this is the way in which we pass our dull moments.

"Father says that if you send us a box, to send him several boxes of Grey's patent molded and linen faced paper collars, No. 14., both standing and turned down. I wish you would go and have your photograph taken, and send it to us with Willie's and a good one of Mamie, I am not so particular about Mamie's because we have one. Our servant has just called us to dinner so I will be obliged to close. Kiss all the children for me. . . . Give my love to all the girls.

"From your loving daughter,
Jessie Coggeshall"[7]

The father wrote a personal letter December 4, 1866, with a brief note attached on the 5th.

Also, on the 5th, Jessie, though stiff and tired from a swollen knee after riding horseback, penned a nine-page descriptive and amusing letter giving details of the burial for the former president of Ecuador, General Juan Flores; the sumptuous seven-course Thanksgiving dinner they hosted; her need for corset steels; the offer of a shrunken head; and the impossibility of training fleas.

HUSBANDLY ADVICE TO MARY

"Quito, Dec. 4th, 1866

"Dear Mary:

"Jessie has written so fully and I send herewith so many notes—jotted down, as matters of business occur to me, that there is but little left to write about. I hope Willie will be pleased with my account of my morning hunt.

"I expected by this time, to have been able to send a liberal remittance home, but I have been compelled to buy so many things in order to subsist—to get along decently—that I am poor. Of course I don't count the things sent you from Quayaquil and the Christmas box, for which I paid over 400 pesos—a peso being

---

[7]William T. Coggeshall Papers, Ohio Historical Society.

worth in American gold, 69 cents. I was seduced into buying about $100 worth of extras for Jessie in Quayaquil which I find nearly useless in Quito. After next month I will have a balance with the Gov't and shall keep you independent as to funds. Have therefore hope and patience.

"I am afraid you do not cultivate a very cheerful spirit. Know you not that cheerfulness is nearly allied to Godliness—my cheerfulness is what makes me so good a fellow. If you lived in Equador you might rationally get the blues, but in Ohio, with your children around—a cheerful fire to warm your toes at—and the privilege of a bottle of hot water at your feet every night, you ought to be as gay as a lark, in spite of the fact that your coughing husband is at the Equator endeavoring to rejoin health and cultivate patience, under many difficulties.

"Lately I bought a horse on credit and nowadays I ride out occasionally with much pleasure. Soon, however, the wet days begin when riding is only practicable very early in the morning.

"Jessie has told you about Thanksgiving. I hope this letter will find you all recovering from a most happy Christmas. You must write us all about it. What we shall do on Christmas is yet a problem, but we are invited to a dinner with the English Minister and most probably will go.

"But think of Christmas with September weather—with flowers in the gardens—potatoes and corn growing in the fields—strawberries, peaches, and pears fresh gathered for dinner. Today at noon the temperature was delightful. I enjoyed genial air very much—but to-night it is cold—and I would very much like a brisk fire at which to toast my feet.

"I have watched the political news from the States with zealous interest and now await the President's Message to Congress with anxiety—unlike any I ever felt at home. There is much talk here about fear of dreadful times in the States but I dispute such probability and declare that the American people are a common sense people—and that prudent counsels will control.

"I hope Father is with you and well and happy. We have written the girls but got no answer. Let me know whether you rec'd my diary of the journey to Quito.

"I hope Willie continues to do well at school and also that Mamie and Hattie get along prosperously. I am sure Prockie flourishes. She is one of the flourishing girls. I wish I had her in Equador. Willie must write oftener. It is good for him and he must write long letters."

"Dec. 5th.

"This is mail day. I intended to write several pages and also write letters to the Gov. and Mrs. Jones, but I caught cold yesterday which settled in my bowels, and I am in too much pain to-day. I can hardly get ready my official dispatches.

"So adieu. Siempre Lo Mismo, with love to all . . .

"Yours
W.T.C."[8]

PRESIDENT'S FUNERAL; ELABORATE THANKSGIVING DINNER; SHRUNKEN HEAD

"Quito, Dec. 5th, 1866

"Dear Mother,

"If this letter is poky and dull I hope you will make some allowances. Yesterday we were horse back riding and this morning I am very stiff and tired. My right leg is very sore and very much swollen just under the knee, because as I sat on my saddle it rubbed against the horse and as my horse was very hard to hold, it took all my strength and attention to attend to him. I am getting to be a very good horsewoman. I can say this without exaggeration because father says that it is really a fact.

"The other day Father bought a beautiful horse, the color is grey. I rode him yesterday and Father borrowed one from a gentleman in the hotel, but after we had ridden about a mile, I concluded to change with Father, because our horse has a trick of cutting up when with other horses. We rode out on a delightful road and the scenery was magnificent, the sun was just setting, and the mountains were tinged with rose color and the clouds looked like one mass of fire.

"Cotopaxi, one of the most beautiful volcanoes of Ecuador, was perfectly magnificent, the snow on its peaks tinged with the sun presented a splendid sight. Cayambe, next to Chimborazo, the highest mountain in South America, also could be seen. We could see almost the whole of the splendid volcano, with its sides and peak covered with snow. You must know by this time that I have no descriptive powers, so I will leave it all to Father.

"Life in Quito is just the same except that last Monday the remains of General Flores arrived from Guayaquil and were buried in the Cathedral with great pomp and ceremony. There was a long procession which I will attempt to describe.

---

[8]William T. Coggeshall Papers, Ohio Historical Society.

"First there marched into the Plaza General, Priests of the College with their pupils arranged with a row of boys on each side of the street; after these came all the Priests of Quito marching in the same manner as the pupils of the College; next came the novices followed by old Priests; next came several officers of the Ecuadorian army mounted on splendid white horses and in full uniform; next came four white horses led by grooms with black on their hats and their horses were covered with black saddle cloths trimmed with silver fringe; next came the funeral car, drawn by four brown mules draped in black the same as the horses; the car was very handsome and very nicely trimmed and in good taste.

"The coffin rested on a base, exposed to full view, with the hat, coat, sword of the dead General resting upon the coffin, the car was trimmed with black cloth and silver fringe. After the corpse were 8 or 9 little girls dressed in black with black lace vails [sic] thrown over their heads; they were arranged on each side of the street.

"Next in order came the sons, sons in law, and the other friends and relatives of the deceased, of which there were a great many. The procession which marched behind the family was a very curious one. It was composed of the soldiers and cavalry of Ecuador with the band which played waltzes and polkas during the ceremony. The whole procession marched to the door of the Cathedral, when the coffin was carried by the three sons, and several friends of the General, on their shoulders, into the building but as I was not inside of the building, I can not tell anything about it, but Father can.

"As last Thursday was Thanksgiving day, Father and I went to work to prepare a dinner. We had bought a turkey some weeks before and the servant had been fattening it for that occasion. So we invited Mr. Gouin and brother and a friend of his with Mr. Aquirre [Aguerre] to take dinner with us and eat roast turkey.

"It was quite an undertaking for us because we had never tried anything of the kind before and did not know how our dinner service would do, but every thing passed off in good style and we had a splendid dinner. We had on the table five kinds of wine, pickled sardines and butter. First was brought soup. After soup came a leg of mutton very nicely cooked and very nice meat, next came the turkey which was perfectly splendid, it was cooked splendidly and was very fat and nice, after turkey came beef, which also was very nice. Then came dessert which I had prepared partly myself, we had pineapple sliced in sugar, stewed peaches, oranges sliced in sugar, a dulce made by the cook, and three kinds of ices, which were exceedingly beautiful, we also had cakes of Quito, and cakes which we bought in Quayaquil, which are put up in boxes and come all the way from England. The first ice which came on the table was in the shape of a mush melon *as perfect as it could be, with the seeds and all.* The next was of frozen milk *and was* a lamb *lying on one side on a large platter, it was not of a very agreeable taste but looked beautiful.* The other *was in the* shape of a melon but was flavored with apple.

"The guests were very much pleased with the sliced oranges because they were entirely new to them prepared in that way. Fruit is as cheap as dirt in this country, *send the servant out with six cents and he will come back with a dozen nice large oranges, another six cents will buy six bananas, if large, if they are small a dozen for a media or six cents; for the same amount of money you can buy a plate full of Brazil nuts.*

"Father is thinking of taking a house in Guapulo *a small village about three or four miles from Quito, situated in a deep ravine, it is warmer than Quito and the water is perfectly splendid. I think it will be very good for Father's health.* Father is much better than when we came here, *his face is fuller, his lungs are much stronger and he does not cough near as much as he did. I am at least two inches taller and much fleshier. Mother, I beg of you to send me a riding hat. I have nothing to wear to ride.*

"*Mother you write very unsatisfactory letters, you do not tell any deaths, marriages or births, you do not say whether the house is fixed or not, if the window is put in or more flowers in the yard. Next time you write let us know all this and tell us what is going on for Christmas, for you must not suppose that because we are away from home and are seeing new faces and acres that we do not care for such things, because if we cannot have any pleasure or enjoy ourselves Christmas, it will give us all the more pleasure to know that you are enjoying yourselves.*

"*Also tell us about the theatre and Opera if there is any. Mother the next time you write you might send me some ribbons and one or two nets and for conscience sake, don't forget to send me two or three dozen pairs of corset steels and to impress it upon your memory allow me to inform you that there are none to be found in Quito, and I am almost cut in two by the ones which I have because they are all broken. Also send me five or six pairs of corsets, No. 20. If you should forget to send the corset steels I am certain that I will have to be sent home in two pieces in a box.*

"And Mother please send us the Harper's *weekly* and the Godey's *lady book regularly, read them yourself and then send them to us,* for we are almost starved for something to read. *If you have sent the box which we told you to send, do not try to send me corsets, corset steels or hat, because it will be an impossibility to send them in a bundle and it will not be best to send another box. Therefore, if you have sent the box which we told you to, do not attempt to send the corsets or hat.*

"A man has just been here with the most wonderful thing I have ever seen in my life. *It is a human head shrunken to the size of your fist. It is done in a most wonderful manner, the bones of the head are taken out also the teeth and eyes, and then the head is shrunken to this small size, by a process known only to a tribe of savage Indians living in Ecuador. The hair is in a perfect state of preservation and about a foot long. The head which I saw today is that of an Indian who was worshipped as a God, by his people. The face is painted in a most hideous manner and I must say that they are a most disgusting thing, but very curious indeed. The man asked a hundred dollars for it, but Father would not buy it for that price.*

"*Tell Cousin George Prout that* it is impossible to train *the fleas in this country but it will give me the greatest pleasure in the world to* send him a small box of these charming insects *if he will be sure and not let his wife know it for fear she will be jealous.*

"*Give my best respects to Mr. Busbey and tell him that if I have time this mail I will write to him but I do not think it is my place to write first. I will also write to his sisters as soon as possible. I wrote to Ed Wasser the last mail, and will answer the rest of my letters this mail.*

"*I am very sorry that Alice has got homesick so soon, and I have that advantage. When I begin to feel homesick, I think it is of no use, I am here and destined to stay, until next July at least and what is the use of fretting myself and Father too.* You need not be alarmed about my playing billiards or cards *on Sunday for I have no cards and I can go nowhere to play billiards.*

"*I have not even the pleasure of the reception to Mr. Flores house now because of their Father's funeral last Monday. Tell Mamie that perhaps Father will rent a piano and then I shall practice three or four hours every day and then she had better be careful or I will get ahead of her. I will enclose a note for Prockie and Hattie. The striped Poncho which we sent in the box is for Hattie, the largest of the scarfs is for Mamie and the other for Prockie. Father has written Willie a description of his hunting expedition, but I think it was the worst thing he could have done. He came home cross, hungry, tired, wet, and with a fever and was sick for a week, but is well now and has promised not to go again if he wants to avoid the Doctor and I intend to lock him up and give him a strong physic. He was in the rain for three days, could get no sleep and had a miserable horse, you can imagine how nicely he would be knocked to pieces by such an adventure. But you need not be worried because he is perfectly well now and it is not very likely that he will do the same thing again. As I said before,* Father is in better health than I have ever seen him and I think that he will be cured.

"I am about the tallest lady in Quito that I know of and I am a general curiosity when I go on the street. The people here call me 'La Senorita Frances de Norte Americana' in English, 'The French Miss of North America.' You can judge of their intelligence. Mr. Gouin told me the other day that the director of the mail to Panama asked him if the mail to Panama went around Cape Horn. This gentleman is very rich. The people also think that they can ride to the United States on a mule. Another person wanted to know if the U.S. was the capitol [sic] of North America. These people whom I have mentioned are all wealthy and of good position in society.

"I can not write any more because it is time for me to dress for dinner and I have written such a long letter that my arm is tired. I hope Willie's hand will soon be well because I am anxious to receive one of his lively letters. Give my love to all my friends and kiss all the children for me.

"When you answer let it be a long letter and tell us lots of news.

"From your true daughter,
Jessie"[9]

---

[9]William T. Coggeshall Papers, Ohio Historical Society.

CHAPTER 12
DEAR LITTLE FOLKS

Christmas in a foreign land made Coggeshall homesick. On December 21 he shed the duties of diplomacy long enough to write a long letter about a beautiful country ride to Willie, 17, Mamie, 11, Hattie, 7, and Prockie, 4. Three days after Christmas he caught up on personal and business matters to Mary. He cautioned her about her own health—her eyes—and suggested tree and fruit plantings for their yard.

RIDE TO EXQUISITE GUAPULO

"Quito, December 21, 1866

"Dear Little Folks:

"I wrote you some weeks ago that Quito is about a mile and a half higher than Columbus—that is, if you could go up above the clouds, in a balloon, a mile and a half you might be as high above the ocean as Quito. But Quito is situated on a high plain and very near it are deep narrow vallies [sic].

"Although near the Equator, that is in the middle of the earth—or midway between the poles, where the sun is very hot and there is no winter, Quito is not a city which enjoys hot weather, and therefore many tropical fruits and flowers do not grow in its gardens and there are no trees except a few orange or lemon, wild cherry and apples or pear, and some stunted tropical trees.

"In the vallies [sic], however, grow fruits and flowers of almost every description. I can give you some idea of these vallies by describing a ride which Jessie and I took a few mornings ago.

"We went to Guapulo, a small village in a deep valley about three miles north of Quito. As soon as we got beyond the roughly paved streets of Quito, we struck a narrow road which led down a steep hill into a wide green plain, from which we had distant views of several mountains whose peaks are covered with snow, which, in a clear day, are brilliantly white and very beautiful in contrast with the bright green of the plains above which they rise.

"After riding about a mile over the grass of the plain, we ascended a hill and at its summit looked down on Guapulo. The village contains a beautiful church which seemed to be immediately under us. I do not know exactly how far, but it seemed to me the church must be 700 or 800 feet below the summit of the hill. The road, roughly paved, is very steep, and winds around the hill in a very picturesque manner.

"North of Guapulo stretches a beautiful valley, broken by many ravines, but cultivated with corn, barley, potatoes and clover—all of which crops are now—(mark it in the month of December)—in the very freshness of luxuriant growth.

"Beyond this valley northward, as seen from the Guapulo hills, rises the great Mountain Cayambe, whose white crown is higher than any other in Equador, except that of Chimborazo. To the southeast may often be seen Antisana, upon which is a town higher than Quito—a village at greater altitude than any other in the world.

"The descent of Guapulo hill is not easy and Miss Jessie was quite uneasy lest her horse might give her a toss over his head. Her discomfort was very much increased, when we were about half way down the hill, by a sudden shower, from which we were obliged to take shelter in the archway of a house situated near the church. Some Indians offered us the shelter of their mud cabin with a stone roof, but we respectfully declined, observing that it was occupied in common by men, women, children, dogs, pigs, and chickens, all of which no doubt, as is the 'fashion' in Equador, imported countless pulgas—fleas.

"In half an hour the shower had passed and we turned off the main road and proceeded, still down hill, along a narrow way, lined with fragrant flowers, by the side of a clear swift flowery brook to a house, of which the keys had been loaned us by the proprietor, because he is anxious to rent it, with the garden which belongs to it. You will be surprised at the price. It is a pleasant, one story house, with 12 or 14 rooms—the garden contains ten or 12 acres and all was offered us for 12 pesos a month, about $9 in American gold.

"In the yard we were met by two Indians, a man and woman—very dark, both with long black hair. The man wore a poncho, short cotton breeches and a straw hat—his legs and arms were bare. The woman was without hat or bonnet, and was clothed only in two pieces of coarse woolen cloth, one of which was wrapped around her waist and hung to her knees—the other crossed over her shoulders and fastened with thorns.

"These people were our guides. They showed us the house and then conducted us to the garden. It is surrounded by high mud walls over which clamber many flower and fruit bearing vines. We recognized as homelike, heliotrope and blackberries. In this garden potatoes, onions, lettuce, clover were under good cultivation and promising good return. Along all the walks roses bloomed and air was sweet with their fragrance, and that of honeysuckles and orange blossoms. We picked ripe oranges, lemons and figs and saw apple, pear, peach and quince trees in bloom. On some of the trees were peaches and quinces nearly ripe. There were tropical fruits of several kinds, the Spanish names of which I cannot recall. In the center of the garden is a large black walnut tree, which in a few weeks will bear fruit exactly like the black walnuts of Ohio.

"Would you not have delighted in such a garden? Where there are so many flowers that though you plucked every day as many as you could carry, they would not be missed? Roses of many different sizes, colors and odors were most abundant but violets, tulips, heliotrope, honeysuckles and many others too numerous to mention were abundant. Suppose you had a nice swing in such a garden, would you not enjoy it? A clear brook flows through it and runs into a court near the house where a pleasant place for washing and bathing is arranged.

"From this garden you look up high hills, which, at a short distance, entirely surround Guapulo. Their sides, though steep, are generally cultivated and the prospect is pleasant. In the valley northward are pleasant sides also, and the gallop to Quito is quite agreeable.

"Now you may say why does not Pa live at Guapulo, in that beautiful garden, instead of Quito? Let me answer. We would be almost entirely deprived of society—we would find difficulty in getting supplies regularly from Quito, and now begins the rainy season. For four months it will rain every day—the mornings are clear and beautiful, but about noon the rain usually begins and the evenings and nights are dreary enough. Now while I write, about 8 o'clock in the evening, the rain is pouring down heavily. I hear it dripping musically from the eaves.

"Near Quito, in a southeasterly direction beyond a very high hill, is the Valley of Chillo, a tropical valley; there are now—December—mosquitoes and snakes there—and all the tropical fruits and flowers flourish. When the rainy season is over we will take a house in Guapulo or Chillo, if we stay in Ecuador.

"This morning, in company with the Secretary of the French Minister, who cannot speak a word of English—we rode to the brow of the hill which overlooks Chillo—about four miles from Quito. The prospect was beautiful. We did not go down into the valley because fear of rain compelled us to return to Quito. Some other day we will visit Chillo, when I will write you all about it.

"Ma, or Willie can read this letter to you and Mamie can look up Quito on the map or globe, and explain to Hattie and Prockie. You must, in return, send me letters about how you get along—what you learn, etc. Ma can also let the Governor's children and Mrs. Ide read this letter to little folks, if she pleases.

"I hope you are well and that you are very good children. Wishing you a very Merry Christmas, and the same for all your amigitas—little friends—

"Good Night—
W.T.C."[1]

BUSINESS ADVICE TO MARY

"Quito, December 28, 1866

"Dear Mary,

"After having written you per last steamer I found I would have difficulty now in forwarding gold and therefore negotiated a draft which I send by this mail to the 1st Nat. Bank Washington, for $500 gold, which if the premium is $40.00 will give you a credit of $700 in greenbacks.

"I have asked the bank to advise you of the am't. of your credit, but to pay Mr. Miller on the house, if you have rec'd nothing from Sessions, you can draw as soon as you get this. You might tell Mr. Sessions that he is authorized by me to pay you and take your receipt for whatever sum may be due me on the Journal notes—if they are paid. If not, ask him how much my interest now is and what he will give you for it in cash.

"We had a frightfully dull Christmas. We had arranged for a picnic dinner in the country. It rained all day—so we dined at home—or en Casa—rather—taking wine to friends at home, hoping all were well and merry. We have learned our Christmas box did not leave Quayaquil till Dec. 13th—In regard to the Quayaquil box I will write the Consul's office and P. (Postmaster), also the Custom house in New York and will get Mr. Prevost to write.

"I am very much obliged to Prockie for her leaves. They are very pleasant reminders. Bless Hattie's blue eyes—Doesn't Pa care

---
[1]William T. Coggeshall Papers, Ohio Historical Society.

for her? Would verily we could see her now. She is one of the brightest and most precious of the jewels in the home casket. Mamie's, Hattie's and Prockie's letters are 'muy bueno'—very good. Willie does well but might do better on a letter, with care. I rejoice to hear that he is doing well. There is a good future before him, if he is a good student and a good boy. Of all things, I hope he shuns bad company and spends his evenings in society which his Mother approves.

"Our life goes on as usual. Jessie will write you about some personal matters. I sent the little folks a long letter with this mail about a visit to a Hacienda. I also send letters to Love, Bascom, Gov. Dennison and Mr. Janney. I have a long one under way for the Gov. and also for Mr. Busbey. Send us the Weekly Journal, from the office regularly. Pay the subscription.

"In the latter part of next month I will send you, or the bank, either gold or another draft.

"I have been much distressed about your eyes. Get shutters on your room window and procure a pair of glasses like those described in a slip enclosed—with gold film.

"I hope most earnestly you saw your Mother ere she departed, if such has been her lot. Her age is so advanced much longer life could not be expected, and therefore we must be schooled, but it would be a consolation great to her to have her children about her and I hope that consolation was vouch-safed her in her last moments.

"You must take special care of your health and be cheerful and grow young again. My health improves and they say here I am 20 years younger than when I came to Quito—but they are a people prone to compliments, and cultivate lying as an accomplishment. My letter to Mr. Janney is very appreciative of Quito. See it.

"At the sale of Neale's effects we bought several articles of comfort and convenience and expect in a few days to be in an independent house, when life here will be more agreeable than now. I will have a stove in my office, or working soon then.

"You write us of many people sick, but of none well and happy. I hope there are some and I hope the sick are well.

"Tell Mrs. Ide [wife of the family doctor] I am meditating a huge letter to her. Hope the Dr. liked his cigars. Today I go with young Neale a few miles on the road to Quayaquil whence he goes to Europe.

"I want the lot in Springfield to be sold to pay King. Let Mower settle up. Don't trouble yourself. People will see in a short time whether Coggeshall can and will pay his debts. Write Mower to have David make out Hook's account and see whether the balance cannot be collected.

"I am sorry you did not get trees. Don't fail to set out a lot in the Spring. Also currant, gooseberry, and other bushes, roses, etc. Willie ought to take lessons in music. I am glad Mamie gets along prosperously. Let her and Hattie go to dancing school if you can, now or in the Spring. We have not got yours, or Willie's or father's photograph, or views of Columbus. You must purchase a sterescope for the views I sent you. Randell and Astor can get you a good one.

"Love to all—kisses for all at home—regards to friends, trusting the Lord keeps you well and happy.

"Yours,
W.T.C."[2]

Though lonesome, Jessie was full of Christmas chatter when she wrote separate letters to her mother and brother Willie on December 29. Besides a Christmas gift from her father, Jessie received three from Senor Gouin, including a riding whip. Senor Gouin, who had accompanied the Coggeshalls on their long horseback and donkey ride over the Andes Mountains from Guayaquil to Quito, was apparently showing Jessie much attention. But nowhere in the Coggeshall letters is his first name mentioned.

The teenager also promised to try to take a parrot home to sister Hattie.

Jessie's descriptions of a free-spending Austrian Count in Quito and of little boys' holiday custom of dressing up like monkeys gave the folks at home a cheerful note on which to end the year.

LONESOME CHRISTMAS

"Quito, December 29th, 1866

"Dear Mother,

"We received your letters of the 24 & 25 of November on Christmas, which helped to cheer us. I never passed such a Christmas and hope I never will again.

"It rained all day as hard as it could pour and it had been raining for four or five days and nights before.

"Before Mr. Neale's death we had arranged to have a grand Christmas dinner in his house, but his death put an end to all our plans; then Father and I thought we would give a dinner to the same persons who were to have been at Mr. Neale's but we had not the heart to do so, as we knew that the remembrance of Mr. Neale's death would spread a gloom over the whole party.

---

[2]William T. Coggeshall Papers, Ohio Historical Society.

"We then concluded to invite Mr. Gouin and his brother to a lunch and go into the country to spend the day; but when Christmas morning came it was raining terrible, so we were obliged to take our dinners at home. I received four Christmas presents: three from Mr. Gouin and one from Father. Mr. Gouin gave me a very beautiful box full of French candies, a lovely bouquet and a riding whip. Father gave me a gold strand for my chimes.

"Since Mr. Neale's death we have got a great many things from his house. His son gave me a trunk for my hats, a parrot which belonged to his Father and several chinese curiosities. He gave Father a tea cady [sic] which came from Japan. We bought a great many things such as chairs, mattresses, wine glasses and dishes. Father also bought a small cupboard of Japanese work.

"I think he [Neale's son] is the biggest fool that ever lived. After they had insulted his Father's remains in the way in which they did, he has gone to Guayaquil and left his father's corpse here in charge of this Government. Instead of going with the remains and attending to their transportation from Quito to Guayaquil he leaves it to strangers who have no regard or respect for his memory. He thinks that if he leaves his Father in Quito, when he gets to Guayaquil, he can go to the theater and enjoy himself generally. It would take too long to tell you of his tricks, but the above will give you an idea of his regard for his father.

"Quito is the same as ever only a little worse; for now we have no receptions at the Flores because Mrs. Flores is sick with the typhoid fever and the doctors say that she can not live; and now the rainy season has fairly begun. It rains every day, sometimes all day and night—it is very cold and we have no fires, but I am willing to stay here because Father is three times as well as when we left home. He goes for days and nights and does not cough at all, and he can walk five times as far without being tired. We ride horseback every day when it is pleasant. Father has a beautiful horse and so have I but mine is not as stylish as Father's. His is grey and mine is roan. You say in your letter that Hattie has had chicken pox. I hope she is well by this time. Tell her that she need not think that we have forgotten her, she will soon find that out when you receive the last box. Tell her that when I come home (which I hope will be next spring) I will try and bring her my parrot. It is dull now because it is in a strange house, and it does not see any of Mr. Neale's folks, but yesterday when Henry Neale and his servant were here it talked all day. It says 'Manuel, Senoro' and several other words, and crys [sic] like a baby in convulsions and laughs splendidly.

"I hope New Year's will be pleasanter than Christmas was. We are going to give a reception to all the Americans in Quito on New Year's night.

"I am very much obliged to Mr. Busbey for his opinion of my last letter although I do not know what one it was. I will try and write to him by this mail. The next mail I will give a full description of the Masquerades which begin today and continue for eight days. If you can send me some new music, Father is thinking of renting a Piano which will be a great consolation for us—during the rainy season.

"The children all speak about their handkerchiefs but you do not mention it whether you like yours or not, I sincerely hope you do. I intend to write a good long letter to Will this mail and to accomplish it I must close this.

"I hope you will go out in company as much as possible and enjoy yourself. You need not be alarmed about Father because I think he is getting along splendidly. I wish you would tell all the girls that if they knew how lonesome I was and how much pleasure it gives me to receive letters they would write every mail.

"Give my love to Grandpa and the girls.

"From your Daughter
Jessie"[3]

FREE-SPENDING AUSTRIAN COUNT; MASKED CELEBRATION

"Quito, December 29th, 1866

"Dear Brother,

"I hope this letter will interest you as much as yours did Father and I. We received it on Christmas day.

"Quito has had a great deal of excitement in the last two months. First, the arrival of an Austrian Count and before it had recovered from this terrible shock, Mr. Neale died. . . . I will endeavor to give some account of the Austrian Count.

"He arrived at Guayaquil and immediately rented the whole of the French Hotel. At dinner he had the band to play for him, and when they were done he gave them $35.00 and engaged them to play every day and until he retired at night. Of course the papers were full of it and it soon reached Quito. The papers described him as being very young, very homely, well educated, and immensely wealthy, his income was a thousand dollars a day and he was a Prince of the Royal blood of Austria. He gave balls and dinners,

---
[3]William T. Coggeshall Papers, Ohio Historical Society.

and hired steamers to take him and his friends on an excursion up the Guayaquil river. His door and the Hotel was always full of beggars, and he is said to have paid over five hundred dollars a day.

"It was soon rumored that he was going to honor Quito with a visit, also he was going as far up Chimborazo as possible, also to the crater of Pichincha.

"One day I was sitting in the Saloon [salon] near the window when I heard horses coming down the street at a great rate. I looked out of the window and got a glimpse of several persons on horseback just going into the hotel. I thought it was just some common travelers and paid no more attention to it. Pretty soon one of our servants came in and said that 'El Condo' had arrived and was in the Hotel and that all the rooms were occupied and he was going to go somewhere else. To be sure I was very much disappointed, but consoled myself by thinking that I should have the pleasure of telling my friends the Flores.

"At dinner Modesto told me that he [the Count] had taken one of the rooms which belonged to Mr. Alarron and that he would stay to dinner, but had already taken a house (which had been offered for $20.00 a month) for $50.00 for fifteen days and that he had paid Mr. Alarron $30.00 for the use of three rooms for two or three hours.

"In the evening there were quite a number of gentlemen in the Saloon [salon] spending the evening with Father and I. Mr. Hurtado [Chilean Minister] and I were playing chess when the servant of the hotel entered and handed me a card on which was written 'Mr. Alfred H. C. Cox.' I soon discovered that this was a gentleman whom I had met in Guayaquil and who was now the Secretary of the Count. Soon after we heard music in the court and our servant told us that the Count had gone to the other house with a band of music.

"The next morning (Sunday) Father and I sent our cards to Mr. Alfred H. C. Cox and in the afternoon I was honored with a visit from the above named gentleman who told me several things about the Count's conduct on the road from Guayaquil to Quito. He said that they were shooting at a shilling in the house where they stopped all night, when the sparks flew on the straw (of which the houses in Ecuador are made) and immediately the house was in a flame, but they succeeded in putting it out. At another place the Count took his pistol and shot a chicken for which they made him pay six dollars.

"On Monday morning our landlady sent my servant to ask me to lend her my napkins, table cloth and dishes to give to the Count because he was going to give a dinner. I told her no, because all our table linen was marked with our name, and I did not think it would be very stylish to see at the Count's table the napkins and tablecloth with the name of the American Minister.

"On Tuesday after Father and I came home from our ride my servant gave me an envelope. I opened and found inside two cards, one with the name—Graff von Anersperg—and the other of his secretary.

"That same evening Father was in Mr. Gouin's store when the Count came in, and immediately asked Father if he was the American Minister and invited him to go to his house the next day to dinner and said that he would call at our house that same evening.

"Father came home while I was playing chess with Mr. Hurtado and told me that the Count would be here very soon. He had been in the room about fifteen minutes when the Count came with his Secretary. He immediately took my place at the chess board and finished the game. He staid [sic] until after eleven o'clock talking with Father and explaining to him his travels in South America. He gave a most interesting account of his trip across the Continent from the Atlantic to the Pacific Ocean.

"The next day Mr. Neale died and of course, Father did not go to the dinner, but the persons who were invited all went (except the Ministers). In the evening I received a splendid bouquet from the Count.

"A week after there was a rumor around town that the Count had no more money, nothing but bills and drafts and that no person would buy his drafts because they were rather suspicious articles. And he left very soon for Guayaquil without going to the crater of Pichincha although he had made up a party to go with him, and neither did he go to Chimborazo. Before he left Mr. Carlos Chinker gave him a large dinner which cost over a thousand dollars. We have heard nothing from him since, and people in Quito have good reason to think that he is a humbug.

"He spoke fourteen languages, so he said, and I know that he spoke English, French, Spanish, and German but all very badly. In his manners he was a perfect Gentleman and was always dressed in good taste.

"You say in your letter that you have a hemorage [sic] of the nose. I hope that you will recover, and when you get enough to make soap, do not send it to Ecuador because it would not sell for 1 cent a cake.

"You need not be alarmed about Father's using profane language, he cannot be demoralized in Ecuador. You and Eva Buttles must not fight because it won't do at all. She will be rather a dangerous enemy. I should like very much to join the skating party but I will be denied that pleasure for this winter.

"When you write again be sure and tell me all about Christmas and your presents.

"Last night we had quite an amusing time with my parrot. I sent over to the Vice President's and borrowed theirs to see if mine would talk. I never heard such a noise in my life. My parrot said everything, swore in Spanish, said 'viente y ados reales,' 'twenty two reales,' 'Dolores, hoy an mol creado,' 'Dolores, so impolite,' scolded as though all the old women in the neighborhood were fighting. It also said a great many words that I could not understand. I intend to teach it to speak English.

"Last night I saw a very funny sight. It is the custom here during holidays for all the little boys to dress up like monkeys with long tails. I saw about a dozen yesterday dressed in this manner; some had their dresses made of two or three colors, one side blue or grey and the other some contrasting color and the part which they draw over their heads, of another color. They ran along the street and when they meet other boys, take their tails and thrash them good.

"Last night Father and I made a riddle, it was as follows:

Q.—How can I (Jessie) be converted into a man?

A.—By striking out one eye (i).[4]

"Can you see how we get the answer?

"I can not write any more because I am very tired. I hope you will be pleased with your Christmas presents.

"From your loving sister,
Jessie Coggeshall"[5]

---

[4]The name Jessie is spelled two ways: Jessie is feminine; Jesse is masculine.
[5]William T. Coggeshall Papers, Ohio Historical Society.

CHAPTER 13
DIPLOMATIC SOCIAL LIFE

JANUARY, FEBRUARY, 1867;
QUITO HIGH SOCIETY

The lonely days of Christmas soon turned to exciting days in January.

Coggeshall's dispatches to the State Department in January were brief. On the 2nd he sent his quarterly report, then on the 9th informed Secretary of State Seward that President Carrion, in accordance with treaty stipulations, had assured him that Ecuador *would* establish a cemetery for Protestants. In a January 20 dispatch he notified Washington that he would "watch attentively" any negotiations regarding "the sale" of the Galapagos Islands and, was "collecting information regarding the Amazon River and its tributaries."

Social life in Quito picked up during the next few weeks despite the rainy season. Jessie's letters glowed with accounts of a masked celebration in the streets; a delectable English dinner she and her father hosted, attended by the cross-eyed Vice-President of Ecuador; her continuing disgust with the Ecuadorians; the good news of her father's improved health; and the frustration of being far from events at home.

What she did not mention in these letters but what was happening was that Senior Gouin was courting her. He owned the largest store in Quito and was one of its wealthiest young men.

CROSS-EYED VICE-PRESIDENT: COGGESHALLS' ENGLISH DINNER

"Quito, January 18th, 1867

"Dear Mother,

"Why do you not write to us? We have not received letters from any of you for two mails. We are very anxious to hear about the two boxes which we have sent home. Life in Quito is just the same as ever; except that the last week we have had a Cosmorama;[1] the price of admission was two reals—in Spanish money; about twenty five cents our money. In the States such a show would not be patronized except by little children.

"There is some prospect now of having a few concerts. Yesterday there arrived at this hotel two or three gentlemen from Guayaquil, one of whom is a magnificent performer on the piano, and I was told this morning that he intended to give a few concerts as soon as he could find a room and a piano. I do not see where he is to get a room unless he rents a convent which I think would be a first rate idea. If he should happen to give a concert I will come out resplendent in a grenadine dress. I have not had it on since I left Guayaquil.

"In my last letter I promised to finish the description of the Innocentes. All the Maskers knew me, and one of them tried to get down on his knees to the 'Senorita de Norte America' but was prevented by a gentleman who was standing by me. One stopped in front of me and made quite a long speech about the 'Senorita America y con su sombrerito blanco.' (The young American lady with her white hat). I listened very quietly until he finished and then said, 'Mil gracias' (a thousand thanks) which raised a laugh among the bystanders at the expense of the masker who immediately left. One of the Maskers gave me a cake of soap, but I knew him and had a great deal of fun about it afterwards. He is the Secretary of the Chilian [sic] Minister. Another whom I did not recognize gave me a piece of paper on which he said was written a piece of poetry in Italian.

"An hour or two later after the Misses Sacarobi had retired, I was sitting in Mr. Gouin's store when all the Maskers went past for the last time; three or four came up to me and began to talk English, the few words which they knew they had picked up somewhere. When they had all stopped talking I said in Spanish 'Muy mal ingles' (very bad English) which caused another laugh. The Misses Sacarobi invited me to sit with them the next night but I

---

[1] "A visual rendition of the most important sights and events of the universe." Tana de Gamez, *International Dictionary,* English and Spanish, Simon and Schuster, New York, 1973, p. 1083.

could not see the fun of setting on a hard table until I was blistered to see a few foolish young men dressed up in foolisher styles so I did not accept their invitation.

"Last Sunday we gave a real English dinner which would have been a perfect success if it had not been for one little incident which spoiled the idea of an English dinner.

"Father had told the Vice President a week before that we were going to give an English dinner the next Sunday and invited him to come in the evening at seven o'clock to take tea and hear them speak English as he is very anxious to learn. He also told him that the following Sunday we would give a dinner to several Ministers and would be very glad to see him at the dinner; and unless the man would make a mistake and come to dinner on the wrong Sunday Father repeated it several times. But on Sunday afternoon about four o'clock what was our amazement, astonishment and horror to see the Vice President walk into the parlor with his stove pipe hat, spike tail coat, white cravat and white gloves. I was so overcome with surprise, anger and disgust and amusement at the mistake that I could hardly treat the poor man with decent politeness.

"Dinner was kept waiting by this awkard piece of stupidity until old General Stagg was almost starved. After dinner General Stagg said to Father, 'How in the name of God did you get the Vice President here.' So as the old man is very deaf Father took him into another room and explained to him the mistake. The old General laughed and said, 'Well my dear sir it is so much the better for you because you will not have to go to the expense of another dinner for him. God bless us all.' This last is a favorite expression of his and he brings it in such peculiar places and at such peculiar times that it has got to be a by word among the Diplomatic Corps.

"But to return to the Vice President. He sat all the evening and played chess with Mr. Reed, an English architect who lives in Quito. Father and I are inclined to think that it was no mistake at all, nothing but a piece of presumption and that he is just fishing for two dinners. If he comes next Sunday I shall be tempted to chuck him out the window. You may think this judgment rather harsh, but if you had lived with these people for six months you would soon discover that all I say is true. I am half inclined to think it a mistake as he is crossed eyed and perhaps his calamity has affected his mind and made him think as well as look cross eyed.

"We had a splendid dinner: everything was English as far as possible and what was not from England was cooked in English or American style. First we had a 'mock turtle soup.' Second, currie with chicken. Third, roast duck; fourth mutton prepared by the cook; fifth roast hare brought from England in a tin can; sixth a *fillet of beef with roast potatoes and salad, this also by the cook . . these were all the meats.*

"For dessert we had 1st plum pudding and English cheese with English crackers, 2nd sliced oranges as we have them at home, 3rd Quince jelly from France which was presented to me on Christmas by Mr. Gouin, 4th sliced pineapple. We then took coffee and adjourned to the saloon where we had English tea with English sugar and English crackers. So you see were were pretty nearly all English.

"One thing almost spoiled my digestion, namely: the Vice President put his knife in his mouth and spoke bad English.

"I am very anxious to go home next spring and if we go to Guayaquil I most probably shall. But if we have a good house in Quito we will stay in Quito all during summer. One thing is certain—that if I go home some one must come out here to stay with Father for it would be perfectly horrible for him to live here alone. He very seldom goes into the street, except on horse back, and he and I spend our evenings alone unless some of our friends favor us with their company. I think it would be expense for nothing to send me home and bring anyone else out here into this frightful, heathenish country—neither do I know of anyone who could come, no one except yourself or Willie, and I would rather that he should become a villain and a drunken sot at home than here.

"To show you what a splendid place Quito is for young men I will tell you its effect upon Henry Neale. Before he left Quito he drank a bottle or two of wine every day because his Father was dead and he had as much money as he pleased; during his Father's life he never gave his son money, probably because he knew he would spend it for liquor. Finding that he could not spend his own money for liquor he used to drink aquardiente, the whiskey of the country, with his Father's servants, then paying the money. He was expelled from the Flores house because he made improper proposals to one of the young ladies. I am not in the least alarmed about Willie because I think he is a much better young man but it makes no difference whether the life of Quito must have some effect upon his morals so it is out of the question as to his coming— as for you it is horrible to think about, it would be a great deal better to save the money and go to Europe with Father when he returns to the United States.

"When you go to Guayaquil you have a miserable little place to live in until you start for Quito. The place is dirty, hot and unhealthy. Then you start for Quito. You have a horrible road until you get there, and when you are there what do you see—beautiful scenery and magnificent mountains outside of the town. You ride into the town and you see on all sides of you sloppy women catching fleas and lice and eating them, men and women performing their natural necessities in the street, scraggy broken-legged broken-backed mules and dirty nasty black naked carrying their loads and their filthy lousy children on their backs.

"I do not tell you this because I want to stay or because I do not want you to travel but it is sickening to think of any person who knows what Quito is and what civilized countries are, coming here. I am very sick at the stomach and almost vomiting as I write about it.

"I will now tell you something which will cheer you a little. Father is stronger, fleshier, and better looking than when he left home, he eats three times as much as I do and after his breakfast and dinner he can neither read, write, walk, talk, or ride simply because he eats so much. Immediately after dinner he lys [sic] down on the sofa and quickly goes to sleep until time for tea, after tea he walks up and down the room to promote digestion, reads a little and goes to bed.

"It is the same thing over and over again every day except that sometimes he takes his breakfast in bed and don't get up until two o'clock in the afternoon as he did the other day and several times before. Almost every evening after dinner I go up to Mr. Flores house to see the young ladies, returning before dark. In this way I learn a great deal of Spanish. I have succeeded so well in Spanish that I intend to begin to study French and Italian, so by the time I come home I will be quite an accomplished young lady.

"I have been amusing myself for some time past making a postage stamp collection, some of which I send to Will. I have a book in which I paste them according to the importance of the countrys [sic] to which they belong. I flatter myself that it is very pretty and interesting. I want Willie to ask Cora Alber to give him some stamps which she has received from her Father if she has any now. Father says that some person asked him to send them postage stamps but he does not remember who it was. I think that if you know of any person who wishes to make a collection you might exchange the extra ones, which I send to Will, with the person and send some to me.

"Father wants to know if the Coggeshall family has starved or run away? If they have all starved we will put mourning on our hats; if they have run away we will illuminate the house and get tight!

"It is very singular that Em nor Dealia have ever answered my letters. They must have received them because they were sent with the letters which were sent from Guayaquil and which you received. I am resolved never to write to them again until they answer my letter. I guess they are ashamed to write for fear they will make mistakes and Father will make fun of them.

"Well I am coming to the end of the paper and it is time to dress for dinner. Tell all my friends that as soon as they answer my letters I will write to them but not until then.

"Give my love to Cousin Prout and his wife and tell him that I am afraid that I cannot send him a box of live fleas because they are too fractious but I am making a collection of dead ones which he can have stuffed and put in his room.

"Tell Mamie hello. Kiss Prockie and Hattie for me, give love to Mrs. Ide, Jones, Lessions and all my friends. This note which I enclose is for Cousin George Prout.

"From your loving daughter,
Jessie"[2]

In January, Coggeshall had the first chance in weeks to go hunting. In three letters to the children he described his effort to shoot a heron; the Ecuadorian method of digging potatoes; and finding obsidian—volcanic glass.

HUNTING TRIP

"Quito, January 23, 1867

"Dear Little Folks:

"I told you I had seen a flock of white Herons north of Quito when I was out riding with Senior Hurtado and that I intended to shoot one. I went to hunt them yesterday with my servant Modesto. The sky was cloudy and the weather cool. Pichincha's crowns were hid in thick mist. About five miles north of the city is a grove of wild cherry trees. There we saw the birds, about 30, feeding on the cherries. I dismounted, crept across two fields, along the hedges and got behind a tree where I had a very fair shot. I fired, birds rose from half a dozen trees and sailed gracefully over my head, but none fell to the ground. I was chagrined but unwilling to give up. I sallied into the field to survey the tree on which I had seen my intended victim. Lo and behold, there he was in the very top lodged in the branches. I called Modesto who climbed the tree and took the prize. I had shot him through the head and in the body at the butt of the wing. He was perfectly white and was about five feet long, or high, from the tip of his bill to his toes—body very small—feathers very beautiful—Jessie will pick the most beautiful and send you. This heron flies very gracefully and is the white bird in Church's picture of the heart of the Andes, sketches near Quito."[3]

---

[2]William T. Coggeshall Papers, Ohio Historical Society.
[3]Ibid.

"January 25th, 1867

"Yesterday I rode up one of the narrow roads leading toward the foot of Pichincha. I passed through a ravine in which are huge rocks thrown out of the volcano many years ago. I saw many beautiful flowers and gathered a boquet [sic]. No garden in Columbus in the month of June could furnish a greater variety of beautiful flowers.

"To-day I rode with Tomoleon Flores to a hacienda southwest of Quito, on high land commanding a charming view of Quito. In the hacienda was a fat old woman who showed us her garden and gave us fruit to eat. She is old, fat, dirty and ugly yet we called her Senorita—Miss, not Senora, Madam—All the women are Senoritas here, except the Indians.

"Returning to Quito we saw men and women in a field digging potatoes. What sort of hoes do you think they use? Their hands. The Senorita of the hacienda sold $7,000 worth of potatoes this year. We also saw, on our way home, many Senoritas bathing and washing clothes, in a swift stream, which we crossed on a high bridge. Every day the women bathe there, indifferent to the gaze of men. They wear very short and very thin skirts in the bath. You would not like to bathe out of doors in Ohio on the 26th day of January. Some of the women were in the water yesterday two or three hours. It gave me the chills to look at them, and think of January in Ohio . . . ."[4]

VOLCANIC RESIDUE

"January 31, 1867

"North of Quito, about three miles, near the foot of Pichincha is a point described as having received the major part of the productions of a volcanic eruption many years ago. Huge rocks are scattered in every direction over many hundreds of acres of ground. This point I visited yesterday and climbed up the mountain, in a deep ravine as far as it was possible to go with my horse. I passed precipices over 100 feet deep where the point of my horse's hoof was not more than four inches from the verge of destruction.

"The mountain with its green and brown shades rose square above me—one side crowned with rocks and sharp points—the other having a few stunted trees and free from rocks. In the water courses I hunted for volcanic curiosities and found many specimens of what is called obsidian—volcanic glass. I will send some home at the first opportunity.

---

[4]William T. Coggeshall Papers, Ohio Historical Society.

> "When upon the mountain I had views of the peaks of Turuargua—of Cayambe and of several others—those named being crowned with snow. I saw men plowing with wooden plows as the Incas did. . . . On the way home being very thirsty I drank of bowl of Chicha, the native liquor—fermented Maize.
>
> "W.T.C."[5]

RIDICULE STARTS

During the rainy season Coggeshall had time to catch up on his dispatches to Washington. Ecuador's promises to establish a Protestant Cemetery continued. The commitment was printed in the official government newspaper *El Nacional* which also carried the responses of all the diplomatic representatives to the government guarantee. Coggeshall sent a copy of the paper to Washington.

After the issue of *El Nacional* was published, some of the natives started taunting the U.S. Minister and Jessie. The little boys who tagged at Jessie's skirts would mock "Protestante, Protestante." They yelled the same epithet at Coggeshall. Some adults did, too. Coggeshall attributed their taunts to ignorance. He was fighting for a principle.

In a February 1 dispatch, Coggeshall informed Secretary of State Seward that Ecuador had "instructed its representative in Rome to protest to His Holiness against the conduct of the Delegado in Quito in regard to the remains of Mr. Neale."

There were also less controversial matters to report. There was talk of "a Congress of the Republics of South America to be held at Lima [Peru]." . . . Ecuador's answer to the United States' offer to re-establish peace between the Allied Republics of South America and Spain, Coggeshall stated, was: "Ecuador awaits the decision of Chile and Peru, especially of Chile." It would be necessary to arrange a peace offer unanimously.

ECUADOR'S DEBT TO U.S.
FOR DAMAGED SHIPS

Coggeshall rejoiced in informing Seward that he had perfected arrangements for Ecuador's second payment on its debt to the United States, due February 27, 1867.

A telephone conversation June 24, 1981, with Milton Gustafson, Chief of Diplomatic Branch, National Archives, Washington, D.C., revealed the nature of the debt. "In 1862 there was a claims convention (treaty) between the United States and Ecuador. Both countries signed a reciprocal agreement. In it, Ecuador was to pay damages in the

---

[5]William T. Coggeshall Papers, Ohio Historical Society.

amount of $94,799.56 to the United States for claims of 14 American citizens against Ecuador for damages in Ecuadorian waters to American cargo ships and other ships. In all, there were eventually nine payments. Coggeshall secured payment of the second installment of $10,533.28 in February, 1867."

The diplomat had convinced the Ecuadorians to try to meet this obligation on time in order to avoid the embarrassment they had experienced by paying late the previous year.

The money was invested by the U.S. Consul in Guayaquil (Ecuador's seaport, business center) in this manner: "Invested the $10,533.28 into Bills on London at 90 days sight [sic], which produced 1572, 2% at 3% Premium valuing the pound Sterling as is the custom in this country at Five Dollars. The said Bill of Exchange payable to the Department of State goes forward in Dispatch No. 30 by the Steamer which sails this afternoon. — L. V. Prevost, U.S. Consul, Guayaquil."[6]

During February Coggeshall wrote that he was becoming "dulled" by Quito life and sought escape. He informed Mary about his plans to go on vacation. Also, for the first time in writing, he lamented his daily cough.

MONEY TO MARY; CONCERN ABOUT CHILDREN

"Quito, February 2, 1867

"Dear Mary,

"Three mails and no letters from home. What's up? We have not heard whether you returned from Illinois, or how your Mother's health is and naturally we are somewhat anxious and perhaps a little vexed. I have been anxious also about Father; and we have desired to know not only whether our first box arrived, but whether you got the Christmas box, also about business. I sent a draft to Washington for $500 and hoped you would get the $1,000 or more from State Journal and could pay the note on the house and have money to spare. On all these matters we are in suspense, as well as regards many others, too 'numerous to mention.'

"Next mail I will send a draft on Washington for $300 gold against which you can draw as you require.

"Next month a gentleman goes from here to the United States and we propose to send a box by him but would like to know first the fate of our other box. I have procured many curiosities and have made some purchases valuable, of which we'll send list when we send the box.

---

[6]William T. Coggeshall Dispatches from Ecuador, 1866–67, U.S. Department of State.

"This is a weary town and a weary life. I am growing dull, duller, dullest—stupid, stupider, stupidest. I vegetate. I don't live—hardly subsist. I eat and sleep all I can, but have little taste or disposition either for reading or writing and am afraid that for want of legitimate exercise I shall forget how to talk. What a calamity in the Coggeshall family! Jessie makes good progress in Spanish, but I get on slowly because I am too indolent to study.

"For the sake of diversion and change I propose to make a trip to Ambato next week with half a dozen friends and visit on our return the Inca palaces near Cotopaxi. We will be gone about a week. Jessie will stay with the Misses Flores.

"Jessie will write you the local news, about our dinners—a concert—a false count and other matters.

"We are in the rainy seasons, but it has not yet 'poured' regularly. When the sun shines the temperature is balmy but on dark days the wind is like the December blasts which sweep over Ohio.

"I have succeeded in getting on order from this Gov't., an advance for the payment of the debt due U.S. Feb. 17th. Last year there was much trouble about it. I advise the Gov't. of my success by this mail and doubt not will be complimented for my attention. We look with interest for comments on the Neale and Priest discussion etc.—both from the U.S. and from England.

"Our papers come very irregularly and the magazines not at all, and we have never been advised whether the handkerchiefs sent you and the girls (at Springfield) and Aunt Eliza (at Massillon) were rec'd.

"I am quite anxious to hear about Willie [now age 17]. I hope he attends school regularly and that he keeps ahead of his classes, also that he spends his evenings at home reading history, biography and travels and doing whatever is in his power to make his Mother happy and proud of him as a dutiful son and promising young man. It is of the utmost importance that he improve his present opportunities and I have faith that he does. I want him to practice writing, so that he will compose readily and correctly. Let him write long letters to Jessie and copy each one carefully, being sure it is correct in every particular when he seals it up.

"I doubt not Mamie is getting to be a famous musician, and I am sure Hattie is a smart little scholar. About Prockie—I don't know what to say—but I know she is mischievous and I hope she knows 'B' from a bull's foot by this time. Mamie must write me all about these matters.

"Fly swiftly round ye wheels of time and bring the welcome day, when once more I can be in the family circle; but, alas, then, little folks may no longer be little folks—but big girls—Enough, I'll get the bluest of the blues if I go on in this strain—ADIOS!!

"We hope your eyes are now all right and that you are fat and hearty—if not fair and forty.

"My health is fair to middling. I am much stronger than when I left Columbus, but still suffer somewhat on account of the thin air and the accursed cough afflicts me more or less every day. My lungs are stronger however than when I first came here. Jessie enjoys excellent health and has grown taller and heavier than when she left the States.

"If the Guayaquil box has not been rec'd. write the Pres't. of Panama R.R. New York and also Wells and Fargo's Express, New York, giving description. It was directed to you and was in Panama (if ever it reached there) in September.

"Love to all—as ever
W.T.C."[7]

In her inimitable, sometimes hilarious style, Jessie described a concert she and her father attended. They sat in the second row behind the "President's seats." In back of them were three ladies dressed in "horrible taste." Jessie wrote every detail of their ornate get-ups.

GAUDY LADIES AT CONCERT

"Quito, February 2, 1867

"Dear Mother,

"I cannot imagine why you do not write to us, there have been three mails more and no letters. Father wishes me to ask if the Coggeshalls have all starved to death or not, because there are a great many pretty 'Senoritas' in Ecuador, and if such is the case we will both of us get married right away. Father will marry one of these pretty 'Senoritas' and I will accept the first chance I have. If you do not wish such a thing to happen, you must write soon.

"Some time ago I wrote to Willie about the German Count. He is now meandering about in the mountains of Ecuador with the police at his heels. While he was here he sold a draft, on a bank in Lima, to a merchant for $1,500 and a few days ago it was discovered that the draft was false.

"Last Sunday night there was a concert, and although it rained as it only can rain in Ecuador Father and I took our umbrellas, big cloaks and went. There were about two hundred persons in the room when we arrived, which is a very large audience indeed for Quito. Father and myself and the Misses Flores had our chairs placed in the row directly behind the chairs reserved for the President and Family which were in the first row.

---

[7]William T. Coggeshall Papers, Ohio Historical Society.

". . . three ladies occupied the seats reserved for the President . . . dressed in such hideous taste it made me sick to look at them.

"One was a young girl very homely and silly—she had on a dress of gray and white barege,[8] a white alpaca cloak trimmed with blue, and her head was decorated in the most singular style. Over the forehead was an immense bow made of dirty blue crepe and green and pink artificial flowers and tinsel cord; the cord passed along each side of her head and held a horrible arrangement placed over two braids of hair which were caught up by what was intended to be a gold comb.

"The lady who was with her was dressed in still worse taste— her dress was black grenadine with small pink flowers, cut low in the neck. Her front hair was combed straight back from her face and shoved with the back hair into a net dotted all over with large wax pearls. On the top of the net was a crown about 4 inches high made of red cotton velvet. This immense structure was also covered with wax pearls, on each side of the crown were two long streamers of red ribbon which were tied behind on the net in a huge bow.

"The sister of the first mentioned lady sat on a side seat with a black shawl over her head and face the whole evening long.

"Three ladies sat behind us, one of whom is a most beautiful woman, the other two were splendidly dressed but are both as ugly as it is possible to be and their clothes were in horrible taste. One, the oldest and fattest, had on a red silk dress made very well. Low necked and short sleeved, her huge arms were decorated with magnificent pearl bracelets with clasps made of splendid emeralds. On her neck she wore a superb pearl necklace. Her hair was dressed in the latest style and her face was covered with about 4 pounds of paint, both white and red. Her sister was dressed after the same style except that her dress was a gay brocade silk and her pearls were more magnificent. Both sisters carried elegant fans and wore white kid gloves.

"The other lady wore a white swiss dress made frightfully and in very bad taste, her jewelry was very beautiful, and on her head she wore a small Parisian hat. Her exceeding beauty is all that saved her from being a perfect dowdy.

"I wore for the first time in Quito my grenadine dress, a red shawl trimmed with white goat's hair fringe, white kid gloves, my hair very plain without any ornament, and I carried a very handsome fan. I was without a jewel of any kind, not even a breast pin.

"The concert was given by a Mr. Sipp, a young man who came to Quito without a cent in his pocket, who pretends to have a splendid reputation and who is a splendid player. He was assisted by a young man, a native of Quito, and who taught himself to play

---

[8] A sheer fabric of silk warp and cotton or worsted filling, often used for veils or dresses.

the piano, and who is a very good player; also by several other persons who played the violin. The violin playing was miserable and the piano was placed in such a bad position that it was not much better.

"Why don't you send me some ribbons in a letter? I can not write any more for the simple reason that I have nothing more to write about.

"Give my love to everybody and tell them that I should like to receive letters once in a while.

"From your daughter,
Jessie Coggeshall"[9]

HOLIDAY TRIP

"Quito, February 7, 1867

"Dear Mary:

"I write you in advance of the regular mail day because I expect to leave Quito tomorrow for 8 or 10 days. I go with Saint Robert, the French Minister, Mr. Gouin and others, to Ambato, not very temperate and abounding in fruits. Mr. G. goes on to Europe. I go to Bonos, then Riobamba, and return slowly, visiting places of interest—Inca palaces, curiosities of volcanoes, earthquakes, etc.

"I take three horses and a mule and two servants, one a cook. I feel strong enough now for such a trip and Quito is so dull a change is desirable. I have wished for some weeks to get away but would not leave till I had settled with the Gov't. for the debt due Feb. 27th.

"I feel now I am entitled to a short play spell, but I go not for play. I go to hunt material for future work, health permitting. I will keep my journal regularly and will write you, or send it you."[10]

– Unsigned –

Coggeshall was doubtless happy to visit historic sights in Ecuador but he might have been equally anxious to get a breather from the controversy over his efforts to secure a Protestant Cemetery. He might get taunts—over the Neale Incident—on the streets from the uneducated in Quito but he had won the respect of the diplomatic corps (except the Pope's Delegate!) and the respect of educated citizens.

---

[9]William T. Coggeshall Papers, Ohio Historical Society.
[10]Ibid.

"Madonna and Child," oil painting from Ecuador, shipped home with U.S. Minister Coggeshall's possessions in the late 1860s. Painting hangs in Springfield, Ohio, Art Center.

—Ramon Salas, 1860

CHAPTER 14
BURIED TREASURE

JEWELS AND SILVER

In February, Coggeshall left Quito for a 10-day holiday. Accompanying him were Chilean Minister Hurtado, store-owner and importer Senior Gouin and French attache Mr. Saint Robert.

Mr. Gouin was going to Europe on a buying trip while the three diplomats set out on an adventure. With horses, mules, and Indian servants they were going to explore some of Ecuador's historic spots near Quito: Inca palaces, lava-covered terrain, rocky crevices, gullies, and other residue from volcanoes and earthquakes. Who knew what they might discover? Coggeshall hoped for material for the novel he planned to write.

At Latacunga, near Quito, lay the ruins of an ancient small community blotted out by volcanic eruption. As the group approached Latacunga, they decided to take a circuitous route, following a footpath that must go somewhere. Coggeshall and his horse were leading. They ventured into a low-lying spot of gray-brown ashes when suddenly, Coggeshall's horse began sinking . . . "the earth was giving way"[1] beneath him. Quickly, his servants circled around to rescue him but their horses began sinking, too. All at once, like a periscope, the top of a gray stone chimney was peering up at them.

The Indians dropped to their knees and began digging with bare hands. The rocky structure was a tiny steeple. The Indians jabbered excitedly. They grabbed their tools and swung pick-axes up and down over their heads, into the rocky, lava-covered terrain. Dig, they did. Dig, and dig, and dig.

---

[1]Interview December 1, 1979, with Chrystal Swan, 27-year housekeeper for Coggeshall's grandson and wife, Ralph and Blanche Busbey.

Suddenly one axe clanked into a pile of pillar-shaped stone and adobe. The group shouted with glee. Then dug faster and faster. They had discovered a Hacienda and, excavating further, realized they had burrowed into a "chancel" (chapel).

Bit by bit, for several days, the human beavers unearthed treasures of ancient art and jewelry. Wide-eyed, they discovered stunning emeralds and gold peeping through cocoons of mucky chunks of centuries-old lava, sealed inside a volcanic lava tube.

Still other treasures awaited them. All there for the taking. With crude hand tools, they stripped layers of lava ash off oddly shaped objects and brought to light rare pieces of solid silver.

It is not known what the total amount of the exquisite cache was, but the part that became Coggeshall's was described by his grandson Ralph:

". . . he obtained items of ancient Spanish, Ecuadorian and Peruvian art, jewels and silverware. According to Ecuadorian art experts, these dated back to the Canare Indians of the Asuay Province, before the Inca conquest of Ecuador in the 15th century.

"The silverware, by its hallmarks, dates back at least to the Spanish conquest of Ecuador in the 17th century.

"The entire Coggeshall collection was shipped to the United States in 1867.

"The collection includes: 10 pieces of ancient jewelry, yellow gold set with emeralds, which show the work of the Canare Indians (now a lost art) of making gold and silver and copper amalgae. The pieces contain more than 150 emeralds in sizes varying from three carats to one-quarter carat, as follows:

"One large bow-knot brooch with pendant containing large emerald of tear-drop shape, in filigree basket of gold. This piece contains over 80 emeralds.

"One bracelet of yellow gold and emeralds, reinforced with sturdy, slender gold wire. Contains over 50 emeralds.

"Two sets of gold, emerald and pearl earrings.

"One set of 5 emerald and gold pins and ancient cuff links.

"One yellow gold ring set with emeralds.

"Two solid silver communion trays, containing hallmarks authentically before the 17th century.

"One solid silver, hand wrought Holy Water Vase.

"One solid silver hand wrought Host Tray.

"One small ruby ring set in gold."[2]

---

[2]Ralph Coggeshall Busbey Papers, in the collection of the author.

Minister Coggeshall did not write the total results of his marvelous discovery in a single letter to Mary. But subsequent letters show that she knew about it and even received some of the jewels. In an April 3, 1867, letter, Jessie coaxed her mother to have her "picture taken wearing the emeralds . . . and with crimped hair."

Ralph Busbey and his wife Blanche gave the small ruby ring to their housekeeper, Chrystal Swan. In a December 1, 1979, interview, Chrystal told that she saw all the Coggeshall jewelry and artifacts from South America; she tried on the brooch with pendant containing 80 emeralds—"it was extremely heavy, it nearly bent me over"—and polished the silver weekly. Ralph gave two of the silver communion plates to a Catholic church in Akron . . . and, "when Coggeshall and his party unearthed the chapel, they found the ruby ring on the little finger of the Virgin Mary."[3]

Today, in most countries of the world, it would be illegal to remove treasures without government permission. But there was no such restriction at that time in Ecuador.

Ancient silver host tray found in buried treasure, 1867.

---

[3]The jewels and silver were not the only treasures shipped home. The priceless items also included 36 watercolors by Ramon Salas, Ecuador's finest watercolorist of the 1860s. Ralph sold nearly all the jewels and artifacts to dealers. One of the two oils shipped home, *Madonna and Child,* is in the Springfield, Ohio, Art Center. Another, *Indian Orange Vendor,* is owned by a Springfield woman.

CHAPTER 15
PREJUDICE CONTINUES

CHURCH/STATE CONTROVERSY GROWS; JESSIE ENGAGED

Gossip—gossip—gossip. It knows no geographic boundaries. Jessie sent gossip galore to her mother: an altercation at the Bolivian diplomat's dance; a scandal about Friedrich Houssarek (Coggeshall's predecessor as U.S. Minister to Ecuador); and complaints by General Stagg, older husband of a Flores daughter, that the Bishop and church excessively usurped wives' daylight hours.

One bit of news Jessie did not include, in the available letters, was about herself. When Senor Gouin returned in early May from a buying trip to Europe, he asked Coggeshall for Jessie's hand. Coggeshall consented. So, Jessie became engaged. The teenager began making plans—happy plans—for her wedding. The Quito nuns did exquisite handwork so she chose them to make her wedding gown and trousseau.

But, back to the local gossip she wrote to her mother.

DRUNKEN NEW GRANADIAN MINISTER

"Quito, March 16, 1867

"Dear Mother,

"I wrote a long letter last mail and must not expect a very long one now. I have had a great deal of sewing to do for the last two or three weeks, and you must not open your eyes as big as saucers when I tell you that next week, I intend to begin to make those drawers which you cut out and put in my trunk.

"Quito is duller than ever, because as Father never goes out in the evening, I do not get to the Flores to spend the evening and when we do not have company or have nothing to read, the evenings are perfectly frightful. The conversations of persons who come to spend the evening are not the most intelligent. All they talk about is the stinginess of [French Minister] Mr. Saint Robert and the ages of the Flores girls and who they will most likely marry. I have exhausted all the librarys [sic] in Quito and a few days ago I took all the old magazines I could find that were in the Legation but I have read all the stories, and am at loss again for something to read. I wish you would send some magazines and particularly the 'Godey,' also some novels with paper covers would be very acceptable.

"This last mail we received no letters from you, but one from Mr. Busbey informed us that you were all well. If you know how provoked and disappointed we are when we receive no letters you would always have some member of the family write every mail. The last mail but one, I received a letter from Delia, and wish you would tell her to write the fashions, and make her letters a little longer. It seems to me that all the Springfield girls are getting married except the Coggeshall girls and they better hurry as they will be old maids before they know it.

"Mamie says in her letter that Father better be careful or when he goes home he will have no wife. I really hope there is no danger.

"I believe that Mary Harvey had entirely captivated Mr. Busbey by her 'clear ringing laugh' as he calls it, in her letter. I hope that Mamie is not jealous. She thought when I left that the field was clear and that he was going to court her, and I should like to know how she takes it now that a rival has come into the field.

"Mother, I begin to feel the need of one or two dresses. My black alpaca dress is beginning to wear out and looks hardly fit for the street and I have grown so much that my sole dress is so short that I can wear it nowhere but in the house, it hardly touches the ground behind and in front gives a fine show of my legs when I walk. I have lengthened it about two inches but it is past all help. I think I shall manage to exist until I get home and then there will be a fine stack of old clothes for Mamie and Hattie. My shoes are getting so old and torn that it will not do to wear a short dress or lift up any dress in the street or Mr. Saint Robert will set me down to be as bad as the Quito Ladies.

"The latest excitement in Quito was a dance given by the Bolivian Minister. None or very few of the first ladies of Quito were invited. The dinner given to the Diplomatic Corps and the Officers of the Government was quite a brilliant affair but the ball afterwards was not quite as brilliant. Several of the gentlemen got drunk and the Minister from New Granada was exceedingly so, and he hugged the ladies, put his legs across their laps, and insulted and fought with almost every man in the room. His example seemed to inspire them all and it was not long before it became nearly a regular melee. This affair has furnished wonder and scandal for the usual period of five days. It was rumored that the Bolivian Minister was going to give another ball for the 'first ladies' of Quito, but this last mail he received news of his wife's death and now he will be spared the mortification of having his invitations to the second ball refused.

"I think that I have written a very gossipy letter and shall close it telling the real, sober, honest truth—that I am sick about and completely disgusted with Ecuador and very anxious to get home again. Love to all and tell Willie to write.

"From your homesick Daughter,
Jessie Coggeshall"[1]

SCANDALOUS HOUSSAREKS; WOMEN'S SUBSERVIENCE TO THE BISHOP

"Quito, April 3, 1867

"Dear Mother,

"The last mail we received enough papers to keep us supplied with reading matter until another mail. The shoes, music and corset steels arrived all safe. The shoes are a little large but are splendid for Quito. You said in one of your letters that you were going to send me a pair of garters. I do not think they could have been sent the same time that the shoes were, for they have not yet arrived.

"The illustrated Harper's Weekly have been examined and read and admired by every gentleman who is in the habit of calling here.

"We gave a dinner yesterday to Mr. Hurtado, the Minister from Chile, Mr. Larrain, his Secretary, [French Minister] Mr. Saint Robert, and a Mr. Hurtado who is a young merchant of Quito and who speaks English very well. The dinner was very nice and it was all a complete success.

"Mr. Saint Robert kept us in a roar the whole time by his queer actions and speeches. Sunday before last, Father and I dined with Mr. Saint Robert and Secretary. He has a french cook and subsequently his dinners are very frenchy but as perfectly delicious

---

[1]William T. Coggeshall Papers, Ohio Historical Society.

although according to the Equadorian idea, are not at all liberal or generous.

"The ladies and gentlemen of Quito have a habit of tying a handkerchief around their heads whether they have anything the matter with them or not. This is one of Mr. Saint Robert's hobbys [sic] and he never loses an opportunity of exposing and ridiculing them. After dinner he stepped out on the balcony and espied a young lady who was standing on a balcony opposite the house with her face tied up in a handkerchief. He immediately called me to come out and see her and although I did not feel at all like getting up I went, out of politeness. After I had been there a minute or two, this young lady went into the house and pretty soon, there were three more who had come out to see the 'Senorita Norte Americana.'

"As I looked up the street I saw a gentleman at the house of the Bolivian Minister looking at me with an Opera glass. I did not give him a chance to look long for I went into the house and did not go out of it again until after dark when we went to the Flores house to spend the evening. This is only a very small specimen of their inpudence and curiosity in Quito.

"You ask in your letter if Mr. Houssarek [former U.S. Minister to Ecuador] was not gay[2] in Quito. From what I hear about him I should think he was gay, and rather too much so for his own comfort, the comfort of his wife, and also that of a lady who did live in Quito with her husband, but when Mr. Houssarek went to Guayaquil she went too.

"As for the lady friends which Father and I have in Quito we have a few and want less. Our evenings are of course very dull but we manage to get through them by reading, talking, drinking tea and entertaining such persons who call. Mr. Houssarek has good reason for looking at Mrs. Prevost's[3] picture with a sneer, for she always protected his wife and took her part. Mrs. Prevost is a very stylish lady who cares a great deal for dress but is not very nice, she is rather sharp and crusty with her husband and is a miserable housekeeper.

"While Mr. Houssarek and his wife were in Quito they were the subjects of the lowest scandal. He was running around with other women and she was seen in the low miserable eating houses of Quito with a young German drinking coffee at the hours not the most respectable.

"I can not very well send a piece of my dress because it is not made up and it will hardly do to cut it but I will examine and see. I

---

[2]Gay in that day meant a flirtatious playboy or ladies' man. It did not mean being homosexual as implied today.
[3]Wife of the U.S. Consul at Guayaquil, L. V. Prevost.

am very glad that you are getting so that you go out in society more. I think your dress must be very pretty and stylish. I should like to have your picture taken in that dress with emeralds and crimped hair.

"Poor little Hattie must have had a hard time of it [chicken pox]. I will write her a letter this mail and try to console her.

"I just now examined my dress and cut off a piece which I send.[4] The dress has never been made up and I shall bring it home in the piece. I bought it in Guayaquil supposing I would have it made but when I got to Quito and saw what a dirty place it was I concluded I had enough dresses to be spoiled here. I have never worn my white alpaca in Quito. My grenadine I wore 3 or 4 times but have always been freezing while I had it on.

"You say in your letters that we should be thankful that we have sunshine. But sunshine is a very rare article here now and it is so cold that Father goes around the house with two or three coats on and I can not wear my calico dresses with any comfort and I now wear my black alpaca every day and even with that I wear my cloth sack or a shawl.

"You made a grand mistake in sending me vocal music for I can not sing any more than a cat and besides I have no piano. Father and I concluded that it would not pay to rent one as we are going to Guayaquil soon.

"The corset steels do splendidly and have some hopes of getting in a whole condition, because there was some danger of my being cut in two. You wish to know if I knit or sew. I made a scarf for Mr. Gouin and a scarf for myself and this week I intend to commence another for Father and I do not think there is any danger of my getting spinal diseases or the consumption from bending over my sewing. I do nearly just as I please, sew, read, knit, talk, walk or play, just when I please. You may think that this is a very enviable life and so I used to think but now I have got over that and don't see it as much as I used to.

"Mrs. Jones asks in her letter what the roofs of the houses are made of, and for special benefit I will describe a Quito house. The roofs are made of tiles, two rows are laid with hollow upwards and one row with the hollow downwards and thus they are interlapped; the walls are built of adobe and are not papered or plastered but covered with a whitewash and are from four to six feet thick; except in the houses of the better class and in very few of them. There are no carpets, the floors being covered with matting. The material for building is brought sometimes for miles on the backs of Indians and women particularly are used for doing such labor.

---

[4] A swatch from Jessie's dress is at the Ohio Historical Society. It is tan pongee imprinted with small daubs of purple encircled with orange.

"The Spanish ladies of Quito are not the most charming creatures in the world. A mother deserts her family to go to the church, and a wife her husband. The ladies get up at four o'clock in the morning and go to the church where they stay until ten or twelve at which time they breakfast and at one or two o'clock they return to the church and do not return to their homes until six or seven in the evening and at eight they are in bed.

"General Stagg who married one of the Flores girls told me that sometimes he did not see his wife for three days at a time, and even then he could not see her unless he went to her mother's room between six and eight o'clock in the evening. He wanted to know of me if that was not domestic. He said that when they were first married he would not permit it but now folks had told him that he had better leave them alone or he would have all the priests and the Bishop too on his back.

"One gentleman complained so openly and publicly of the desertion of his wife that the Bishop heard of it and sending for him reprimanded him very severely and told him not to let him hear of such a thing again or he would be excommunicated. This is domestic bliss in Ecuador.

"Father tells me to say that the Plaza which you see in your photographs, filled with trees, is Plaza Mayor the principal Plaza of Quito where all the exquisites of Quito walk on Sunday and in the evenings after dinner.

"This dinner which we gave and which I told you about was given in honor of your birthday although rather late. We intended to give it to the Flores the same week of your birthday but we received news of the death of Carlos Klinker, a young man who left Quito to go to Europe but was taken sick in Panama of yellow fever and died in New York. We have not had any rain for three or four days and I think the dry season is beginning.

"Mr. Saint Robert has promised to teach us to play 'Whist' and now we have some means of keeping ourselves from dying of dullness.

"I have not been to the Flores house for more than a week. Yesterday General Stagg was here to dinner and enjoyed it hugely but it is a horrible bore to have him here because he is so deaf. Father was obliged to talk so loud that he got nervous and during the whole evening he talked so loud that I was almost deafened by the noise.

"Last night Father was telling Mr. Saint Robert about making speeches and sitting up late at night reading the political campaigns and about you making hot punch for him late at night. Mr. Saint Robert was full of pity for you and said that it was enough to kill any man or woman and that he was going to Columbus to pity and console you.

"As I have a great deal of writing to do both for myself and Father it is time to close this or my poor stock of writing material will be exhausted. I intend to write also to Mamie and Hattie.

"From your daughter,
Jessie Coggeshall"[5]

RIDICULE INCREASES

That was people gossip, over-the-back-fence. Then there was political gossip—the kind that hurts. More and more criticism kept flying Coggeshall's way, and Jessie could not always escape it. The Neale Incident continued to have repercussions.

Ridicule of the Coggeshalls as Protestants was a topic of gossip among Ecuadorians. Nasty little boys spit at Coggeshall's heels—and at Jessie's. The controversy over the U.S. Minister's determination to secure a cemetery for Protestants raged—loudly among the ignorant peasants, quietly among the more informed and finally, in print from the ecclesiastics.

After his holiday and amazing discovery of the lava-covered jewels, Coggeshall returned to Quito with improved health and a new zest for continuing his fight to get Christian burial rights and a cemetery for non-Catholics.

ANOTHER BISHOP PROTESTS

The gains Coggeshall had made hit a snag when another Bishop raised a loud protest. This time it was the Bishop of Cuenca protesting. He was from President Carrion's home province.

Coggeshall's few diplomatic dispatches for March and April relayed to Washington the growing rancor. He sent copies of *El Nacional* for both months with his dispatches.

In March, *El Nacional* carried the diplomatic corps' appreciation to Ecuador for its promise "to establish a Protestant Pantheon" . . . "which," Coggeshall added, "I persistently urged but which the treaty disregarded for 25 years."

But prejudice continued. In April, Coggeshall reported that the Bishop of Cuenca, "violently protested Christian burial and a cemetery for Protestants."

The diplomat enclosed another copy of *El Nacional* containing the Bishop's objection. The Ecuadorian government, however, affirmed that "The Minister of Foreign Affairs does not shirk the responsibility he has assumed" (to establish a Protestant Cemetery).

[5]William T. Coggeshall Papers, Ohio Historical Society.

In his dispatch to the State Department Coggeshall continued: "The new British chargé d'affaires has arrived—Frederick Hamilton. The family of the late chargé, Col. Neale, determined that his remains shall be buried at Quito. The new chargé will execute this trust. That will bring the question of the burial place for Protestants to a practical and determinate issue. I say this because, notwithstanding its promises, and proclamations, public and private, the Government has not yet set apart any particular locality."

Four months after Colonel Neale died in December his body was still not buried.

After the Bishop of Cuenca's protest appeared in *El Nacional,* criticism of Coggeshall and Jessie became more public—still mostly from the uneducated but, disappointingly, also from some Quito citizens who professed to be friends of the two Americans. Increasingly, little boys and even adults, mocked them as being "Protestante, Protestante." They knew they were whispered about. Little children sometimes threw pebbles at their horses' hooves.

WORRY OVER WILLIE

Coggeshall wanted to leave Quito. Another strong Bishop was against him. The weather was getting chilly. His health was up and down. And, he'd learned that his son Willie had been bitten by a dog. He missed the family terribly.

Coggeshall's diary notes tell the story, interspersed with household accounts: "MAY 1, 1867. Better but confined to bed . . . speculated on novel. MAY 4. Up all day—letter from home—*horrible news about Willie* [bitten by a dog]. *Rabies probable*. . . . Got $50 of Gouin—sold 2 barrels of wine for $60—cost $42. WED., MAY 5. Sold Gouin 6 tins fish at 2.50—2 lobster $1—one cheese 3.50 = 20.50—health improved—taking cod liver oil. Gouin debt $5 for chandelier."[6]

The diplomat had much business, as did most citizens of Quito, with his future son-in-law.

On May 17, Coggeshall wrote the State Department requesting permission to go to Lima (Peru) and Santiago (Chile) during the following September and October. The two-month leave would enable him to sightsee through the Andes Mountains, give him a change of scenery and gain a perspective on his work. Besides, it would be useful to see other capitals in neighboring South American countries. He noted that he would "be compelled to return to Quito by the end of October because," after that, "the mule paths of Ecuador are very dangerous."

---

[6]William T. Coggeshall Papers, Ohio Historical Society.

Jessie's lace handkerchief.

In the same dispatch, the U.S. Minister congratulated the State Department on completing negotiations with Russia for purchase of the Alaskan Islands (purchased March 30, 1867, for $7,200,000). Secretary of State Seward had crusaded in favor of the acquisition against such great opposition that his campaign was branded "Seward's Folly."

Worry over Willie continued in the diary: "WED., MAY 22. Wrote letter to Shellabarger—also to Busbey. . . wrote letter to father. Much troubled about Willie. Fear news. FRI., MAY 24. Jessie bot [sic] laces in convents $10 [Jessie was preparing her trousseau]—much distressed about Willie. MAY 26. Weak today—rather dull. Rain in afternoon. At this time take no wine, but much brandy."[7]

A succession of diary notes describe Coggeshall's struggle with his lungs: "SAT., JUNE 1, 1867. Up but very weak. SUN., 2nd. Went to dinner at Gouin's—smoked a cigarette—sick—vomited dinner. TUES., 4. Worse. WED., 5. Unable to sit up. THU., 13. Examination by Drs. Espinosa, Satoncajon and Gandoro. Say a tubercular cavern is forming in my lungs. SUN., JUNE 16, 1867. Dreadful sick—pluck gave way. 1st time in life. MON., 17. Little better but determined to get out of Quito."[8]

---
[7]William T. Coggeshall Papers, Ohio Historical Society.
[8]Ibid.

Up to this time, the 42-year-old diplomat had written all his letters to Mary himself and penned his own dispatches. But for the first time, on June 1, 1867, his brief dispatch was in Jessie's handwriting. He signed it. The dispatch informed Washington of the death of U.S. Consul L. V. Prevost at Guayaquil and Coggeshall's appointment of his successor, E. Lee.

In the next dispatch, dated June 18, Coggeshall relayed the decision of Chile that the United States not mediate the war between South American countries and Spain. Spain had invaded Valparaiso (Chile) and Callao (Peru) "without filing the prescriptions of the right of war."[9]

He warned of the possibility and the threat of war in Ecuador, led by Colombian President Tomas Mosquera who had been seeking an excuse to invade the Ecuadorian east border.[10] "That was a possibility until Monday when received news that there had been a revolution in Colombia and Mosquera was in the hands of his enemies."[11]

SITE SELECTED FOR PROTESTANT CEMETERY

On June 18 Coggeshall announced that Ecuador had finally selected a site for "Protestant burial." Jessie wrote the important message at her father's dictation at his bedside . . . "the condition of my health is such that my visit to Guayaquil is indefinitely postponed." Coggeshall signed the dispatch in wavering script.

A heartbreaking letter from Jessie on June 19 explained the reason for her father's few dispatches since May and his unsteady signature:

CRITICAL ILLNESS

"Quito, June 19, 1867

"Dear Mother,

"Ever since the last mail Father has been very sick, and for two or three days very dangerously so. But now he is better and this week we expect to go to Guapulo,[12] a small place near Quito but much lower and warmer—with stronger air. The Doctor says that Father's right lung and a part of the left are in perfect health and that they are strong enough, with proper care, to prevent the

---

[9]William T. Coggeshall Dispatches from Ecuador, 1866-67, U.S. Department of State.
[10]Until the early 1820s Quito had been a province in the United States of Colombia. Mosquera wanted it back.
[11]Mosquera was exiled.
[12]The same beautiful country place the Coggeshalls had visited and described in an earlier letter.

advance of the disease. He has been examined by three of the most eminent physicians in Ecuador and they all agree on that one point of the health of the right and a portion of the left lung. The left lung is diseased near the shoulder in the same place as Grand Mother's. The Doctors say that there is now being formed what they call a cavern, that is, as I understand it, that the tubicles are drying up and coming out. Father spits the most horrible phlegm that it is possible to imagine. This is necessary, as the physicians say, and it is their object to give him strength enough to throw out this matter. As the air of Quito is so close it tires him very much to breathe and for that reason I think that it will do more good for him to make a change of air and scene.

"I did my best in the nursing line but never having had any experience I am afraid it was some nursing but if will and desire are worth anything or go any way toward making a person feel comfortable, I think it was not wanting on my part. The principle difficulty is the want of nice delicate food, but, such things are not to be found in this God forsaken country and the cooks here can not understand why a sick person can not eat broth seasoned with onions, turnips, garlic, and every other kind of vegetable that Father does not like.

"You can only imagine how disgusted he must be when his breakfast is brought to him with everything tasting and smelling of onion. We finally succeeded in getting some beef stew made with nothing but pepper and salt and which he ate with great relish. For the first few days the Doctors would not permit him to eat jellies of any kind or take any acids, but now they permit him to eat jelly but will not let him take any other acid into his stomach. It seems impossible to make them understand here that he is not like the people of Quito, who all have stomachs like an ox and can eat anything, and one of their delicacies is fleas on which they seem to grow fat.

"Father is firm in the belief that once out of Quito with stronger air, that in two days he will be able to ride horseback. You will now see that it is impossible for me to come home this summer. I could not think of leaving Father as he is now, although it will be very embarrassing and annoying for me to live in Quito. You know for what reason. Nobody knows what a disappointment it is for me, but then I have the consolation of knowing that when I do go home it will be for some time, and very probably Father will go also, but you must not expect to see us this year.

"You must tell Florence Wetmore and all my other friends why I can not write and tell them also that as soon as we are settled in Guapulo I will write to all.

"I wish you could send me some patterns of short dresses and tell me the latest styles. Also send us some of the *Harper's paper* bound novels and stories; also keep on sending collars but a little larger than the last one. The shoes are very large but capitol for the streets of Quito. I want now a couple of pairs of garters and fine walking shoes, a little smaller than the shoes. You might also send me some more gloves but of lighter shades. I wish you could send me a couple of nice new style nets. All these things which I have mentioned you can send in your letters.

"Last mail we forgot to speak about Hattie's birthday which was in May. We now send her much love and are very sorry that we can not send some more substantial birthday present. Neither have forgotten that Willie's birthday comes on the 22nd day of June. Also much love to him and hopes that he will enjoy himself on this his eighteenth birthday. I expected to spend my sixteenth birthday in Columbus but that hope has fallen to ground and nothing is left for me to do but to 'grin and bear it.'

"This little place called Guapulo is the same of which Father wrote so long a description, and the same garden which he enjoyed so much is attached to the house which we have hopes of renting.

"There is nothing new in Quito except that last week there were rumors that the Government had discovered a conspiracy and there was some danger of a revolution. I think that it would be a good diversion to see a good revolution although I am not so wicked as to hope there will be one, but if there is I want to see it. There are going to be several marriages in Quito soon which is something so extraordinary that all Quito is on tip toe but as I am not invited to any of them and have a wholesome disgust of marriage in general, it makes no difference who marries and makes a fool of themselves.

"You need not be worried about Father because he is now much better, has a good appetite and as I said before, when he gets where he will have something to look at besides his dull room and this horrible, cold, nasty, windy, stinking Quito, he will be much better. The last two or three days he has been sitting up in a large easy chair in my room and even this small change livened him up and he was much better afterwards.

"Give best regards to Mr. Busbey both from Father and myself and also to the Governor and family and to all our friends.

"With much love from Father to all the children, to yourself, Grandfather and the girls and the same from me.

"I remain as ever,

"Your affectionate daughter,
Jessie Coggeshall."[13]

---

[13]William T. Coggeshall Papers, Ohio Historical Society.

TREACHEROUS MOVE TO GUAPULO

The difficulty of moving from Quito to Guapulo seemed insurmountable. Promise after promise was broken for the hacienda the Coggeshalls wanted. So they had to settle for a low spot a mile from Quito in which the American Legation, home, office, everything was housed in what Jessie described as an 18-foot, flea-infested, road-level, square "cellar." Rent was $20.00 a month. But, the necessity for stronger air for Coggeshall made them rent it.

Meanwhile, their diplomatic friends pursued getting the spacious farmhouse and gardens in Guapulo and, after a few days, succeeded in renting it for $16.00 per month.

Indian women with babies in their arms carried much of the Coggeshall's "goods and chattels" on their backs, "each woman costing the same as a donkey."

On moving day the ailing diplomat was able to walk from the ground-level hovel to mount a borrowed carriage. It was his first carriage ride in Ecuador. At a deep ravine which the carriage could not cross, he was to transfer to a sedan chair. The Indian bearers of the chair, however, would not move until they had been paid, and the Coggeshalls' money was in Quito.

Tired and weak, the diplomat solved the impasse by borrowing a reale from one Indian, giving it to the most stubborn of the four, and promising each man double pay upon reaching Guapulo.

Once in Guapulo, in the midst of stronger air, beautiful scenery, pure water, a cook, two servants, a horse and a mule, Coggeshall's health improved. And the father and daughter no longer heard "Protestante, Protestante."

There was another unwritten difficulty about moving to Guapulo. Jessie wouldn't get to see her fiancee, Senor Gouin, as often, but preparation for their nuptials could continue unabated. The nuns were already at work on Jessie's trousseau and Senor Gouin could easily ride the three miles to Guapulo. They planned to be married in August.

"The Exiles" recapped their moving ordeal in a letter to the family back in Columbus:

A STRANGE AND EVENTFUL HISTORY

"Guapulo, July 1, 1867

"Dear Folks at Home,

"We wrote you by last mail that we expected in a few days to get into the country at Guapulo. We were grievously disappointed. The Colombian had the place and was unwilling to give it up. We

have passed through a series of queer vicissitudes. First when we were ready to go to Guayaquil and should have started in a day or two, came the sad news of the death of the U.S. Consul, our friend Mr. Prevost, with whose family we expected to live. Of course we had no home and were compelled to make other arrangements. This delayed us. Meanwhile Father fell sick and grew worse and worse until he became very ill. When intending to go to Guayaquil we had given up our rooms in the hotel. They were engaged by other parties. These parties wanted them; the landlord was uneasy. Under these circumstances a friend went to the Colombian Minister on one Thursday and his Secretary said the house in Guapulo would be vacated on Saturday and we could occupy it on Monday. The keys would be sent us on Sunday. No keys came but we prepared to move on Monday. We got all ready but no report from the Minister. Father was suspicious and sent a note to Guapulo. The Minister replied that he was not ready to go out then and he could not tell when he would go. So we gave up Guapulo for the time being. Afterward Father thought that some influences might be brought to bear upon the Colombian Minister and he sent for the Bolivian Minister—his friend.

"The Bolivian came promptly and after explanations visited the Colombian. In half an hour he returned and reported that the Colombian had that day vacated the house but with a condition that after ten or fifteen days he should have it again if he desired it, but in consideration of Father's illness he would forego this condition and leave the whole matter with the proprietor. The Chilian Minister was in our room at that time. He started immediately to visit the proprietor and make arrangements for the house. He was denied admittance. He went a second time and was denied again.

"We then sent a note written in Spanish explaining that the Colombian had surrendered his condition and we expected the house. The servant brought back word that an answer would be given us the next morning at ten o'clock. At that time a note came stating that we could not have the premises because he intended to occupy it himself. The disappointment was sad. Father felt it to be indispensable to his recovery that he should have a lower and warmer atmosphere than that of Quito.

"Move we must out of the hotel. So we cast about for a house in a valley about a mile south of Quito and one grade lower. We sent for a native friend and he hunted a house for us and returned saying he had rented one excellent. Jessie went to see it, and reported it dirty, gloomy and full of fleas. But necessity of better air was such that we determined to take the risk of dirt and fleas.

"The rooms we got there were on the ground floor, the floors being actually the earth paved and covered with thin dirty carpet.

We were content for the time being with the promise of pleasant quarters on the second story after a week.

"We moved, and such a moving. We moved on Willie's birthday—the 22nd day of June. Our servant superintended a horde of Indians, dirty, lousy, stinking witches who carried the heaviest furniture on their backs over a mile, at the same time taking a bottle or piece of crockery in their hands, one taking a whole waiter full of bottles. The expense was about $4.00.

"The rooms, when we got there, we found to be, excepting one, in the middle of the house fronting the street, utterly uninhabitable; at $20.00 a month. We were compelled to buy a bed, a looking glass, candlesticks, lamps and chairs. The furniture we found consisted of one round table and two square ones. In this room about 18 feet square, low ceiling and ground floor, very much like a cellar, we received company, ate, slept, etcetera, a brilliant site for the American Legation.

"Father was very weak when we went there, and had to be borne to and from the carriage which our friends the Flores were kind enough to lend us. This was the first carriage ride Father ever took in Ecuador. But not withstanding all the unpleasant surroundings the air was pure and stronger than that of Quito, and Father had good water to drink—the first in Ecuador, and he gained strength from the first day.

"We soon found we were doomed to another disappointment. We sent to the proprietor asking him when we could have the rooms upstairs when he sent back word saying that we could not have them at all for he intended to occupy them himself. What to do now was the question. Live long in that cellar we could not, though it had good air and pleasant rooms around it. But it had no sunshine and was dreary.

"While we were pondering what to do and hunting another house, the Doctor brought the good news that he had had a conversation with the proprietor of the house at Guapulo and he believed that on the following day word would be sent us that we could occupy the house. Much to our satisfaction on the following evening two daughters of the proprietor and two female friends visited us. We received them with much attention in our cellar and they gave us the gratifying assurance that on the following Monday we could move to Guapulo. We thanked them and treated them to wine and tried to content ourselves in our cellar for the short time we were required to stay.

"The next day the proprietor called and in conversation with him we found we could have the house on Friday. Immediately preparations were made for moving and on Thursday a considerable amount of our goods and chattels went out on the backs of Indian women and donkeys each woman carrying before her a baby wrapped up so that it looked like an image, nothing being visible except its head. We gave each one 20 cents a trip and a reale to the lot—for Chichua. They had to be paid in advance or they would not move a step. That is the custom here. The price for a donkey is the same as that for a woman. The secret of our success is explained in the fact that the Colombian Minister has been recalled—he must go back to New Granada. We are constrained to believe that he played us false as to the matter of his surrendering his condition.

"On Friday preparations were made for final departure from the old cellar. Our cook would not go to Guapulo and we had to get another. One day we had no dinner and were obliged to send to a restaurant for a beef steak. We found a colored woman of good reputation, who has a mother and two children. Of course we feed them all.

"We sent for the Flores carriage to take Father as near Guapulo as it was possible to drive. We found it broken but another was promised us. At the appointed hour two carriages came. We took one belonging to Mr. Jijon, a comfortable family coach. Father was able to walk from the cellar to the carriage.

"There is a wide unimproved road to Guapulo. After you leave Quito, it is good for horses and mules but difficult for carriages. The driver pushed ahead, however, until he came to a deep ravine. Here we expected to meet a servant with a sedan chair [to carry Coggeshall across the ravine], but no servant, no chair; it was somewhere back in Quito. We sent him back to hasten it forward. It came in an hour and a half on the shoulders of four Indians.

"Father got in the chair and we were all ready to start when the Indians declared they would not move a step unless paid in advance. We had no money, and there we were in the broad highway in the hot sun. Father in the chair and Jessie on foot. Our money was back in Quito. So we told the Indians but no avail. Finally the matter was arranged, by borrowing a real from one of the Indians and giving it to another, the most furious of the four and by promising each double price when we reached Guapulo. Then the Indians took the chair upon their shoulders and we journeyed. After a short distance we were compelled to descend a very steep hill on a winding, steep road. It was a severe trial for Father but he bore it well and soon recovered from the fatigue after we reached Guapulo. Jessie walked along side in the hot sun, over the rough stones. This is the worst ride Father ever took.

"We have been at Guapulo now three days. Every day Father has gained strength. The water is delicious, pure as crystal, the air is balmy. He sits in the open air nearly all day, walks about occasionally, surrounded by birds, flowers, trees and pleasant vistas and will in a few days be able to mount his horse and ride anywhere about the country. We pay $16.00 a month for the house and garden which we described in a letter to the children. We have a cook and two servants, one male and one female, a horse and a mule. We are compelled to send to Quito for every thing we want though corn and potatoes are cultivated around us and the Indians have chicken and eggs and milk and vegetables, but are so superstitious they will not sell them here even at Quito prices.

"We hope you will be interested in this strange and eventful history and will console with the miseries and disappointments of The Exiles."[14]

On Monday, July 1, Coggeshall jotted in his diary:" . . . improving—a great mistake I did not come to Guapulo long ago. July 2. Walked about today, better than for 4 weeks or more."[15]

On July 3, Jessie poured out the gravity of her father's illness and her anguishing battle as his nurse in a poignant letter to Willie:

JESSIE'S 19-DAY VIGIL

"Guapulo near Quito
July 3, 1867

"Dear Brother Will,

"I was provoked at your last letter because it was so short and unsatisfactory—why don't you write something about your diversions, where you go and who with—who and what—you see new. It is not very pleasant to receive such short letters. You should write your letters so as to correspond in length with the distance.

"You can not imagine how disappointed I was at not being able to come home this year. But I think I would much rather stay with Father than to go home and know that he was here alone in bad health in this horrible miserable God forsaken country. When Father was so sick I was obliged to be with him all the time. I had no friend on whom I could depend, and, with the exception of two, I watched every night alone with him for more than three weeks. I did not have my clothes off for more than two weeks and it was not until we came here that I slept in a regular bed. You may be sure it was very trying for me, who have no experience in sick rooms and know nothing about nursing.

"The day that he began to get better and the Doctors were more encouraged I was so nervous that I did not know whether to laugh or cry and I almost cried whenever any person asked me how Father was. Although I had not shed a tear when Father was

---

[14]William T. Coggeshall Papers, Ohio Historical Society.
[15]Ibid.

so dangerously ill, this day when he was so much better, I went into my own room and cried myself almost sick.

"It will be impossible for me to come home because Father feels and says that if I had not been here he would have been in his grave now for the want of proper attention. He can not make these people understand and he would have died from neglect. You must not think too much about the disappointment, but do as I do now—think about or speak about it but make up your mind that it is 'all for the best' as the old man said when the dog ran away with his dinner.

"There was quite an excitement in Quito last week caused by the death and burial of the Bishop of Quito. He died of cholera omorbus (?) [sic] caused by eating ices, made by the nuns. They say that he had not eaten meat for more than twenty years and had so weakened himself by abstinence and doing penance that he had no strength to resist the disease.

"The burial was conducted in such a manner as is only possible in Ecuador. The corpse was dressed in the Bishop's dress, placed bolt-upright, in a large chair gayly ornamented, the staff was put in his hand and the Bishop's cap on his head. In this manner the corpse of the 'Santo Obispo' was carried on the shoulders of Indians and paraded around the Plaza exposed to the gaze of the ignorant savage creatures who thronged the Plaza to see the 'show'. If you know of anything more horrible than this in any country which pretends to be civilized just mention it.

"Will, you must not let Mother get so 'triste' as they say in Spanish. If she is not inclined to go to Sandusky as Father tells her to do, you and Mollie must coax, persuade, and scold until she consents to go.

"I am going to pay you in your own by writing a dull, short letter. Give my love to all the girls and best regards to all inquiring friends of the other sex and best best regards for Mr. Busbey and ask him if he now has time to enjoy more of the society of that very pleasant young lady Miss _____. I want you to read or tell him this when he and Mary H are together.

"Good-bye
From your affectionate sister
Jessie."[16]

Coggeshall coughed his way through six weeks of "dangerous" illness. At times he nearly choked. The Quito doctors could only try to keep him comfortable while his body threw off the sputum from the tubercle in his lung. But his tired body did throw it off. Throughout feverish days and nights Coggeshall might have thought of his mother

---
[16]William T. Coggeshall Papers, Ohio Historical Society.

who had had tuberculosis also in the left lung. But, she had not had a tropical climate in which to fight the disease. Once past the crisis, the doctors gave the diplomat hope of healing. He anticipated riding his horse again . . . in a few days.

On July 3, Coggeshall was stronger but still dictated his letter to Mary.

CHEER UP, MARY

"Guapulo near Quito
July 3, 1867

"Dear Mary,

"I am strong enough today to write a letter in my own hand but as there is a good deal of writing to be done, deem it better to dictate.

"We were grieved at several things in your last letter, especially at your condition of mind and your indisposition for society. You must change. You had a great deal better be what Mamie calls 'a gay and illustrated' wife than a moody one. Go out with the children. Get a carriage occasionally and take a trip into the country—have company at the house and go to other people's houses. I am glad you went over to Springfield and to the Busbey's. Now suppose you make a trip to the Lakes and visit your relatives and friends there. It will do you great good. Leave Willie and Mollie at home to take care of the house or shut it up and take the whole lot.

"Next mail I will send you a draft for $300.00. I have sent you $1,200 since February 7th but you have only acknowledged the first draft for $300. Pay Seltzer. The piano was $400 and there was the cover and stool. $8.00 I believe. When I left home there was just about $100 due him. You will find the papers all in my desk, his original bill and everything. Governor Dennison writes me that there were yet $64.00 due on the Deshler notes. I can't understand how or why the sum is so large. In my bank book you will find the record of the check which I gave Deshler a day or two before I left home. I have written Governor Dennison to investigate the whole matter and pay what he thinks right and that you will give him a check for the whole amount.

"In regard to that sewer matter you had better join with the neighbors in the construction of a sewer in the alley, at the same time get Mrs. Marion to join you in building a sewer from the privy and all the water from the house and everywhere will run into it. Your other plan I do not approve. It is right that you should build a gutter in the alley as the street commissioner directs. When you do that put a stone to lead the water away from the spout at the end of the house in the alley.

"You must not now be particularly concerned about my health. I gain strength every day. My general condition is good. I have only to recover from the weakening effects of the discharge from my lung which is now about completed and with care and vaccine the Doctor says further deposit can be nearly if not wholly arrested. The climate where we are now is very agreeable. The air is much purer and stronger than that of Quito. I breathe with perfect ease, which I never did in Quito.

"Tomorrow is the glorious 4th. We shall spend it without fire works, but not without the recollections and impressions that belong to it, and many regrets that we are not among the friends who appreciate and enjoy it.

"We rejoice that the children keep in good health and that Willie is trying to make a man of himself. You must pay attention to Mamie. The trip to Sandusky would be good for her. Tell Willie not to worry about clothes. What he gets in his head is of much more importance than what he has on his back. After a while he shall be rigged out to his heart's content. If they would fit him I could send him a couple of fine suits from here which I don't wear.

"We sent last week to Guayaquil a box of curiosities. Quito needlework and some jewels. We will send you a list by the next mail of what is in it. It will be forwarded from Guayaquil by the Consul to Panama, Welles and Fargo's Express and will be brought by the American Express to New York. Send one of the handkerchiefs in the box to Sarah.

"Quito is now duller than ever it seems. There is but one Minister, one Consul and one Secretary with whom we have intercourse in the Diplomatic circle, and a half a dozen other friends complete our list. We live at Guapulo almost like hermits but is not as dull as Quito, because have trees and flowers and birds for companions, good air and good water. I do not feel that I will ever live another day in Quito. 'I had rather dwell in the midst of alarms than in this horrible place.'

"You can have some idea of mail arrangements in South America when we tell you that our files of Government papers for October, November and February came last week; also one or two State Journals as old as November. The difficulty is not at Washington but at the local post offices in South America. I want you to subscribe for me and have sent from the office postage paid, care of U.S. Consul, Panama, the Semi-weekly New York Tribune and 'Every Saturday monthly post' published in Boston by Ticknor & Co. Also buy and send through the Department 'Howell's Venetian Life.'

"Jessie got her shoes, gloves and would be thankful for more. Send the garters, but not quite so large as the shoes. Love to all the *children, regards to all our friends hoping they are well and happy. Love to you from Father and daughter.*

"As ever
William"[17]

Also on July 3, the U.S. Minister dictated a dispatch to Secretary of State Seward: "There is no political news of importance unless the dissolution of the Diplomatic Corps be of interest. Six months ago England, France, Rome and the United States, Chile, Peru, Bolivia and the Columbian States were represented by Envoys, Ministers or Consuls General. Now there is but one Envoy at the Capitol and but one Minister, myself. France is represented by the Secretary of the Legation and so also is Peru. These, including the Nuncio, constitute the Diplomatic Corps."[18]

There is no explanation why the senior members of the Diplomatic Corps had dwindled from eight to three.

ANOTHER BLOW ABOUT CEMETERY

The U.S. Minister was optimistic about his improved health and hoped his letter to Mary would cheer her. He kept recording his improving health: "SAT., JULY 6. On horseback 3/4 hour. SUN., JULY 7. Walked in garden—cough less. MON., JULY 8. Frequency of cough much less. No medicine. Gaining flesh. TUES. 9. Strength improving. WED. 10. Rode in fields. FRI. 12. When in open air cough very little. Have no chills now."[19]

Then his work suffered a reversal which threatened to undo his progress toward a Protestant Cemetery. It had seemed so near to becoming a reality. The thought of achieving the cemetery against great cultural odds had kept Coggeshall determined in spite of his illness. His spirits had soared when he learned that Willie was past the threat of rabies and when he himself had thwarted six weeks of "dangerous" illness. Now he had only to complete his primary mission in Ecuador—overcoming a centuries-old prejudice that Protestants were "heretics" unworthy of being buried in "consecrated ground."

On July 16, 1867 he informed Washington:

"Hon. William H. Seward,
"The establishment of a Protestant Cemetery has met with another check. The Supreme Government selected an appropriate

---

[17]William T. Coggeshall Papers, Ohio Historical Society.
[18]William T. Coggeshall Dispatches from Ecuador, 1866-67, U.S. Department of State.
[19]William T. Coggeshall Papers, Ohio Historical Society.

site and was prepared to put it in proper order. This property belongs to the Municipal Corporation. Several influential members of the Municipal Council refused their consent to use the property for the purpose desired. The remains of British Charge Neale are still here and, by order of his family, are to be buried here. His successor arrives soon and will take charge of the interment. If the Government does not soon act decisively, the interment of Mr. Neale must settle the question of the Protestant burial ground and bring it to a final issue.

"Your obedient Servant,
W. T. Coggeshall."[20]

The U.S. Minister began coughing violently as he finished dictating the dispatch. He must have felt great heartbreak as he signed his name. Once again he was so near yet so far from securing a Cemetery for Protestants.

Coggeshall then penciled a brief diary note: "JULY 16. Wrote Dispatches. Gave Gouin draft for $520. Not so well."

CHEERFUL DESPITE DEFEAT

In the letters to Mary that are available, nowhere did Coggeshall (or Jessie) mention the persecution they endured because of his stand on a Protestant Cemetery. However, the newspapers of the United States carried brief notices of the discrimination against the American officials.

But it was not Coggeshall's nature to be depressed. He was a fighter—even against seemingly impossible odds in Ecuador. That is, until this last news of another rejection of a site for the Protestant Cemetery.

While his dispatch of July 16 told of the refusal by the Municipal Council, he did not reveal this to his family in Ohio in a July 17 letter.

"Guapulo near Quito
July 17, 1867

"Dear Mary:

"Your letter dated May 2nd (June intended) gave us much distress. You must have had the blues frightfully when you wrote it. The world was upside down and everything going wrong. Miller acted meanly but I wonder you did not earlier get the money from Washington. I wrote you it was there and I can not comprehend why when you know there is money to your credit in Washington and you need it immediately, you do not draw for it and put the

---

[20] William T. Coggeshall Dispatches from Ecuador, 1866-67, U.S. Department of State.

draft in the Columbus bank and get the money. I send with this mail to the Washington bank a draft for $300.00 and will direct the Cashier to forward the proceeds to you by express. I suppose you make your deposits and keep your regular bank account? I probably shall not be able to send you any more money for two months more because I must pay that $2,000 note; so make your calculations accordingly. We will have to live on credit here. I shall make such arrangements as will enable me to pay Miller all that is due on the house in January next.

"Your last letter dated June 13th was a great relief. It was cheerful and hopeful—the kind we like to read. I am glad Sarah is coming to make you a visit. You tell her I say she must make you tote her around to all the sights and scenes and curiosities of Columbus. I was very much pleased with Mary Davey's letter. It was well written, sensible and in good taste. Jessie will answer it next mail.

"I think you did well on the house though perhaps you undertook too much. The kitchen cellar stairs must be a great improvement—it was wise to do it. I suppose you have a padlock door and keep them securely locked. I think you do wrong in using kerosene instead of gas. I would not have it about the house if I were there. It is dangerous and unhealthy. I advise you to give it up and use the gas.

"I send you Mr. Manner's letter, giving up the business in Springfield. It shows the debts I have. If anything can be collected apply it to them. As soon as I get through with Washington note and straightened up, I will square them all off. You would have done better to have paid Seltzer and some others than to have given Father that $200.00 but perhaps he was importunate. Pay Seltzer if it is possible without embarrassing yourself. I do not understand whether your grocery bill is paid or not. McCollin & Co. have behaved like gentlemen and will not lose by it. There was a great deal of old lumber, magazines and so forth in the cellar when I came away. Two or three barrels of Genius of the West[21] etcetera. I shall never bind them or do anything else with them. Pick out the pamphlets from among them and put them on your shelves upstairs and sell the rest of them. What won't sell in the periodical store send to the paper mill at so much per pound. Save the Ladies Repository if there are any among them or anything else you think is worth keeping.

"I am glad Willie takes an interest in the yard. He seems to be doing very well. I rejoice at it. Only he must be careful about smoking and not let the habit grow on him. In his letter to me he asks for clothes.

---

[21]William T. Coggeshall Papers, Ohio Historical Society.

"As soon as we get a fair opportunity we intend to send back a good many things we brought here which were of no use to us. In that box will be many things useful to Willie. The box we wrote you about the last mail did not get to Guayaquil in time for that steamer. The gentleman to whom it was entrusted, stopping on the way at different towns. It will probably go by this steamer. You will open your eyes when you open it. You have not written a word about the hammocks. Have you hung them? Properly put up they must be a great diversion to the children. You wrote something about having a sink in the kitchen with pipes to the cistern. It would be a great improvement to get the cistern pump out of the yard and not over it. The play may be feasible, if you put the sink on the alley in order to discharge the refuse water into it.

"I have passed in the last six weeks through a terrible ordeal, but I passed, and Jessie says my health is better now than it was before I was taken to my bed. I have the consumption, that's a fact, but only in a small portion of the upper and outer part of the left lung. My right lung and two thirds of the left are perfectly healthy, sound in every respect, therefore, I do not intend that tubercle shall kill me for a dozen years hence, at least I gain strength now every day and my doctors say that re-establishment of health is possible. Ah! Probable. With good food, careful exercise and little 'worry.' We are more contented now than we have been at any time in Ecuador. We do our own marketing and buy what suits us. Jessie superintends the cooking and we have better meals than we ever had in Quito. We want you to send us some recipes, namely: viz: pancakes, cookies, biscuits for stewing mutton, for corn cakes, doughnuts, and any others you may think useful.

"You write about my coming home. It is out of the question. I wouldn't if I could and I couldn't if I would. It would be dangerous in the extreme for me to undertake the passage of Chimborazo. My desires are strong enough for the home circle, home society, home attentions but I know my duty and I cultivate contentment in each with the hope of future reward. I have had enough of dragging poverty, and how or where could I enjoy the chance of relief from it which is now before me, should I resign my present position. This is the view you must take and not sentimentalize over impossibilities. Your deprivations are nothing to ours and you must be cheerful and not work yourself into imaginary frenzy as you did about the Frenchman [Senor Gouin who wrote Mary that he wanted to marry Jessie]. It was a lucky chance that you sent him a positive letter.

"We enjoy delicious mornings and evenings, we spend as much time as we can out doors during the day and as soon as I am a little stronger we intend to cultivate the garden. There is about half an acre we can put into vegetables, etc. I have sent to the Agricultural Department for an assortment of seeds.

"Sometimes in the calm starlight it would be most delightful to have the home circle around us. We talk about it and sigh and try to think how you may be engaged at home.

"Don't push Mamie. She needs air and exercise more than books or music. She will die before she is sixteen years of age unless her physical system is built up and her nervous and intellectual [system] is kept in restraint.

"We join in love to the children and Mary. I will try to answer Willie's letter next mail. Regards to our friends and sincere hope that this letter will find you all well and happy.

"As ever,
William"[22]

Coggeshall ended his day on Wednesday, July 17 with this diary entry: "Sent quarterly report to Govt—sent [U.S. Consul in Guayaquil] Lee $500—Washington bank $300—wrote wife—very tired and depressed."[23] His writing trailed off. This was the last diary note William Coggeshall would make.

On July 20, 1867, the U.S. Minister and Jessie swung in their hammocks in their serene country garden in the valley below Quito. Coggeshall dictated a letter to the family while Jessie wrote.

LAST LETTER

"Guapulo near Quito
July 20, 1867

"Dear Folks:

"We have some curious experiences in our new country home. The proprietor of the 'hacienda' [farm] and his wife reside here during the most of the dry season. A few nights ago they paid us a visit. They had many questions to ask about 'Norte America.' The Senor wanted to know whether the true name of the great Republic was North America or the United States. He knew there was such a city as New York but asked what was the name of the Capitol [sic]. When told that the revenue of the United States last year was five hundred millions he held up his hands in awful astonishment. The Senorita desired to know if the United States had a President or an Emperor. After a while we had tea. They were urged to partake and with some persuasion consented. It was their first experience. The Senorita desired to know what tea was. She did not know whether it was vegetable or mineral or

---

[22]William T. Coggeshall Papers, Ohio Historical Society.
[23]Ibid.

where it came from. When told it was leaf she was very curious to know how it grew and whether on such trees as there are in Ecuador.

"Now these are wealthy people. Have 'haciendas' in the country and 'casas' (houses) in the city, and are ranked in good society.

"We have swung a hammock in a sheltered corridor on the north side of the house where we have a view of the garden. If you could see me lying in it now swinging gently and dictating these lines to Jessie, you would be greatly amused. I hope you enjoy the luxury of your hammock. The water ripples gently near me, the sun shines brightly upon the foliage around me, and I feel much more like dreaming than dictating.

"You would be amused at our experiments for the production of Yankee dishes. In Quito we were excluded from the kitchen and we took Ecuadorian cookery. Here we control the kitchen and we have good roast beef and mashed potatoes and have this morning arrived at the dignity of fried mush for breakfast.

"Oh, how you would enjoy the starlight which prevails every clear night about one hour after the sun disappears over a high hill to the west of us. Our valley is deep and narrow. We look up into a lofty dome, deep blue and stuffed with brilliant stars—very brilliant, twinkling stars. The air is calm and balmy and from the other side of the valley comes to us the loud roar of a swift stream as it rushes over its rocky bed. When there is moonlight we watch the luminary as it comes up above the hills, with calm pleasure enjoy its placid influence until it rides high into the heavens."[24]

Suddenly, Coggeshall stopped dictating. He bent over double with a choking, coughing spell. Jessie dropped her paper and pencil and called the servants. They came running and carried her father to his bed. Modesto rushed on horseback to Quito to get the doctor.

The diplomat had suffered a severe relapse. He had had plenty of two ingredients the doctor prescribed to get well—good food, careful exercise—but how much of the third, 'little worry,' is unknown.

It had been a week since the bad news that the Municipal Council had rejected a site for the Protestant Cemetery.

---

[24]William T. Coggeshall Papers, Ohio Historical Society

CHAPTER 16
PERSECUTION

The letter of July 20, 1867, to his wife Mary was the last William Coggeshall would write or dictate. Despite the warmer country air of Guapulo, ravages of the "disease of the lung" were finally weakening the U.S. Minister.

He kept brief diaries nearly to the end, but during the last week of July his condition deteriorated rapidly. With close diplomatic friends, Ecuadorian state officials and brave young Jessie at his bedside, Colonel William T. Coggeshall died of tuberculosis on Wednesday, August 2, 1867, at 9:00 a.m., a month short of his 43rd birthday. He had been in Ecuador exactly one year.

The U.S. Minister's last directive was that Jessie go to live with the family of the late ex-president of Ecuador, General Juan Flores.

In shock, as her father slipped away, Jessie clung to him tenaciously until Chilean Minister Hurtado gently lifted her arms from around her father's neck and led her to the garden where the soft, whirring wind in the trees caused the young girl to look up and, between sobs, offer a prayer toward the place of her father's last words in his last letter, "into the heavens."

WHERE TO BURY COGGESHALL

Where would the U.S. Minister be buried? Would William T. Coggeshall's body be allowed a Christian burial—and entrance into a Catholic church through the front door? Or would the Papal Nuncio and the Ecuadorian Government be at "swords' points" over disposition of the U.S. Minister's remains as they still were over the body of British Minister Neale?

Eight months earlier Coggeshall's protestations, supported by the other foreign representatives, succeeded in getting Mr. Neale's body taken into the Catholic church by the front entrance. Further, the Ecuadorian government promised to establish a Protestant Cemetery in Quito. But when Coggeshall died, the site was not yet selected.

Answers about the burial came quickly. Upon learning of Coggeshall's death, the Ecuadorian government sent a police officer to the Guapulo residence to express sympathy and give assurance that proper funeral honors would be accorded the deceased U.S. Minister.

The day after Coggeshall died Mr. Hurtado had the U.S. Minister's body removed to his own home, the Chilean Legation in Quito, and reported in letters to Mary:

"Quito
August 3, 1867

"Honorable U.S. Minister died of pulmonary consumption. . . .

"His body was brought to my house and thence carried to the place of deposit till the protestant cemetery is finished.

"An inventory of books, papers and other articles was made out in my presence and the things were put in my house.

"Mr. Coggeshall's personal effects remain in possession of his daughter, the only individual of his family who was with him."[1]

Protestant rites were conducted in Mr. Hurtado's house before Coggeshall's body was temporarily placed in an anteroom in the Church of Tejar near Mr. Neale's coffin.

"Mrs. W. T. Coggeshall

"Quito
17th August 1867

"Madam,

. . . "Referring you to my letter of 3rd instant, the contents of which I herewith confirm, I have the honour to inform you, that on the fourth of the same, the ceremonies of burial according to the rite of the church of England, were performed at my house over the body of Mr. Coggeshall, your lamented husband. His mortal remains were removed from thence with all due honors to the place destined for their reception until the completion of the protestant burial, which will be in a few days more.

"Miss Jessie is well and continues to reside with the highly respectable family of the widow of Gen. Flores, former President of this Republic.

---

[1] William T. Coggeshall Papers, Ohio Historical Society.

"I have, Madam, the honour to subscribe myself most respectfully,

"Your obt. humble Servant,
J. Nicolas Hurtado."[2]

Then, the diplomat sketched the entire occurrence in a letter to his Chilean Legation in Washington.

"Legation of Chile in U.S.
Wash. 4 Sept., 1867

"At 10 minutes of 9 the Honorable Mr. W. T. Coggeshall, Minister Resident of the United States of America, died in a country place near Guapulo, August 2, 1867.

"The Equatorian government had already received the news, and sent the Chief of Police to his house in Guapulo, to inform the undersigned of the just participation of everybody in grief of the daughter, colleagues and friends of Mr. Coggeshall, who are mourning his premature end, of his intention to render proper funeral honors to the mortal remains of the U.S. Representative and of his disposal to do what he could in the deplorable case.

"Mr. Coggeshall's daughter and . . . the undersigned give sincere thanks to the Equatorian government for its noble and worthy conduct, and is sure the United States Government will duly appreciate the discharged token of esteem and friendship.

"As the protestant cemetery is not finished, the undersigned thinks the Government ought to have Mr. Coggeshall's coffin put in the same place with Mr. Neale's, the British Chargé, till the cemetery is finished.

". . . The funeral ceremonies will take place on Sunday the 4th instant, when the body will be taken to the house of the undersigned and thence at 11 o'clock a.m. to the place of deposit designated by the government.

"J. Nicolas Hurtado."[3]

It was sadly ironic that Coggeshall's own death rather than Neale's forced the Ecuadorian government to "act decisively" and "settle the question of the Protestant burial ground and bring it to a final issue."[4]

JESSIE ALONE

Jessie was now alone in a foreign country. According to her father's last wish, she went to live with the Flores family to wait through

---

[2] William T. Coggeshall Papers, Ohio Historical Society.
[3] Ibid.
[4] See pp. 211–12.

the agony of weeks before her father would be "properly" buried in the Protestant Cemetery.

When Coggeshall died, Jessie's life changed overnight. She was betrothed to Mr. Gouin and was to have married him in August but her father's unexpected death delayed that. Jessie became acutely homesick. She had to make a decision. Should she become the wife of a rich young merchant and remain in South America or should she heed her homesickness and return to Ohio?

While pondering this dilemma the teenager continued to conduct herself as a dignified representative of the United States. During her father's last months, "Jessie was practically in charge of the Legation."[5] Now, she made preparations to keep all her father's official documents and personal belongings in order.

Finally, on Sunday, September 4th, a month after his death, the Coggeshall funeral was held. The diplomat's body was removed from the vault at the Catholic church and taken to Chilean Minister Hurtado's house. At 11:00 a.m. the Chief of Police of Quito, Ecuadorian government officials, diplomatic representatives, the Flores family, Mr. Gouin and grieving Jessie accompanied the casket, borne on the shoulders of servants, down a dusty street to the edge of Quito where a small plot of ground was cordoned off by a log fence. A small hand-painted sign in front read "Protestante." The procession was a somber contrast to the usual Ecuadorian funeral festivities.

Armed guards stood at the burial plot while Senor Hurtado conducted a brief graveside service and Jessie, sobbing quietly, bade a final goodbye to her father.

The plot for which U.S. Minister Coggeshall had fought, consecrated Protestant burial ground, ironically became his resting place.

When Mary received word in the middle of July that Coggeshall was dangerously ill, she suspected that her husband would not live long. According to family legend she asked trusted family friend, William Harrison Busbey,[6] if he would go to South America to look after Jessie and, in case of Coggeshall's death, to bring his body and Jessie home to Ohio. Busbey, who had been city editor of Coggeshall's *Ohio State Journal*, was 27 and single and was free to embark on a mission of mercy.

Busbey repeated the Coggeshalls' journey to Ecuador—by steamer and clipper ship to Guayaquil and then on horseback across the Andes Mountains to Quito. He arrived the day after Coggeshall was buried.

---

[5]*Dictionary of American Biography*, Vol. II, Brearly to Cushing, edited by Allen Johnson and Dumas Malone, Charles Scribner's Sons, New York, 1957, p. 272.
[6]Great-uncle of the author.

The good samaritan had left Columbus with good intentions, soon to be frustrated. Somehow, the Quitoans detained Jessie after her father's burial. Despite Busbey's pleadings and diplomacy, in a few weeks he finally gave up and dejectedly left Ecuador to return to the United States, alone.

COGGESHALL'S REMAINS IN WAREHOUSE

The full reason for the Ecuadorian detainment of Jessie is not clear but it is believed to be linked to an upheaval in the Papal Nuncio's office, referred to in the Coggeshall biography in the *Dictionary of American Biography:* "Coggeshall's body was at first buried in consecrated ground but, when the clerical revolution occurred soon afterward, was disinterred and placed in a public warehouse."

In death, Coggeshall's adversaries in the priesthood stifled the government's provision for Christian burial of Protestants.[7]

JESSIE AND FIANCEE

Mr. Busbey left Quito shortly before yellow fever spread to epidemic proportions throughout Ecuador. In Jessie's last available letter, October 19, 1867, for the first time she mentions what the author grew up hearing—that she was engaged to a handsome young South American.

> "Quito, October 19, 1867
>
> "Dearest Mother,
>
> > "I received your letter with a mixture of pain and pleasure. Pain because it brought up remembrances, and pleasure because it gave me very good advice and gave me some hope of seeing you all soon.
> >
> > "The day after I received your letter, I had an interview with Mr. Gouin and translated your letter as well as possible. He said he could not wait and spoke in very strong language and I answered him quite as strongly and told him it was better that it should be finished at once and have no more discussions.
> >
> > "He left me perfectly furious after telling me and saying that he had been deceived by you, by Father and by me. You know very well what a temper I have and that to hear any one say one word

---

[7]An inquiry from the author to Ecuador seeking information about what happened shed no light re: the "clerical revolution," but it is known that the Catholic clergy was exceedingly powerful. The government offices were unable to document why Coggeshall's body was moved from the Protestant Cemetery to a warehouse. Nor was a reason given for detaining Jessie. There was little precise record keeping in Ecuador during the mid-1800s.

against Father is enough to make me forget everything. But nevertheless, I answered as a lady should answer such an insult.

"I immediately returned everything, even a dirty collar which he gave me, a hat and scarf which he presented, too, but he sold them to the Misses Flores. Everything I had I was obliged to return.

"This morning his brother came to visit and inquire what I had said and what had passed between us. He said his brother was almost crazy, that he eats nothing, does not sleep. . . . Also, has the idea that there is somebody in Quito who had influence over me and that I had once an engagement with Mr. Busbey in Columbus! I assured him that nothing had ever passed between Mr. Busbey and myself and my opinions and resolutions come from me and that I am independent enough to decide for myself without influence of anyone.

"He [the brother] said that perhaps it would be consolation for him [Senor Gouin] to visit me. I answered him that if his brother chose to visit me as a friend I should be very glad to receive him but, if he came with hopes, and as a lover, I could not receive him. I told him that I was very sorry and it pained me very much to know his brother was in such a state and if he could console him and change his affection for me, I will be very much obliged to him. He said that it was my place to console him. I said no, that from the moment his brother said to me that there could not exist even friendship between us, I could not say anything nor have anything to do with him.

"I beg of you Mother, to answer this last letter of Mr. Gouin very carefully and, so as not to compromise me . . . and sustain me in my decision.

"Also, please give orders to Mr. Lee [American Consul in Guayaquil] or some one to pay immediately the accounts [at his store]. I do not wish to be indebted to Mr. Gouin for anything.

"I received a letter from Mrs. Lee full of kindness and offering to do anything possible for me.

"I am very well in health and my friends could not be kinder. . . . I am selling my things as fast as possible so as to be ready to start any moment.

"I beg of you Mother not to worry about me and if my letters should not reach you regularly, do not be surprised because the steamers are at quarantine in Guayaquil.

"Tell dear Bro. Willie I will write next mail. Give regards to all friends and kiss all the children for me.

"From
Your loving daughter,
Jessie."[8]

---

[8]William T. Coggeshall Papers, Ohio Historical Society.

Jessie had made her decision. She jilted Senor Gouin. She wanted to go home.

JESSIE GOING HOME

Jessie had done all she could to get her father's diplomatic documents in order. She was satisfied that whoever succeeded him could carry on. Now, she was selling their few possessions as rapidly as possible.

The young American longed to leave Ecuador. She had been distraught when Mr. Busbey's request to take her home had been denied. But now that the clerical revolution had occurred and her father's body had been disinterred from the Protestant Cemetery and stashed in a warehouse—oh, the humiliation of it all—maybe, the common folk of Quito would let her alone and their taunts would subside. She could not wait to leave the "horrid place."

It was difficult to bide her time until the yellow fever quarantine was lifted. Finally, the ships at Guayaquil were free to sail. Jessie prepared to leave Quito.

The Flores sisters helped her pack. Antonio Flores and Chilean Minister Nicolas Hurtado secured horses, donkeys and provisions for the trip. Senor Gouin came to say goodbye but did not ride with her. He had escorted her and Coggeshall on their first trip over the Andes. But not on this last. He was a rejected lover. Jessie had forsaken him.

Saying goodbye to the Flores household was hard. They had been the young girl's only family for several months and she had grown to love them. Jessie hugged and kissed each of them, mounted her horse, and riding off, waved a tearful but smiling farewell.

It was late November, 1867. The Flores brother and a servant accompanied Jessie on the 240-mile journey back over the Andes Mountains to the port city of Guayaquil. At long last, the young woman was going home.

The Andes Mountains seemed to echo Jessie's joy as she and her horse gingerly picked their way back over them. There were still high winds, deep crevices and flea-infested Tambos for lodging. But the discomforts paled in the prospect of what was waiting at journey's end.

As they approached Guayaquil and saw the masts of the ships in the harbor, Jessie's heart beat harder and her horse trotted faster. In only four short days she would board the sailing vessel for home.

U.S. Consul and Mrs. Lee hosted the tired but exhilarated girl and her companions. Senor Flores would stay in Guayaquil to put Jessie on the steamer and see that she was safely on her way.

The travelers arrived in Guayaquil December 30th. The ship would sail January 3rd, 1868. New Year's passed quickly. Jessie was exhausted but happy. She was going home. Her stomach was upset with expectation.

She retired early the night of January 2nd so she would be fresh to board the steamer the next morning to sail home.

On January 3rd Jessie awoke early—not from excitement, but from the need to stop choking. Almost fainting, she grabbed the wash bowl . . . vomited . . . her forehead was hot. She called Mrs. Lee, who came running with her husband. The Lees summoned a doctor who gave a dire diagnosis: Jessie had yellow fever.

Jessie's ship sailed at 2:00 p.m. without her.

Senor Flores was distraught. He and his sisters had been close friends of Jessie's since she arrived in Ecuador. She had been their charge since her father died five months earlier and was like his little sister. The Floreses wanted nothing more than to see her—this young girl—no longer alone; to be reunited with her family.

Senor Flores changed his plans to attend to business in Guayaquil and stood by Jessie's bed each day. He did not have to do so many days. In one short week, Jessie succumbed. The brave little ambassadress of the United States died at the age of 16, on January 10, 1868.

WHERE TO BURY JESSIE

Would there be an altercation about burying Jessie? Would Christian burial in consecrated ground be possible? Yes, because in Guayaquil there *was* a Protestant Cemetery, established due to Jessie's father's efforts.

Jessie's funeral was a solemn occasion. This young American girl, hardly known in Guayaquil, had only seven people at her funeral: Consul and Mrs. Lee, their cook and servant, Senor Flores, his servant and the Chief of the Guayaquil Police.

Mr. Lee read a brief scripture passage from the *Bible* and Senor Flores gave an emotional eulogy over Jessie's casket. It was just a plain wooden box, but inside it was beautiful.

Jessie had packed two exquisite things in her trunk—her linen and lace wedding gown and emeralds which her father had unearthed at Latacunga.

Jessie was buried in both—her wedding gown and her emeralds.

On January 24, 1868, Consul Lee sent a touching report on the fate of Jessie to Secretary of State William H. Seward.

> "U.S. Consulate
> QUAYAQUIL
> January 24, 1868
>
> "Hon. William H. Seward
> Secretary of State
> Washington, D.C.
>
> "It is my painful duty to announce the death of Miss Jessie Coggeshall, daughter of the late Minister at Quito.
>
> "This most interesting young lady came to Ecuador with her father, and after his death remained until recently in the interior, with the object of avoiding the risk of the epidemic which was prevailing here (yellow fever).
>
> "As mortality had sensibly diminished, and the port was declared healthy by the Sanitary authorities, it was supposed she could pass through here on her trip to the States in impunity. She arrived here on the 30th Ult, was attacked with the fever on the 3rd inst., the day I had made arrangements for her departure on the Panama steamer, and on the 10th she died.
>
> "Hardly yet arrived at the age of womanhood, in a foreign land, far from home and kindred, amongst people of different religion and education, with few sympathizers but such as her own gentle character had inspired, she had found an untimely grave.
>
> "This event alone would naturally cause much painful impressions, but when connected with the apprehension that her remains may not repose free from desecration and disturbance, it is grievous to contemplate. She was interred in what is called the Protestant Cemetery.
>
> > "I have the honor to remain,
> > Your most obedient servant,
> > E. Lee
> > [American Consul in Guayaquil]."[9]

Coggeshall's efforts had not been in vain. His dear, beloved daughter was buried in a Protestant Cemetery. But, unlike her father's fate, Jessie's remains were not disturbed and rested in the Protestant Cemetery two-and-one-half years.

---

[9] William T. Coggeshall Dispatches from Ecuador, 1866–67, U.S. Department of State.

CHAPTER 17
DOUBLE BURIAL

The news of Jessie's death so stunned Mary that her hair literally turned white overnight. She had lost her husband William five months previously. Now, her oldest daughter Jessie would never be back in her loving arms.

Jessie had been the victim of an Ecuadorian internal political struggle. For no apparent reason, the Quito government had detained the teenager. Mr. Busbey had failed to bring Jessie home before yellow fever struck Ecuador.

And fate had been cruel to William Coggeshall. He had had improved health and hopes of recovery until his months-long effort to get a Protestant Cemetery was halted by the Municipal Council which owned the property for the proposed site. They refused to relinquish the property for burial of non-Catholics. Another blow came from worry at home—whether Willie would get rabies. The two shocks took their toll. Coggeshall sank soon after them.

The inscrutable, faraway land had claimed Mary's two loved ones; she could do nothing about that fate. But she would not allow the foreign nation to have a permanent victory. She would fight to bring their bodies home to the United States for proper burial in the family plot in Columbus' Green Lawn Cemetery. There, they would lie in their rightful place alongside the graves of the Coggeshall babies, Turner and Martha.

Mary appealed to her Congressman, James A. Garfield. (He later became President.) In a letter of March 5, 1868, Garfield replied to Mary's appeal to get the bodies out of Ecuador: "You have my deepest sympathy for the great bereavement which has befallen you, and anything I can do to aid you will be most cheerfully done. I will see the

Fortieth Congress, U.S.

HOUSE OF REPRESENTATIVES.

Washington, D.C. March 5. 1868.

Dear Madam,

On my return to the city a few days since, after an absence of two weeks, I found your favor of Feb 21st awaiting me — You have my deepest sympathy for the great bereavement which has befallen you — and anything I can do to aid you, will be most cheerfully done — I will see the other representatives from

Ohio, and we will try to devise some means of serving you. In the excitement attending the conflict between the President and Congress it is difficult to get any favors from the Executive Departments - but I hope we shall be able to do something for you -

With kindest regards
I am Very Truly Yours,
J. A. Garfield

Mrs. W. T. Coggeshall
Columbus Ohio.

Congressman James A. Garfield letter to Mary Coggeshall. He later became President.

other representatives from Ohio and we will try to devise some means of serving you."[1]

The State Department also wanted to bring the Coggeshall bodies back to the United States. But in the days of travel by horses and steamships, such a maneuver was both costly and time-consuming. William Coggeshall's casket would have to be carried on the shoulders of Ecuadorian servants over the 240-mile danger-ridden precipices of the snow-capped Andes Mountains and through valleys of dense, jungle foliage. Jessie's coffin would have to be disinterred at Guayaquil; both bodies put aboard a steamer, switched to a railroad to cross Panama, loaded into another steamer on the Atlantic Ocean, then sail for New York. Congress would have to vote funds, government red tape would take time, and implementation would have to go through diplomatic channels—through another U.S. Minister appointed to Ecuador.

Finally, three years after Coggeshall's death, Mary's efforts were successful. The father's and daughter's remains returned to the United States at "public expense." Family legend tells that Senor Gouin, Jessie's former fiancee, accompanied the coffins. Three years after rejection by his sweetheart, Senor Gouin remained faithful to his unrequited, lost love, escorting her body back to her home on another continent.

This last fact was a tale the author's romantic appetite feasted on while growing up.

Another cousin, Dr. Mary Harbage of Kettering, Ohio, tells the tale of Jessie's South American fiancee bringing her body back to American soil. Mary has a childhood memory of being taken by her mother to an upstairs bedroom in Prockie's home in South Vienna, Ohio, to see some of Jessie's clothes laid out on the bed. Some were from her trousseau. Mary said, "They were glittery and lacy. There were jewels and I saw some emeralds, too. It was like peeking into fairyland."[2]

FINAL RESTING PLACE

On Wednesday, October 18, 1870, Mary Coggeshall rose early to go to the State House in Columbus. As she dressed, she recalled the happiness of the earlier day in February, 1861, when she had gone to the Ohio Capitol with William and Jessie to greet President-elect Abraham Lincoln.

---

[1] Letter to "Mrs. W. T. Coggeshall" from "J. A. Garfield," March 5, 1868, in the collection of the author.
[2] Mary has Jessie's black lace mantilla with hood which ties with black velvet ribbons.

Now she would again be with William and Jessie—sealed in their plain, wooden caskets.

Many times Mary had had to be brave. This day she might have to be the bravest. She and the children—Willie, 21; Mamie, 14; Hattie, 10; and Prockie, 8—rode quietly in a carriage to the State Capitol where a vast crowd had gathered. The governor's office had made the plans for a double funeral. The October 19, 1870, *Ohio State Journal*, which Coggeshall formerly owned, described the solemn occasion:

FUNERAL OF MR. COGGESHALL

"The unusual spectacle in our city of a funeral procession headed by two hearses, recalled to the mind of every observer yesterday the story of two eventful lives. The foreign looking burial cases, the long line of carriages filled with our leading citizens, the pallbearers taken from among our most distinguished men, showed that the occasion was no ordinary one. So much, that our people thought of the strange tale of a prominent citizen who left them years ago and of the stranger fate of his beautiful daughter, that none asked any questions in regard to the procession.

"It was eminently fit that our citizens should in this way honor the memory of W. T. Coggeshall, U.S. Minister to Ecuador, because as Minister he did so much that we as Americans are proud of, and it was beautifully appropriate that our Fathers and Mothers and their sons and daughters should honor the memory of Jessie Coggeshall, the Columbus school girl who became in so short a time a heroic woman, her girlhood changing when occasion required, when persecution, that we cannot understand, threatened her, to the greatest womanhood.

"In addition to the sorrow for the dead, and the sympathy for the bereaved family, there was another emotion ruling all these people who rode in that procession and who stood on our streets and in the doorways as spectators and this was something like triumph at the thought that the two-years-dead[3] were, away from the land where they had lived so long, among friends that the bodies over which governments had contended, after the triumph of all principle at stake, after receiving honors at the hands of South American officials, were now to receive funeral honors at the hands of friends and be laid in our own beautiful Green Lawn.

"And why this feeling? Let the brief story of the lives of the deceased answer.

"Mr. Coggeshall, after twenty years duty as a newspaper man, Reporter, Correspondent and Editor, after accepting leading positions on the Press of Cincinnati, Columbus, Cleveland and Akron,

---

[3]William T. Coggeshall had been dead three years.

after sending out a number of books to the public, after years of hard work in the field of politics, in June, 1866, accepted the appointment of U.S. Minister to Ecuador. He had just retired from the editorial control of the *Ohio State Journal* on account of ill health, and went abroad with the hope of becoming strong enough for the active work he had been engaged in all of his life. He was at that time about 42 years of age and had mapped out work enough to occupy him two more years. He left the country in July, 1866, his daughter, Jessie, then about 15 years of age, accompanying him.

"The new Minister arrived in due time in Quito and was received by the government officials with the usual pompous formalities. There was little to do in the usual light, but Mr. Coggeshall had been in place only a few months when an American citizen who died a Protestant was denied a Christian burial."[4]

"The Minister protested and, as a representative of the U.S. government, took force with the ruling parties and pressed his claim for the establishment of a Protestant cemetery. This meant revolutionizing things and the plea was sneered at. Opposition grew threatening and pretended friends became treacherous. The struggle ended—to the approval of the government—and just as this decisive step had received the approval of the government, and just as other steps were taken, to secure the rights of American citizens in Ecuador, Mr. Coggeshall was incapacitated and beseiged by illness. This terminated fatally August 2, 1867, and the Ecuadorian government reports how the U.S. Minister became leered at by the citizens he had so well defended. The remains were denied (permanent) burial and were interred in a warehouse and there guarded by friends.

"His daughter, placed as her father thought safest, under the guardianship of trusted friends, faced that even these friends could not protect her against the machinations of her father's and her country's enemies.

"She was persecuted because she was a Protestant, she was threatened because she cared more for her mother's wishes than for the commands of men in authority. She was detained for months when her heart longed for home. Under these circumstances she behaved as should the daughter of an American Minister. Retained the official papers collected about by her friends and finally triumphed. Though denied the company of a gentleman who went for her by direction of relatives here, she finally started for home in December '67. She made the perilous journey over the mountains to the coast but died at Quayaquil of yellow fever just as her house in this city was brightening up to receive her, and just as the hearts of her young friends were planning in their love for her, and their pride of her doings, a hearty welcome.

---

[4]Mr. Cashmore died the same week as British Consul Colonel Edward St. John Neale; in mid-December, 1866.

"At Quayaquil, she was among friends. Mr. Lee, American Consul, saw that she was tenderly cared for in her illness, and the remains interred in the Protestant Cemetery in Quayaquil.

"Last winter the Congress of the U.S. had appropriated funds to remove the remains of Mr. Coggeshall and daughter to this country and arrangements were made. Last Spring, Col. Whig of Kentucky, was appointed Minister to Ecuador and on his departure for Quito was instructed to see that the arrangements for removal were carried out.

"He found that the good work instituted by Mr. Coggeshall had been carried forward by Mr. Fredrick Hamilton, Minister at Quito for Great Britain, who succeeded Mr. Neale, who died about the same time as the deceased.[5]

"Col. Whig had the remains disinterred and forwarded to New York in care of the State Department at Washington. They were received in this city on Saturday night and were interred in Green Lawn Cemetery yesterday with much demonstration of popular respect and love as communities pay only to the most deserving."

Colonel William T. Coggeshall and Jessie were home at last.

---

[5]Mr. Neale died eight months before Colonel Coggeshall.

Portrait of Col. William T. Coggeshall painted posthumously by J. H. Witt, 1871.

EPILOGUE

Prockie's son, Ralph Coggeshall Busbey, told stories about his mother's difficulties stemming from her unusually long and historically rooted name—Emancipation Proclamation.

During the two-and-one-half years from her birth until the Confederate capital of Richmond fell to the Union Army ("I will not name her until Richmond falls," her father had said) the baby was called "Girlie."

TRADES HER NAME

During childhood Emancipation tried to give her name away. Many amusing incidents occurred resulting from the taunts of other children. They would stop her, tease her, and force her to say, "Emancipation Proclamation of Independence Constitution Amendments" before they would release her, embarrassed and hurt. So, one morning Emancipation traded her name with another girl—she became Lilly Dale. But, in a short time, she heard the words "Emancipation Proclamation" sung to the tune of "Old Hundred" and decided that it didn't sound so bad after all. So, she hunted up Lilly Dale, traded back for her original name and was proud of it ever afterwards.

Emancipation Proclamation's first-grade teacher in Columbus said, "That's too long a name for such a little girl. I'll just call you 'Prockie.'"

One day when a band led a procession of flag-bearers past her elementary school, the children asked the teacher what the celebration was for. The teacher replied, "It's Emancipation Proclamation Day." Prockie got up, said, "That's for me," left her seat, and went out and marched with them. She thought they were celebrating her birthday.

"Prockie" remained the nickname for Emancipation Proclamation Coggeshall all her life.

As she grew to adulthood she signed her name "E. Prockie" but for official papers she always had to sign her full name with 34 letters.

When Prockie was 21 she became a paid assistant to her mother Mary who was postmaster at Westerville, Ohio. One day Mary received this letter addressed to the "Postmaster of Westerville:"

"THE UNITED STATES MAIL
Cincinnati, O.
Sept. 7, 1884

"Dear Madam:

How in the world did your assistant come to have such a name as was given her? Were names Scarce when she was born? The wife of a P.M. in Pickaway County was named America Adelaide Victoria, but Emancipation Proclamation takes the cake.

"Yours truly,
The U.S. Mail."[1]

OUTSTANDING SOLOIST

Prockie had a beautiful soprano voice. Her reputation as a soloist took her to unexpected heights. After two years as a student at Otterbein University (now Otterbein College), Westerville, Ohio, "Miss E. Prockie Coggeshall" became the "Instructor in Voice Culture" for the University. She was in great demand to sing at conferences and meetings throughout Ohio.

MARRIAGE

The young swains of Westerville did not win Prockie's heart but the author's great-uncle did.

On June 28, 1888, Prockie married "Addie," Thomas Addison Busbey,[2] at her home in Westerville, Ohio. The wedding invitation read:

---

[1] The letter was on an official United States letterhead illustrating the old "Paterson" locomotive and mail train, a mail carrier on foot, and mail bags being tossed out of stage coaches.

[2] T. Addison Busbey was the youngest brother of William Harrison Busbey who was city editor of the *Ohio State Journal* when Coggeshall published it in 1865, and, who made the unsuccessful attempt to bring Jessie back from Ecuador. They were two of the five Busbey brothers of South Vienna, called "Ohio's Most Famous Journalistic Family."

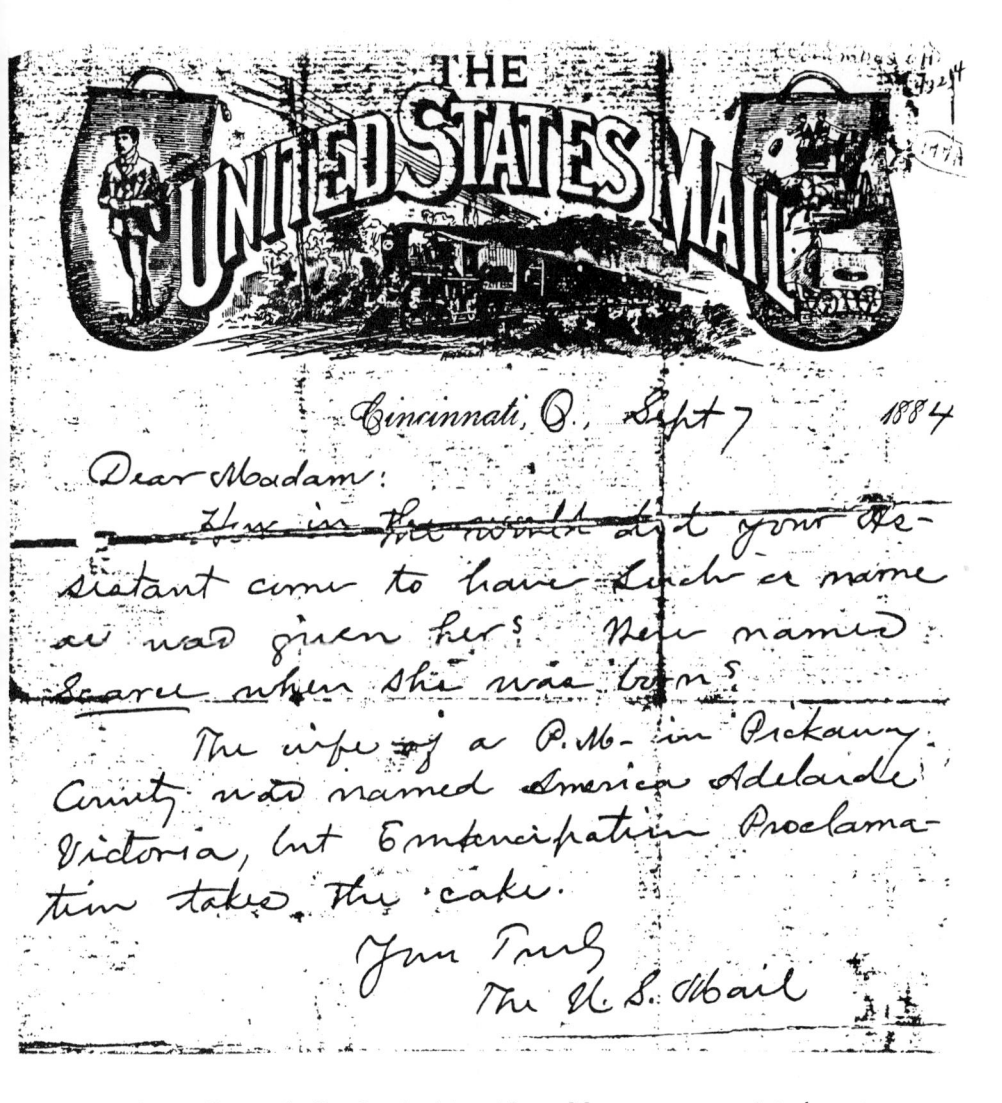

> **THE UNITED STATES MAIL**
>
> Cincinnati, O., Sept 7   1884
>
> Dear Madam:
>
> How in the world did your Assistant come to have such a name as was given her? Were names scarce when she was born?
>
> The wife of a P. M. in Pickaway County was named America Adelaide Victoria, but Emancipation Proclamation takes the cake.
>
> Yours Truly
> The U. S. Mail

After Coggeshall's death, his widow, Mary, was appointed postmaster at Westerville, Ohio. Daughter, Prockie, became her assistant at $100 a year. This letter of 1884 from "The U.S. Mail" inquires how Emancipation Proclamation got her name.

"Mrs. M. M. Coggeshall
requests the pleasure of your company at the
marriage of her daughter
E. Prockie
and
T. A. Busbey
at her residence, 55 W. College Avenue,
Thursday, June 28th, 1888.
Ceremony at 1 P.M.
Westerville,
Ohio."

    Several of Prockie's wedding presents are intact: a silver pie server decorated with a bird design; a cocoa pitcher made in Holland; and a rare plaque, "Love's Awakening," sculpted by the famous 19th century sculptor Lorado Taft. He was a friend of the bridegroom.

    Prockie sang at her own wedding. She stepped to the front door so the curious neighbors filling the yard could hear her sing "Oh, Promise Me." Newspapers country-wide reported her wedding.

    Later, in Chicago, Prockie was soloist for the Thomas Orchestra, the forerunner of the Chicago Symphony Orchestra.

    Busbey, an Ohioan from South Vienna, was editor of the *Railway Age* magazine in Chicago. They had one son, Ralph Coggeshall Busbey. His mother's complete name—Emancipation Proclamation Coggeshall Busbey—appeared on Ralph's birth certificate. In 1908 Busbey moved his family back to South Vienna.

    Prockie was the only one of the seven Coggeshall children to live past the age of 50. She died October 3, 1913, at South Vienna, Ohio, at age 51 of "sudden shock and severe asthma." An innovator, she even orchestrated her own funeral. In deference to her preference for white, everything at her funeral was white: the casket, the hearse, the horses. Her husband, son, and other male relatives wore white neckties; the pallbearers, white gloves; and the ladies wore white dresses. . . . The banks and all business houses were closed during the hour of the funeral held at the South Vienna Christian Church. After the services, the horse-drawn hearse, followed by a wagonload of flowers, took Prockie's body to the South Vienna Cemetery.

    On her tombstone Emancipation Proclamation Coggeshall Busbey's name is inscribed simply "E. Prockie Busbey."

    Prockie never really knew her father. Colonel Coggeshall died when she was four. But during her lifetime Emancipation Proclamation Coggeshall Busbey paid homage to the cause for which she was named

Mrs. M. M. Coggeshall

requests the pleasure of your company at the

marriage of her daughter

E. Prockie

and

T. A. Busbey,

at her residence, 55 W. College Avenue,

Thursday, June 28th, 1888.

Ceremony at 1 P. M.

Westerville,

Ohio.

Prockie, Emancipation Proclamation Coggeshall at age 17, painted by J. H. Witt, 1879. Prockie's wedding invitation.

Prockie's wedding gifts: cocoa pitcher from Holland and silver pie server.

"Love's Awakening," original plaque by sculptor Lorado Taft, friend of the bridegroom. Taft's gift to Emancipation Proclamation and T. Addison Busbey for their wedding June 28, 1888, in the author's possession.

Prockie, Emancipation Proclamation Coggeshall Busbey, and 13-month-old son, Ralph Coggeshall Busbey, June 11, 1891.

and the moment it represented in history for her father, her father's president and the nation. Herself the symbol of the triumph of that cause, she traveled the country singing, "The Nation's Jubilee," the prize-winning song celebrating the end of the Civil War.[3] Prockie would explain her connection with the war, then, in her beautiful voice, end her concerts with the song:

"THE NATION'S JUBILEE

Verse I: "Fling out the Nation's starry flag
In Glory on the air;
The ancient flag of Freedom still,
No star is missing there;
The Lord of Hosts hath given the word,
The People all are free;
The Jubilee hath sounded forth
The Nation's Liberty.

Chorus: "Shout! Our redemption's come,
Our Nation now is free;
Echo the chorus wide,
Proclaim the Jubilee!
Echo the chorus wide,
Proclaim the Jubilee!

Verse II: "The Dove of Peace is brooding o'er
The desolated earth,
And flowers are springing in the light
Of Freedom's second birth!
Then from the field of battle call
Our noble Vet'rans home:
Ring out the joyous bells and greet
The Heroes as they come.

Verse III: "The hosts of proud oppressors now,
Are whelmed in endless night;
And dusky brows of millions wear,
The crown of freedom's light.
Proclaim the triumph thru the world,
And shout from pole to pole;
Eternal be the boon for all,
The birthright of a Soul.

---

[3] Contest sponsored by *Demorest's Magazine*, 39 Beekman St., New York City; prize $100. Music by Konrad Truer; lyrics by Carlos Wilcox. Prockie's copy of "The Nation's Jubilee" is in the collection of the author.

Verse IV: "Then fling the Nation's banner out,
In glory on the air;
The spotless Flag of Freedom now—
No star is missing there;
While Justice and Eternal Truth
Mankind exulting see;
We'll shout our Country's joyous song,
The Nation's Jubilee."

Colonel William T. Coggeshall and his family may be counted among the true patriots of the 19th century in American history.

Prockie's tombstone.

Ralph Coggeshall Busbey displays his mother Prockie's (Emancipation Proclamation Coggeshall Busbey) copy of prize-winning Civil War song, "The Nation's Jubilee," with which she ended her concerts.

Coggeshall burial plot, Green Lawn Cemetery—Columbus, Ohio

Hattie	Turner	Wm. T.	Mary	Jessie	Martha	Willie
1860–	1853–	(father)	(mother)	1851–	3/1865–	1849–
1883	1855	1824–	1826–	1868	6/1866	1896
		1867	1915			

Immediately in front of these markers are markers for Mamie (1856–1896) and her husband Lyman Scovil and son, Lyman, Jr. Prockie (1862–1913) is buried at South Vienna, Ohio, with her husband T. Addison Busbey. Mary Coggeshall outlived her eight brothers and sisters, her husband, and her seven children.

Busbey Family picture at home of Prockie (Coggeshall) and T. Addison Busbey, 1045 Wilcox St., Chicago, August 16, 1903.

Bottom step: Busbey Children—Ralph, 13 (Prockie's son and Coggeshall's grandson), Gertrude, L. White Jr., Horace.

Second step: Prockie (Emancipation Proclamation Coggeshall Busbey).

Third step: Alma (wife of Charles), Mary Coggeshall (widow of Colonel Coggeshall), Katherine (wife of L. White).

Five Busbey brothers of South Vienna, Ohio

Fourth Step: T. (Thomas) Addison (Prockie's husband and Coggeshall's son-in-law), Charles Sumner, William Harrison (tried to bring Jessie home from Ecuador).

Standing left: L. (Leroy) White

Standing right: Hamilton

The five Busbey brothers were called Ohio's most famous journalistic family. One of them, T. Addison, was Prockie's husband and Col. Coggeshall's son-in-law.

BIBLIOGRAPHY

UNPUBLISHED MATERIAL: PAPERS, DIARIES, SPEECHES, SCRAPBOOKS

BUS.   Busbey, Ralph Coggeshall. Papers, speeches, scrapbooks, in the collection of the author.

COG.   Coggeshall, Mary. Papers, in the collection of the author.

Coggeshall, William T. Diaries, papers, notebooks, in the collection of the author. Includes Civil War Diary (copy) and original Diary of Journey from Guayaquil to Quito, 1866.

Coggeshall, William T. William T. Coggeshall Papers, The Ohio Historical Society.

LETTERS

BUS.   Busbey, Ralph Coggeshall. 1956-59, in the collection of the author.

COG.   Coggeshall, Jessie. 1866-67, William T. Coggeshall Papers, The Ohio Historical Society.

Coggeshall, Mary. February 25, 1908, letter, in the collection of the author.

Coggeshall, William T. Letters spanning 1850s and 1860s, William T. Coggeshall Papers, The Ohio Historical Society.

INTERVIEWS

BEC.   Becker, John. Librarian, Otterbein College, Westerville, Ohio. 1979.

GUS.   Gustafson, Milton. Chief, Diplomatic Branch, National Archives, Washington, D.C. (by telephone). 1981.

HAN.   Hancock, Dr. Harold. Chairman History and Political Science Department, Otterbein College, Westerville, Ohio, and Professor of History, University of Delaware. 1979.

HAR.   Harbage, Dr. Mary. Professor Emeritus of Education, Wright State University, Dayton, Ohio. 1979-81.

SWA.   Swan, Chrystal. 27-year housekeeper to Ralph Coggeshall Busbey and wife Blanche. 1979.

PICTURES

BUS.   Busbey, Ralph Coggeshall. Papers, in the collection of the author.

HAR.   Harbage, Dr. Mary. Professor Emeritus of Education, Wright State University, Dayton, Ohio.

KOC.   Koch, Freda Postle. Collection: the author.

OHI.   Ohio Historical Society.

DISPATCHES

COG.   Coggeshall, William T. Dispatches from Ecuador 1866-67, United States Department of State.

PUBLISHED WORKS

AND.   Andrews, E. Benjamin. *History of the United States*, Vol. III. Chas. Scribner's Sons, New York, 1926.

ANG.   Angle, Paul M. *Lincoln Day by Day*, 1854-1861, Abraham Lincoln Association, Springfield, Ill., 1933.

BUS.   Busbey, Ralph C. *Columbus Dispatch Magazine*, November, 1958.

CIN.   *Cincinnati Star*. February 9, 1908.

COG.   Coggeshall, William T. *Easy Warren and His Cotemporaries* [sic], Redfield, 110-112 Nassau St., New York, 1854.

Coggeshall, William T. *Home Hits and Hints,* Redfield, 34 Beekman St., New York, 1859.

Coggeshall, William T. *Lincoln Memorial,* Ohio State Journal, Columbus, Ohio, 1865.

deG.   deGamez, Tana. *International Dictionary of English and Spanish,* Simon and Schuster, New York, 1973.

GAL.   Galbreath, Chas. B. *History of Ohio,* American Historical Society, Vol. II, Chicago and New York, 1925.

HAY.   Hayes, Melvin L. *Mr. Lincoln Runs for President,* The Citadel Press, New York, 1960.

JOH.   Johnson, Allen and Dumas Malone, editors. *Dictionary of American Biography,* Vol. II, Brearly to Cushing, Chas. Scribner's Sons, New York, 1957.

KIM.   Kimmel, Stanley. *Mr. Lincoln's Washington,* Bramhall House, New York, 1957.

LAN.   Langer, William L. *Encyclopedia of World History,* Houghton Mifflin Co., Boston, 1940.

MIE.   Miers, Earl Schenck. *Lincoln Day by Day, 1809–1865,* Vol. III, 1861–1865; C. Percy Powell, Lincoln Sesquicentennial Commission, Washington, 1960.

MOO.   Moore, Frank, editor. *The Rebellion Record, A Diary of American Events,* Arno Press, a New York Times Co., New York, 1977.

NBC.   NBC-TV. *The Lincoln Conspiracy,* May 16, 1978.

NYE.   Nye, Russel Blaine. *Society and Culture in America, 1830-1860,* Harper & Row, New York, Evanston, San Francisco, London, 1974.

OHI.   Ohio Year Book 1966. Ohioana Library.

RAN.   Randall, J. G. *Lincoln the President—Springfield to Gettysburg,* Dodd, Mead & Co., New York, 1946.

RAN.   Random House Dictionary.

RHO.   Rhodes, James A. and Dean Jauchius. *The Trial of Mary Todd Lincoln,* The Bobbs-Merrill Co., Indianapolis, Ind., 1959.

ROW.   Rowan, Richard Wilmer, with Robert G. Deindorfer. *Secret Service,* Hawthorn Books, Inc., New York, 1967.

SAN.   Sandburg, Carl. *Abraham Lincoln, The Prairie Years and the War Years,* Harcourt, Brace & World, New York, 1954.

SHA.   Shaw, Albert. *Abraham Lincoln, The Year of His Election,* The Review of Reviews Corporation, 1929.

SPR.   Springfield (Ohio) Daily Sun. February 8, 1908.

THO.   Thomas, Benjamin P. *Abraham Lincoln,* Alfred A. Knopf, New York City, 1952.

WHI.   Whipple, T. Herbert. *Gallery of Western Portraits,* Chicago, 1852.

APPENDIX

In the Name and by the Authority of **THE STATE OF OHIO,**

SALMON P. CHASE,
GOVERNOR OF SAID STATE,

To All who shall see these Presents, Greeting:

Know Ye, That whereas a vacancy has occured in the office of State Librarian, by the expiration of the term of Richard Mr. Taylor.

Therefore, By virtue of the power vested in me by the Constitution and Laws of said State, I do Appoint and hereby COMMISSION William T. Coggeshall to be State Librarian authorizing and empowering him to execute and discharge all and singular the duties appertaining to said office, and to enjoy all the privileges and immunities thereof, until the 1st day of the present Assembly and until his successor shall be appointed and qualified agreeably to the Constitution and Laws of Ohio State.

In Testimony Whereof, I have hereunto set my name, and caused the Great Seal of the State of Ohio to be affixed, at Columbus, the 21st day of May, in the year of our Lord one thousand eight hundred and fifty-six, and in the eightieth year of the Independence of the United States of America.

S. P. Chase
Secretary of State.

By the Governor.
G. W. Baker

(Ohio Historical Society)

CITY OF CHICAGO -- Board of Health

OFFICE OF THE PRESIDENT, BOARD OF HEALTH

CERTIFICATE OF BIRTH   D. S. 122471

ORIGINAL
STATE OF ILLINOIS
DWIGHT H. GREEN, Governor
Department of Public Health
Division of Vital Statistics

Registration 3104
Dist. No.
Primary 3104
Dist. No.

1. PLACE OF BIRTH
County of Cook
Chicago

2. FULL NAME AT BIRTH Ralph Coggeshall Busbey

3. Sex Male
4. Twin, Triplet, or other? (To be answered only in the event of plural birth)
5. Number in order of birth
6. Legitimate? Yes
7. Date of birth May 12 1900

FATHER
8. Full Name Thomas Addison Busbey
9. Residence at time of this birth 49 N Ashland, Chicago, Ill.
10. Color White
11. Age at time of this birth 32 yr.
12. Birthplace (City or Place) South Vienna
    (Name State, if in U.S.) Clark County, Ohio
    (Name Country, if Foreign)
13. Occupation Editor "Railway Age"
    (Nature of Industry)

MOTHER
14. Full Maiden Name Emancipation Proclamation Coggeshall Busbey
15. Residence at time of this birth 49 N Ashland, Chicago, Ill.
16. Color White
17. Age at time of this birth 28 yr.
18. Birthplace (City or Place) Springfield
    (Name State, if in U.S.) Clark County, Ohio
    (Name Country, if Foreign)
19. Occupation Housewife
    (Nature of Industry)

20. (a) Number of children born to this mother at the time of and including this birth One
    (b) Number of children living at the time of and including this birth One

Portion of Ralph Coggeshall Busbey's birth certificate shows his mother Prockie's complete name.

252

"Indian Orange Vendor," by Ramon Salas, 1860, Quito, Ecuador.

United States of America
Department of State

To all to whom these Presents shall come, Greeting:

Know Ye, that the bearer hereof William F. Coggeshall, Esquire, Minister Resident of the United States to the Republic of Ecuador, is now proceeding thither accompanied by his Suite —

These are therefore to request all whom it may concern, to permit him to pass freely, without let or molestation, and to extend to him all such friendly aid and protection as would be extended to Minister Resident of Foreign Governments resorting to the United States.

In Testimony Whereof, I, William H. Seward, Secretary of State of the United States of America, have hereunto set my hand and caused the seal of this Department to be affixed at Washington, this twenty-second day of May, A.D. 1866 and of the Independence of the United States the Ninetieth.

William H. Seward

(Ohio Historical Society)

INDEX

Absentee ballots, the first, 79–82
Akron, Ohio, 16–17
Alaskan Islands, purchase of, 199
Albany Evening Journal, 37
Amazon River, 129, 173
American problems in Ecuador, 127–28
Antietam Creek, 63, 69, 70, 76
Anti-Spanish League problems, 108, 124, 180
Appomattox Court House, Virginia, 74, 83

Bates, Edward, 60
Bird Islands, 108
Bishop of Cuenca, 197–98
Bishop of Quito
   controversy over Neale burial, 145–47
   funeral, 208
   power over women, 196
Blair, Montgomery, 77
   disagreement with Stanton, 61, 62
Bolivia, 107–08, 124
Booth, John Wilkes, 84–85
Brazil, 107, 129
Bull fights, 124, 132–34
Bull Run/Manassas Junction, 58, 66, 67, 69, 71, 76
Busbey, Ralph Coggeshall, v, vi, 60, 75, 79, 86
   Civil War song, 244
   family picture, 246
   mother's birth, 75–78
   mother's problem name, 235, 238
   treasure, list of, 188–89
   with mother Prockie, 241

Busbey, T. (Thomas) Addison, 236, 238–40, 246
Busbey, William Harrison, 104–05, 135, 147, 149, 158, 165, 168, 192, 199, 202, 208, 222, 246
   journey to take Jessie home, 220–21
Cameron, Simon, 60, 67
Carrion, Geronimo, President of Ecuador, 124, 197
Cincinnati Commercial, 107
Chase, Salmon P., 2, 24, 55, 60, 64, 72, 77, 102
   appointed Chief Justice, 64
   bitter toward Lincoln, 63
   friction in Lincoln Cabinet, 59–62
   Secretary of Treasury, 55
Chicago Tribune, 2
Chile, 107–08, 124, 129–30, 180, 198, 200
Civil War, 51–74
Clay, General Cassius, 54, 57
Coggeshall, Emancipation Proclamation (Prockie)
   at double burial, 231
   birth, how named, 75–78
   father sails to Ecuador, 105
   home in South Vienna, 230
   letters from father to children, 161–64, 178–80
   postal assistant, 236–37
   trades name, 235
   vocalist, marriage, funeral, 236, 238–43
Coggeshall, Harriet Eliza (Hattie), 27, 77, 182, 195, 197, 245
   at double burial, 231

father sails to Ecuador, 105
letters from father to children, 161-64 178-80
Coggeshall, Jessie Austrace
  birth, 22
  journey to Quito, 105-07, 108-21
  letters from Quito
    bishop's power over women, 196
    Bolivian Minister's Ball, 192-93
    bull fights, 132-34
    burial, 227-33
    controversy over Neale burial, 141-46
    cross-eyed vice president, 175-76
    disgust with Quito, 176-77
    eccentric diplomats, 135-38
    extravagant Austrian Count, 168-70
    father's death, 217-19
    gaudy ladies at concert, 183-84
    jilts fiancee, 221-23
    lonesome Christmas, 166-68
    President's funeral, 155-56
    Quito customs, 151-53
    scandalous Houssareks, 194
    Thanksgiving dinner, 156-57
    trousseau items, 199, 224, 230
Coggeshall, Mary
  absentee ballots, role in first, 79-82
  and assassination attempt on Lincoln, 33-38
  appointed postmaster, 236-37
  children: Willie, 21, Jessie, 22, Turner, 22, 23, Mary (Mamie), 23, Harriet (Hattie), 27, Emancipation Proclamation (Prockie), 75-78, Martha, 101
  double burial, 230-33
  effort to bring bodies home, 227-30
  gift from ex-president of Hungary, 23
  husband/Lincoln meeting April 14, 1865, 84
  husband, letters from, 149-50, 153-55, 164-66, 181-83, 185, 203-07, 209-11, 212-15, 215-16
  husband sails to Ecuador, 104-05
  husband's death, 218-19
  Jessie, letters from, 132-35, 143-47, 151-53, 155-59, 166-68, 174-78, 183-85, 191-93, 193-97, 200-02, 221-22

Jessie's death, 227
Lincoln, Columbus reception for, 1, 3, 4, 9, 10
longevity, 245
marriage, 17
Prockie, wedding invitation for, 239
Coggeshall, Mary Marie (Mamie), 23, 182
  at double burial, 231
  father sails to Ecuador, 105
  health, 215
  letters from father to children, 161-64, 178-80
Coggeshall, Martha, 101, 104, 227, 245
Coggeshall, Turner, 22, 23, 227, 245
Coggeshall, William Turner
  and Abraham Lincoln
    appointed bodyguard by, 37
    as escort in Columbus, 1, 4-9
    Emancipation Proclamation, 75-78
    eulogy, 97, 98
    in secret service for, 37, 59
    military aide to, 55, 57, 58, 59
    on funeral train, 86-94
    on inaugural train, 11-38
    saves from assassination, 35, 36
    with, before assassination, 84
  books authored
    Easy Warren and His Cotemporaries (sic), 22
    Frontier Life, 29
    Home Hits and Hints, 23
    Lincoln Memorial, 86-98, 101
    Poets and Poetry of the West, 27, 28
  childhood, 11, 12
  lecturer
    on miscellaneous subjects, 27, 29
    on temperance, 18, 19
  Librarian for Ohio, 24
  magazines, index, editor or publisher of
    Genius of the West (publisher), 24, 25, 213
    Index to Ohio Laws and Resolutions, 1845-1857, 29
    The Newspaper Record of 1856, 29
    Ohio Education Monthly, 27
  marriage, 17
  newspapers associated with
    A Wit, A Wag, and A Painter, 17
    (Cincinnati) Daily Queen City, 19

Cincinnati Daily Times, 20, 23
Cincinnati Gazette, 20, 77, 102
Louisville Courier (won contest), 21
Ohio Temperance Artisan, 17
Poughkeepsie Blacksmith, 19
Teetotal Mechanic, 17
Western Fountain (publisher), 21
newspapers correspondent for
  Boston Commonwealth, 23
  Boston New Englander, 20
  Cincinnati Columbian and Great West, 23
  New York Times, 23
  New York Tribune, 20
  Ohio State Journal (publisher), 77
    see also *Ohio State Journal*
  Ohio Statesman, 23
  Springfield (Ohio) *Press Republic* (publisher), 75, 77, 79, 80
prints first absentee ballots, 79, 80
publisher, temperance papers and magazines, 16-19, 21
role in first absentee ballots, 79-82
secretary to ex-president of Hungary, Louis Kossuth, 23, 24
secretary to three Ohio governors: Dennison, 1; Chase, 24; Cox, 101
smallpox, 59
U.S. Minister to Ecuador
  advice to Mary, 149-50, 153-55, 164-66, 181-83, 209-11
  American problems, 127-28
  burial in Columbus, 230-33, 245
  cheerful despite defeat, 212-15
  concern about children, 181-82
  controversy over Neale burial, 141-47, 150-51, 197-98
  critical illness, 200-202
  death, 217
  finds treasure, 187-89
  first diplomatic speech, 123-24
  format of dispatches to Secretary of State Seward, 123
  hunting trips, 178-80
  journey to Quito, 101-21
  last letter, 215-16
  Latin American problems, 129-30
  move to Guapulo, 203-07
  Protestant Cemetery fight, 148-49, 150-51, 173, 180, 197-98, 200, 219, 225
  remains in warehouse, 221
Coggeshall, Willie West, 21, 22, 182
  at double burial, 231
  bitten by dog, 198-99, 211, 227
  father sails to Ecuador, 105
  father's clothes, 210
  letters from father to children, 161-64, 178-80
  letters from Jessie, 135-38, 168-71, 207-08
Colombia/New Granada, 107, 129, 200
Columbus Dispatch Magazine, 86
Columbus, Ohio
  double burial at, 227-33
  reception for Lincoln, 1-10
Cotopaxi volcano, 118-19, 121
Cox, Governor Jacob D., 101, 102

Davis, Jefferson, 53, 60, 61
Dennison, William, Governor of Ohio, 1, 52-54, 61, 69, 70, 74, 77
  advises Mary on bills, 209
  greets Lincoln, 3
  letter from Lincoln, 56
  Postmaster General, 72, 102
Douglas, Stephen A., 2, 8, 38

Ecuador, history of, 107-08
Election of 1864, 79, 82
El Nacional, 129, 180, 197-98
Emancipation Proclamation
  Coggeshall's, 75-78
  Lincoln's, 75-77

Flores, Antonio, 120-21, 141
  gives Jessie emerald, 134
  last service for Jessie, 223-24
Flores, General Juan, President of Ecuador, 111, 141, 153, 155-56, 217-18
Ford Theatre, 84
Fort Sumter, South Carolina, 53
Fremont, General John Charles, 77

Gage, Frances Dana, 27
Galapagos Islands, 129-30, 173
Gallagher, William D., 20, 24, 27
Garfield, James A., 72, 227-30
Gettysburg Address, 63, 98
Godey's Lady's Book, 134, 157

Gouin, Senor
  birthday gifts to Jessie, 134
  brings Jessie home, 230
  Christmas gifts for Jessie, 167
  Coggeshall accounts, 198, 212
  courting Jessie, 173
  dinner guest, 156
  engaged to Jessie, 191, 203, 214
  guide over Andes Mountains, 110–13, 116–17, 120
  jilted by Jessie, 220–23
  scarf from Jessie, 195
Grant, General Ulysses S., 62, 72, 74, 78

Harper's Weekly, 157, 193, 201
Houssarek, Friedrich, 101–02, 191, 194
Hurtado, J. Nicholas, Chilean Minister, 144, 147, 170, 193
  on Coggeshall's death, 217–20
  trip with Coggeshall, 187

Inca Indians, 103, 120, 127, 180, 187

Jackson, Stonewall, 67, 68
Johnson, President Andrew, 64, 72, 85, 96, 102–03, 106, 124

Kossuth, Louis, ex-president of Hungary, 22–24

La America Latina, 124
Ladies Repository, The, 27, 213
Lamon Ward, 34, 35
Lee, General Robert E., 62, 67–71, 74, 78
Lincoln, Abraham
  appoints Coggeshall as bodyguard, 37
  assassinated, 84
  assassination attempt, 33–37
  Coggeshall eulogy, 97–98
  Columbus reception, 1, 3–10
  controversy over McClellan, 64–72
  elected president, 2
  first inaugural address, 37, 38
  friction in Cabinet, 59–62
  funeral trip, 85–96
  Gettysburg address, 62, 63, 98
  humor, 51, 52
  inaugural train route and speeches, 13, 14, 21, 23, 29, 30–32
  Mary Coggeshall letter re Lincoln and Coggeshall, 39–49
  re-elected president, 82
  religious faith, 51
  suggests Coggeshall head Secret Service, 59
  trust, 59
Lincoln, Mary Todd, 3, 34, 61, 96
Lincoln, Robert, 3, 96
Lincoln, Tad, 3, 96
Lincoln, Willie, 3, 87, 93, 96

McClellan, General George B.
  controversy over, 64–70
  dismissed by Lincoln, 70, 71
  his own story, 70–72
  presidential candidate, 70, 79, 82
McDowell, General Irvin, 58, 67
Meade, General George G., 62
Medill, Joseph, 2
Mt. Chimborazo, 108, 112, 115, 116–17, 214

Neale, Colonel Edward St. John, British Consul to Ecuador, controversy over his burial, 141–51
New York Times, 23, 33, 34, 86, 150–51
New York Tribune, 20, 23, 86, 210

Ohio State Journal, 1, 73, 101, 104, 105, 181, 210, 220
  Coggeshall, publisher, 77, 86–89
  Columbus reception for Lincoln, 4–9
  double burial, 231–33
  special edition day Lincoln died, 86

Papal Nuncio (Delegado of the Pope)
  Coggeshall protests to Pope, 180
  controversy over Neale burial, 142–47, 185, 217, 221
Pendleton, George W., 79
Peru, 107–08, 124, 130, 180, 198, 200
Pope, General John, 76
Press Republic, Springfield, Ohio, 75, 77, 79–80
Prockie, *see also Emancipation Proclamation Coggeshall*
Protestant Cemetery fight, 141–51, 173, 180, 185, 197–98, 200, 219, 232-33
Railway Age, 238
Richmond, Virginia, 55, 58, 63, 67, 68, 71, 75–78, 235
  conquered, 83

Secret Service, 37, 59, 64, 75, 105
Seward, William E., Senator, 2, 30, 61, 77, 106
  against Emancipation Proclamation, 77
  bitterness toward Lincoln, 60
  controversy over Neale burial, 141-51
  disagrees with Lincoln, 63, 77
  form of Coggeshall dispatches from Ecuador, 123
  Jessie's death, 225
  offered Secretary of State post, 60
  Protestant Cemetery fight, 148-51, 173, 180, 211-12
  Seward's Folly, 199
Shellabarger, Samuel, 79-81
Shellabarger, Samuel, Jr., 81-82
Sherman, Senator John, 102
Springfield (Ohio) *Press Republic*, 75, 77, 79, 80

Stanton, Edwin M., 52, 60, 67, 71, 76, 77
  disagrees with Blair, 61
  disagrees with Lincoln, 62
  disagrees with McClellan, 67
  praises Lincoln, 62
  Secretary of War, 55

Temperance, 16-19
Toledo Blade, 52

Venezuela, 107, 108

W.C.T.U., Women's Christian Temperance Union, 22
Wells Fargo & Co., 149, 183, 210

Zouaves, 13, 55, 57

ABOUT THE AUTHOR

Freda Postle Koch loves history for what it means to the present. Descended from two pioneer families in Central Ohio, she grew up hearing dramatic stories about her ancestors. In adulthood she discovered that one distant cousin, William Coggeshall, a famous journalist, saved Lincoln from an assassination attempt. The details had never been told. She fell heir to the documentation.

Her research uncovered papers and letters revealing that Coggeshall's wife and a daughter were equally heroic, both here and in diplomatic service abroad.

Koch's sense of family and history drove her to write this book; to preserve the Coggeshalls' strong thread in the tapestry of American history.

Koch is a graduate of Ohio State University; formerly with *Time Magazine* and a newspaper columnist; broadcaster in Chicago, Boston, Oklahoma; past national president of The American Council for Better Broadcasts; and currently, is a host/producer for "Everybody's Talking," WCVO-FM, Gahanna/Columbus.

The author and her husband, Melvin, have a son and two daughters. Like her cousin Coggeshall, one daughter, Katharine, is an American diplomat.

Koch's trademark is hats. She has 93.